The
Vest
Pocket
Controller

THE
VEST
POCKET
CONTROLLER

Steven M. Bragg

WILEY

John Wiley & Sons, Inc.

For general information on our other products and services or for technical support, please contact our Customer Care Department within the United States at (800) 762-2974, outside the United States at (317) 572-3993 or fax (317) 572-4002.

Wiley also publishes its books in a variety of electronic formats. Some content that appears in print may not be available in electronic books. For more information about Wiley products, visit our web site at www.wiley.com.

Library of Congress Cataloging-in-Publication Data
Bragg, Steven M.
   The vest pocket controller/Steven M. Bragg.
      p. cm.
   Includes index.
   ISBN 978-0-470-59373-8 (pbk.)
  1. Managerial accounting. 2. Corporations–Accounting.
  3. Accounting. I. Title.
  HF5657.4.B723 2010
  658.15'11–dc22

                                                    2009051056

Printed in the United States of America

10 9 8 7 6 5 4 3 2 1

CONTENTS

PART II   ACCOUNTING MANAGEMENT   131

PART V PUBLIC COMPANY ACCOUNTING 379

PREFACE

*T*his is a handy pocket problem solver for the controller. It covers the multitude of areas that a controller may address during the working day — accounting standards, management issues, financial analysis, controls, and even how to handle a variety of public company issues. It does so with hundreds of concise explanations that are supported by a multitude of examples, tables, charts, and ratios. The layout is designed for quick comprehension of such questions as:

- Should I report revenue at gross or net?
- What are the different types of marketable securities, and how do I account for them?
- How do I use the FIFO and LIFO inventory valuation methods?
- How do I account for bond discounts and premiums?
- How do I record a treasury stock transaction?
- When is a lease a capital lease?
- How do I convert foreign currency transactions into the home currency?
- How do I achieve a fast close?
- How do I set up cash sweeping or notional pooling?
- How do I create a perpetual inventory system?
- What exemptions are available for stock registrations?
- How do I create a throughput analysis model?
- How do I set long-range prices?
- How do I create a spend analysis system?
- Should I lease an asset or buy it?
- What controls should I implement for the core accounting systems?

Part I (Chapters 1–8) covers the most heavily used GAAP accounting standards. These standards are segregated into the topics of revenue recognition, investments, inventory, fixed assets, debt, stockholders' equity, leases, and foreign currency accounting. Numerous explanatory examples are intermingled with the text.

Part II (Chapters 9–14) addresses a number of management areas that a controller is likely to encounter. These include a discussion of the steps needed to close the books, the banking structures needed to marshal cash into the proper investments, how to accelerate the collection of receivables, what can be done to minimize the investment in inventory, what types of debt are available, and how to register equity for sale.

Part III (Chapters 15–18) delves into a variety of financial analysis topics, with a particular focus on bottleneck analysis, how to set prices correctly, and how to reduce costs. Chapter 18 contains a number of the metrics that a controller is most likely to need, along with helpful examples.

Part IV (Chapters 19–21) describes the primary control systems that a controller needs to ensure that transactions are as error-free as possible. It also describes a comprehensive budgeting system and how to analyze capital budgeting proposals so that only truly necessary assets are acquired.

Part V (Chapters 22–23) covers a number of the more common reports that must be filed periodically with the SEC as well as the accounting issues that are specific to the public company: earnings per share, interim reporting, and segment reporting.

Throughout, *The Vest Pocket Controller* has been structured to provide concise answers to the questions that a controller is most likely to encounter during a typical business day. Keep it handy for easy reference and daily use.

ABOUT THE AUTHOR

Steven Bragg, CPA, has been the chief financial officer or controller of four companies as well as a consulting manager at Ernst & Young and auditor at Deloitte & Touche. He received a master's degree in finance from Bentley College, an MBA from Babson College, and a bachelor's degree in economics from the University of Maine. He has been the two-time president of the Colorado Mountain Club and is an avid alpine skier, mountain biker, and certified master diver. Mr. Bragg resides in Centennial, Colorado. He has written the following books through John Wiley & Sons except where indicated:

Accounting and Finance for Your Small Business
Accounting Best Practices
Accounting Control Best Practices
Accounting Policies and Procedures Manual
Advanced Accounting Systems (Institute of Internal Auditors)
Billing and Collections Best Practices
Business Ratios and Formulas
The Controller's Function
Controller's Guide to Costing
Controller's Guide to Planning and Controlling Operations
Controller's Guide: Roles and Responsibilities for the New Controller
Controllership
Cost Accounting
Cost Reduction Analysis
Essentials of Payroll
Fast Close
Financial Analysis
GAAP Guide
GAAP Policies and Procedures Manual
GAAS Guide
Inventory Accounting
Inventory Best Practices
Investor Relations
Just-in-Time Accounting
Management Accounting Best Practices
Managing Explosive Corporate Growth
Mergers and Acquisitions

The New CFO Financial Leadership Manual
Outsourcing
Payroll Accounting
Payroll Best Practices
Revenue Recognition
Run the Rockies (CMC Press)
Running a Public Company
Sales and Operations for Your Small Business
The Ultimate Accountants' Reference
The Vest Pocket Controller
Throughput Accounting
Treasury Management

FREE ONLINE RESOURCES BY STEVE BRAGG

Mr. Bragg Steve issues a free accounting best practices podcast. You can sign up for it at www.accountingtools.com, or access it through iTunes.

PART I

ACCOUNTING STANDARDS

CHAPTER 1

REVENUE RECOGNITION

When Can I Report Revenue at Gross Instead of Net?

*R*eporting on a "gross" basis is appropriate when the entity takes ownership of the goods being sold to its customers, with the risks and rewards of ownership accruing to it. For example, if the entity runs the risk of obsolescence or spoilage during the period it holds the merchandise, gross reporting would normally be appropriate. However, if the entity merely acts as an agent for the buyer or seller from which it earns a commission, "net" reporting would be more appropriate. These factors are indicators that revenue should be recorded at its gross amount:

- The company that is the primary obligor in the arrangement is the company responsible for the fulfillment of the order, including the acceptability of the product or service to the customer.
- The company has general inventory risk. This exists if a company takes title to a product before the product is ordered by a customer or will take title to the product if the customer returns it.
- The company has physical loss inventory risk. This exists if the title to the product is transferred to the company at the shipping point and then transferred to the customer upon delivery.
- The company establishes the selling price.
- The company changes the product or performs part of the service.
- The company has multiple suppliers for the product or service ordered by the customer.
- The company is involved in determining the nature, type, characteristics, or specifications of the product or service by the customer.
- The company has credit risk for the amount billed to the customer. This exists if the company must pay

the supplier irrespective of whether the customer has paid.

A company should record revenue at its net value if a preponderance of the preceding bullet points were not the case, and especially if it is being paid what is in essence a commission.

How Does the Installment Method Work?

Under the *installment method*, revenue recognition is deferred until the period of cash collection. The seller recognizes both revenues and cost of sales at the time of the sale; however, the related gross profit is deferred to those periods in which cash is collected. The installment method can be used in most sales transactions for which payment is to be made through periodic installments over an extended period of time and the collectibility of the sales price cannot be reasonably estimated. This method is applicable to the sales of real estate, heavy equipment, home furnishings, and other merchandise sold on an installment basis. The six to use in accounting for sales under the installment method are presented next.

1. During the current year, record sales and cost of sales in the regular manner. Record installment sales transactions separately from other sales. Set up installment accounts receivable identified by the year of sale (e.g., Installment Accounts Receivable—2010).
2. Record cash collections from installment accounts receivable. Cash receipts must be properly identified as to the year in which the receivable arose.
3. At the end of the current year, transfer installment sales revenue and installment cost of sales to deferred gross profit properly identified by the year of sale. Compute the current year's gross profit rate on installment sales as follows:

$$\text{Gross profit rate} = 1 - \left(\frac{\text{Cost of installment sales}}{\text{Installment sales revenue}} \right)$$

Alternatively, the gross profit rate can be computed as follows:

$$\text{Gross profit rate} = \frac{\text{Installment sales revenue} - \text{Cost of installment sales}}{\text{Installment sales revenue}}$$

4. Apply the current year's gross profit rate to the cash collections from the current year's installment sales

to compute the realized gross profit from the current year's installment sales.

Realized gross profit =
> Cash collections from current year's installment sales × Current year's gross profit rate

5. Separately apply each of the previous years' gross profit rates to cash collections from those years' installment sales to compute the realized gross profit from each of the previous years' installment sales.

Realized gross profit =
> Cash collections from previous years' installment sales × Previous years' gross profit rate

6. Defer the current year's unrealized gross profit to future years. The deferred gross profit to carry forward to future years is computed as follows:

Deferred gross profit (2010) =
> Ending balance installment account receivable (2010) × Gross profit rate (2010)

Can I Recognize Revenue When There Is a Right of Return?

A company can record revenue from a sales transaction at the time of the sale if all of the next conditions are met, and the company must accrue any estimated losses (such as warranty or sales returns) at the same time:

- The sale price is fixed on the sale date.
- The buyer is obligated to pay the seller.
- The buyer's payment obligation would not be changed if the product is subsequently damaged or destroyed.
- The seller does not have significant future performance obligations connected to the sale.
- The amount of future returns can be reasonably estimated.

When Can I Record Bill-and-Hold Sales?

In a *bill-and-hold* situation, a company bills its customer but stores the sold goods on behalf of the customer. This scenario presents a high risk for fraud, since customers may not agree to or be aware of the sales. Accordingly, all of the next factors must be present before a bill-and-hold transaction can be recorded as revenue:

- ○ The customer requests this arrangement.
- ○ The customer has a substantial business purpose for doing so.
- ○ There is a fixed delivery schedule to the customer.
- ○ The goods are both segregated and ready for shipment.

How Does the Percentage-of-Completion Method Work?

The principal method for recognizing revenue under a long-term construction contract is the *percentage-of-completion method*. It recognizes income as work on a contract (or group of closely related contracts) progresses. The recognition of revenues and profits is related to costs incurred in providing the services required under the contract.

Under this method, work in progress (WIP) is accumulated in the accounting records. If the cumulative billings to date under the contract exceed the amount of the WIP plus the portion of the contract's estimated gross profit attributable to that WIP, the contractor recognizes a current liability captioned "billings in excess of costs and estimated earnings." This liability recognizes the remaining obligation of the contractor to complete additional work prior to recognizing the excess billing as revenue.

If the reverse is true — that is, the accumulated WIP and gross profit earned exceed billings to date — the contractor recognizes a current asset captioned "costs and estimated earnings in excess of billings." This asset represents the portion of the contractor's revenues under the contract that have been earned but not yet billed under the contract provisions. Where more than one contract exists, these assets and liabilities are determined on a project-by-project basis, with the accumulated assets and liabilities being separately stated on the balance sheet. Assets and liabilities are not offset unless a right of offset exists. Thus, the net debit balances for certain contracts are not ordinarily offset against net credit balances for other contracts.

How Does the Completed-Contract Method Work?

The *completed-contract method* recognizes income only when a construction contract is complete or substantially complete. It is most commonly used for shorter-duration contracts or when it is not possible to use the percentage-of-completion method.

Under this method, contract costs and related billings are accumulated in the accounting records and reported as deferred items on the balance sheet until the project is complete or substantially complete. A contract is regarded as substantially complete if remaining costs of completion are immaterial. When the accumulated costs (WIP) exceed the related billings, the excess is presented as a current asset (inventory account). If billings exceed related costs, the difference is presented as a current liability. This determination is also made on a project-by-project basis with the accumulated assets and liabilities being stated separately on the balance sheet. An excess of accumulated costs over related billings is presented as a current asset, and in most cases an excess of accumulated billings over related costs is presented as a current liability.

 ## What Types of Pricing Arrangements Are Used in Contracts?

There are four types of contracts based on their pricing arrangements.

1. *Fixed-price contracts.* Contracts for which the price is not usually subject to adjustment because of costs incurred by the contractor. The contractor bears the risks of cost overruns.
2. *Time-and-materials contracts.* Contracts that provide for payments to the contractor based on direct labor hours at fixed rates and the contractor's cost of materials.
3. *Cost-type contracts.* Contracts that provide for reimbursement of allowable or otherwise defined costs incurred plus a fee representing profits.
4. *Unit-price contracts.* Contracts under which the contractor is paid a specified amount for every unit of work performed.

EXAMPLE

Domino Construction Inc. enters into a government contract to construct an early warning radar dome. The contract amount is for $1,900,000, on which Domino expects to incur costs of $1,750,000 and earn
(Continued)

(Continued)
a profit of $150,000. Costs expected to be incurred on
the project are:

Concrete pad	175,000
Pad installation labor	100,000
Radar dome	1,150,000
Dome installation labor	325,000
Total cost	1,750,000

This is a two-month project, where a concrete pad
is installed during the first month and a prefabri-
cated dome is assembled on the pad during the
second month. To comply with bank loan agreements,
complete generally accepted accounting principles
(GAAP)–basis financial statements are prepared by
Domino at each month-end. Domino encounters problems pouring the concrete pad, requiring its removal
and reinstallation. The extra cost incurred is $175,000.
During the second month, in order to meet the completion deadline, Domino spends an extra $35,000 on
overtime for the dome construction crew. Domino
records different billable amounts and profits under
these five contract scenarios:

1. *Fixed-price contract.* At the end of the first month of
   work, Domino has already lost all of its profit and
   expects to incur an additional loss of $25,000. It
   then incurs an additional loss of $35,000 in the sec-
   ond month. Domino issues one billing upon completion of the project. Its calculation of losses on
   the contract is presented next.

	Month 1	Month 2
Total billing at completion	1,900,000	1,900,000
– Expected total costs	(1,750,000)	(1,925,000)
– Additional costs	(175,000)	(35,000)
+ Loss already recorded	—	25,000
= Loss to record in current period	(25,000)	(35,000)

2. *Cost plus fixed fee.* Domino completes the same
   project but bills it to the government at cost at the
   end of each month and also bills a $150,000 fixed
   fee at the end of the project that is essentially a
   project management fee and which comprises all

of Domino's profit. The project completion entry follows.

	Month 1	Month 2	Totals
Expected material costs	175,000	1,150,000	1,325,000
+ Additional material costs	175,000	–	175,000
+ Expected labor costs	100,000	325,000	425,000
+ Additional labor costs	–	35,000	35,000
+ Fixed fee	–	150,000	150,000
= Total billing	450,000	1,660,000	2,110,000

3. *Cost plus award.* Domino completes the same cost-plus-fixed-fee contract just described but also bills the government an additional $50,000 for achieving the stipulated construction deadline, resulting in a total profit of $200,000. The project completion entry is presented next.

	Month 1	Month 2	Totals
Expected material costs	175,000	1,150,000	1,325,000
+ Additional material costs	175,000	–	175,000
+ Expected labor costs	100,000	325,000	425,000
+ Additional labor costs	–	35,000	35,000
+ Fixed fee	–	150,000	150,000
+ Timely completion bonus	–	50,000	50,000
= Total billing	450,000	1,710,000	2,160,000

4. *Time-and-materials contract with no spending cap.* Domino completes the same project but bills all costs incurred at the end of each month to the government. The additional material cost of the concrete pad is billed at cost, while the overtime incurred is billed at a standard hourly rate with a 25% markup. Domino's profit is contained within the markup on its labor billings. Domino records a profit on the project of $115,000 on total billings of $2,075,000. Its calculation of profits on the contract is:

	Month 1	Month 2	Totals
Expected material costs	175,000	1,150,000	1,325,000
+ Additional material costs	175,000	–	175,000

(Continued)

(*Continued*)

	Month 1	Month 2	Totals
+ Expected labor costs	100,000	325,000	425,000
+ Additional labor costs	–	35,000	35,000
+ 25% profit on labor costs billed	25,000	90,000	115,000
= Total billing	475,000	1,600,000	2,075,000

5. *Time-and-materials contract with spending cap.* Domino completes the same time-and-materials project just described, but the contract authorization is divided into two task orders: one authorizing a spending cap of $450,000 on the concrete pad installation while the other caps spending on the radar dome at $1,500,000. Domino records a loss of $10,000 on total billings of $1,950,000. Its calculation of profits on the contract is:

	Month 1	Month 2	Totals
Expected material costs	175,000	1,150,000	1,325,000
+ Additional material costs	175,000	–	175,000
+ Expected labor costs	100,000	325,000	425,000
+ Additional labor costs	–	35,000	35,000
+ 25% profit on labor costs billed	25,000	90,000	115,000
– Spending cap limitation	(25,000)	(100,000)	(125,000)
= Total billing	450,000	1,500,000	1,950,000

 How Do I Account for Contract Losses?

When the current estimate of total contract costs exceeds the current estimate of total contract revenues, a provision for the entire loss on the entire contract is made. Losses are recognized in the period in which they become evident. The loss is computed on the basis of the total estimated costs to complete the contract, including the contract costs incurred to date plus estimated costs (use the same elements as contract costs incurred) to complete. The loss is presented as a separately captioned current liability on the balance sheet.

In any year when a percentage-of-completion contract has an expected loss, the amount of the loss reported in that year is computed in this way:

Reported loss =

Total expected loss + All profit previously recognized

How Do I Account for Additional Claims under a Contract?

Claims represent amounts in excess of the agreed-on contract price that a contractor seeks to collect from customers for unanticipated additional costs. The recognition of additional contract revenue relating to claims is appropriate if it is probable that the claim will result in additional revenue and if the amount can be estimated reliably. All of the next four conditions must exist in order for the probable and estimable requirements to be satisfied.

1. The contract or other evidence provides a legal basis for the claim.
2. Additional costs are not the result of deficiencies in the contractor's performance.
3. Additional costs are identifiable and reasonable.
4. The evidence supporting the claim is objective and verifiable, not based on management's "feel" for the situation or on unsupported representations.

How Does the Deposit Method Work?

The *deposit method* is used in a real estate sale where the sale is, in substance, the sale of an option and not real estate. The seller does not recognize any profit and does not record a receivable. Cash received from the buyer (initial and continuing investments) is reported as a deposit on the contract. However, some cash may be received that is not subject to refund, such as interest on the unrecorded principal. These amounts are used to offset any carrying charges on the property. If the interest collected on the unrecorded receivable is refundable, the seller records this interest as a deposit before the sale is completed and then includes it as a part of the initial investment once the sale is consummated. If deposits on retail land sales eventually are recognized as sales, the interest portion of the deposit is recognized separately as interest income. For contracts that are canceled, the nonrefundable amounts are recognized as income and the refundable amounts are returned to the depositor at the time of cancellation.

EXAMPLE

Elbrus Investments enters into two separate property acquisition transactions with the Buena Vista Land Company.

1. Elbrus pays a $50,000 deposit and promises to pay an additional $800,000 to buy land and a building in an area not yet properly zoned for the facility Elbrus intends to construct. Final acquisition of the property is contingent upon these zoning changes. Buena Vista does not record the receivable, and records the deposit with the following entry:

Cash	50,000	
Customer deposits		50,000

   Part of the purchase agreement stipulates that Buena Vista will retain all interest earned on the deposit and that 10% of the deposit is nonrefundable. Buena Vista earns 5% interest on Elbrus's deposit over a period of four months, resulting in $208 of interest income that is offset against the property tax expenses of the property with the next entry:

Cash	208	
Property tax expense		208

   Immediately thereafter, the required zoning changes are turned down, and Elbrus cancels the sales contract. Buena Vista returns the refundable portion of the deposit to Elbrus and records the nonrefundable portion as income with this entry:

Customer deposits	50,000	
Income from contract cancellation		10,000
Cash		40,000

2. Elbrus pays a $40,000 deposit on land owned and being improved by Buena Vista. Elbrus immediately begins paying $5,000/month under a four-year, 7% loan agreement totaling $212,000 of principal payments and agrees to pay an additional $350,000 at closing, subject to the land being approved for residential construction. After two

months, Buena Vista has earned $167 of refundable interest income on Elbrus's deposit and has been paid $7,689 of refundable principal and $2,311 of refundable interest on the debt. Buena Vista records these events with the next entry.

Cash	10,167	
Customer deposits		10,167

The land is approved for residential construction, triggering sale of the property. Buena Vista's basis in the property is $520,000. Buena Vista uses the next entry to describe completion of the sale.

Cash	350,000	
Note receivable	204,311	
Customer deposits	50,167	
Gain on asset sale		84,478
Land		520,000

 ## How Do I Account for Installation Fees?

A fee may be charged to install equipment. If customers normally cannot purchase the equipment in a separate transaction, the installation fee is considered an advance charge for future services. The fee is recognized as revenue over the estimated service period. The costs of installation and the installed equipment are amortized over the period the equipment is expected to generate revenue. If customers normally can purchase the equipment in a separate transaction, the installation fee is part of a product transaction that is accounted for separately as such.

EXAMPLE

Vintner Corporation has invented a nitrogen injection device for resealing opened wine bottles, which it calls NitroSeal. The device is especially useful for restaurants, which can seal wine bottles opened for customers who want to take home unfinished wine. Because the NitroSeal device is massive, Vintner pays

(*Continued*)

(*Continued*)

a third party to install each unit for a fixed fee of $200, charging restaurants a $300 nonrefundable installation fee plus a monthly fee for a 20-month cancelable contract. The initial entries to record an installation charge from a supplier and related installation billing to a customer are:

Installation asset	200	
Accounts payable		200
Accounts receivable	300	
Unearned installation fees (liability)		300

Vintner recognizes the installation revenue and associated installation expense for each installation in 1/20 increments to match the contract length, each with this entry:

Unearned installation fees	15	
Installation revenue		15
Installation expense	10	
Installation asset		10

A customer cancels its contract with Vintner after 5 months. As a result, Vintner accelerates all remaining amortization on the installation asset and recognizes all remaining unearned installation fees at once, using the next entries.

Unearned installation fees	225	
Installation revenue		225
Installation expense	150	
Installation asset		150

If the service contract had included a clause for a refundable installation fee, then cancelation after five months would still have resulted in immediate acceleration of amortization on the installation asset. However, the unearned installation revenue could not be recognized. Instead, this entry would have recorded the return of the installation fee:

Unearned installation fees	225	
Cash		225

What Recognition Methods Can I Use for Service Billings?

Once a transaction is determined to be a service transaction, one of four methods is used to recognize revenue. The method chosen is to be based on the nature and extent of the service(s) to be performed.

1. *Specific performance method.* This method is used when performance consists of the execution of a single act. Revenue is recognized at the time the act takes place. For example, a stockbroker records sales commissions as revenue upon the sale of a client's investment.

2. *Proportional performance method.* This method is used when performance consists of a number of identical or similar acts.

   a. If the service transaction involves a specified number of identical or similar acts, an equal amount of revenue is recorded for each act performed.
   b. If the service transaction involves a specified number of defined but not identical or similar acts, the revenue recognized for each act is based on this formula:

   $$\frac{\text{Direct cost of individual act}}{\text{Total estimated direct costs of the transaction}}$$
   $$\times \text{ Total revenues from complete transaction}$$

   c. If the service transaction involves an unspecified number of acts over a fixed time period for performance, revenue is recognized over the period during which the acts will be performed by using the straight-line method unless a better method of relating revenue and performance is appropriate.

EXAMPLE

The Cheyenne Snow Removal Company enters into a contract with the Western Office Tower to plow its parking lot. The contract states that Cheyenne will receive a fixed payment of $500 to clear Western's central parking lot whenever snowfall exceeds two inches. Following an unusually snowy winter, Western elects to cap its snow removal costs by tying Cheyenne into an annual $18,000 fixed price for snow removal, no matter how many snowstorms occur. Snowfall is not

(Continued)

(Continued)

predictable by month and can occur over as much as a six-month period. Western pays the full amount in advance, resulting in the next entry by Cheyenne.

Cash	18,000	
Customer advances		18,000

Although Cheyenne could recognize revenue on a straight-line basis through the contract period, it chooses to tie recognition more closely to actual performance with the proportional performance method. Its total estimated direct cost through the contract period is likely to be $12,600, based on its average costs in previous years. There is one snowstorm in October, which costs Cheyenne $350 for snow removal under the Western contract. Cheyenne's revenue recognition calculation in October is

$$\frac{\$350 \text{ direct cost}}{\$12,600 \text{ total direct cost}} \times \$18,000 \text{ total revenue}$$
$$= \$500 \text{ revenue recognition}$$

Thus, Cheyenne recognizes a gross margin of $150 during the month. By the end of February, Cheyenne has conducted snow removal 28 times at the same margin, resulting in revenue recognition of $14,000 and a gross margin of $4,200. Cheyenne's cumulative entry for all performance under the Western contract to date is:

Customer advances	14,000	
Direct labor expense	9,800	
Revenue		14,000
Cash		9,800

In March, Cheyenne removes snow 12 more times at a cost of $4,200. Its initial revenue recognition calculation during this month is

$$\frac{\$4,200 \text{ direct cost}}{\$12,600 \text{ total direct cost}} \times \$18,000 \text{ total revenue}$$
$$= \$6,000 \text{ revenue recognition}$$

However, this would result in total revenue recognition of $20,000, which exceeds the contract fixed fee by $2,000. Accordingly, Cheyenne only recognizes sufficient revenue to maximize the contract cap, resulting in a loss of $200 for the month.

Customer advances	4,000	
Direct labor expense	4,200	
Revenue		4,000
Cash		4,200

3. *Completed performance method.* This method is used when more than one act must be performed and when the final act is so significant to the entire transaction taken as a whole that performance cannot be considered to have taken place until the performance of that final act occurs.

4. *Collection method.* This method is used in circumstances when there is a significant degree of uncertainty surrounding the collection of service revenue. Under this method, revenue is not recognized until the cash is collected.

How Do I Record Revenue for Franchise Sales?

Revenue is recognized, with a provision for bad debts, when the franchisor has substantially performed all material services or conditions. Only when revenue is collected over an extended period of time and collectibility cannot be predicted in advance would the use of the installment method of revenue recognition be appropriate. Substantial performance means:

○ The franchisor has no remaining obligation to either refund cash or forgive any unpaid balance due.
○ Substantially all initial services required by the agreement have been performed.
○ No material obligations or conditions remain.

If initial franchise fees are large compared to services rendered and continuing franchise fees are small compared to services to be rendered, a portion of the initial fee is deferred in an amount sufficient to cover the costs of future services plus a reasonable profit, after considering the impact of the continuing franchise fee.

EXAMPLE

Shanghai Oriental Cuisine sells a Quack's Roast Duck franchise to Toledo Restaurants. The franchise is renewable after two years. The initial franchise fee is $50,000, plus a fixed fee of $500 per month. In exchange, Shanghai provides staff training, vendor relations support, and site selection consulting. Each month thereafter, Shanghai provides $1,000 of free local advertising. Shanghai's typical gross margin on franchise start-up sales is 25%.

Because the monthly fee does not cover the cost of monthly services provided, Shanghai defers a portion of the initial franchise fee and amortizes it over the two-year life of the franchise agreement, using the next calculation.

Cost of monthly services provided $1000 × 24 months	= $24,000
÷ Markup to equal standard 25% gross margin	= .75
= Estimated revenue required to offset monthly services provided	= $32,000
Less: Monthly billing to franchise $500 × 24 months	= $12,000
= Amount of initial franchise fee to be deferred	= $20,000

Shanghai's entry to record the franchise fee deferral follows.

Franchise fee revenue	20,000	
Unearned franchise fees (liability)		20,000

Shanghai recognizes 1/24 of the unearned franchise fee liability during each month of the franchise period on a straight-line basis, which amounts to $833.33 per month.

CHAPTER 2

INVESTMENT ACCOUNTING

 ### Which Securities Are Designated as Marketable Equity Securities?

Marketable securities are investments that can be easily liquidated through an organized exchange, such as the New York Stock Exchange. If a company also holds securities that are intended for the control of another entity, these securities should be segregated as a long-term investment. Marketable securities must be grouped into one of three categories at the time of purchase and reevaluated periodically to see if they still belong in the designated categories:

1. *Available for sale.* This category includes both debt and equity securities. It contains those securities that do not readily fall into either of the next two categories. It can include investments in other companies that comprise less than 20% of total ownership.
2. *Held to maturity.* This category includes only debt securities for which the company has both the intent and the ability to hold them until their time of maturity.
3. *Trading securities.* This category includes both debt and equity securities that the company intends to sell in the short term for a profit. It can include investments in other companies comprising less than 20% of total ownership.

What Is the Accounting for Marketable Equity Securities?

Available-for-sale securities are reported on the balance sheet at their fair value, while unrealized gains and losses are charged to an equity account and reported in other comprehensive income in the current period. The balance in the equity account is eliminated only upon sale of the underlying securities. If a permanent reduction in the value of an individual security occurs, the unrealized loss is charged against earnings, resulting in a new and lower cost basis in the remaining investment. Any subsequent increase in the value of such an investment above the new cost basis cannot be formally recognized in earnings until the related security is sold, and so the interim gains will be temporarily parked in the unrealized gains account in the equity section of the balance sheet.

All interest, realized gains or losses, and debt amortization for available-for-sale securities are recognized within the continuing operations section of the income statement. The listing of these securities on the balance sheet under either current or long-term assets is dependent on their ability to be liquidated in the short term and to be available for disposition within that time frame, unencumbered by any obligations.

The amortized cost of *held-to-maturity* securities is recorded on the balance sheet. These securities are likely to be listed on the balance sheet as long-term assets. If marketable securities are shifted into the held-to-maturity category from debt securities in the available-for-sale category, their unrealized holding gain or loss should continue to be stored in the equity section while being gradually amortized down to zero over the remaining life of each security.

Trading securities are recorded on the balance sheet at their fair value. This type of security is always positioned in the balance sheet as a current asset.

EXAMPLE

AVAILABLE-FOR-SALE TRANSACTIONS

The Arabian Knights Security Company has purchased $100,000 of equity securities, which it does not intend to sell in the short term for profit, and therefore designates as available for sale. Its initial entry to record the transaction is:

	Debit	Credit
Investments—available for sale	$100,000	
Cash		$100,000

After a month, the fair market value of the securities drops by $15,000, but management considers the loss to be a temporary decline, and so does not record a loss in current earnings. However, it must still alter the value of the investment on the balance sheet to show its fair value, and report the loss in Other Comprehensive Income, which requires this entry:

	Debit	Credit
Unrealized loss on security investment (reported in Other Comprehensive Income)	$15,000	
Investments—available for sale		$15,000

Management then obtains additional information indicating that the loss is likely to be a permanent one, so it then recognizes the loss with this entry:

	Debit	Credit
Loss on equity securities	$15,000	
Unrealized loss on security investment (reported in Other Comprehensive Income)		$15,000

Another month passes by and the fair value of the investment rises by $3,500. Since this gain exceeds the value of the newly written-down investment, management cannot recognize it, even though the new value of the investment would still be less than its original amount. Instead, this entry is used to adjust the investment value on the balance sheet:

	Debit	Credit
Investments—available for sale	$3,500	
Unrealized gain on security investment (recorded in Other Comprehensive Income)		$3,500

EXAMPLE

TRADING TRANSACTIONS

The Arabian Knights Security Company purchases $50,000 of equity securities that it intends to trade for a profit in the short term. Given its intentions, these
(Continued)

(*Continued*)
securities are added to the corporate portfolio of trading securities with this entry:

	Debit	Credit
Investments—held for trading	$50,000	
Cash		$50,000

After two months, the fair value of these trading securities declines by $3,500. The company recognizes the change in current earnings with this entry:

	Debit	Credit
Loss on security investment	$3,500	
Investments—held for trading		$3,500

Later in the year, the fair value of the securities experiences a sudden surge, resulting in a value increase of $5,750. The company records the change with this entry:

	Debit	Credit
Investments—held for trading	$5,750	
Gain on security investments		$5,750

What Is the Accounting for Transfers between Available-for-Sale and Trading Investments?

An investment designated as a trading security can be shifted into the available for sale portfolio of investments with no recognition of a gain or loss on the value of the investment, since this type of investment should have been adjusted to its fair value in each reporting period already. If a gain or loss has arisen since the last adjustment to fair value, this amount should be recognized at the time of the designation change.

If an investment designated as an available-for-sale security is shifted into the trading portfolio of investments, any gain or loss required to immediately adjust its value to fair value should be made at once. This entry should include an adjustment from any prior write-down in value that may have occurred when securities were classified as available for sale.

EXAMPLE

TRANSFER FROM THE TRADING PORTFOLIO TO THE AVAILABLE-FOR-SALE PORTFOLIO

The Arabian Knights Security Company owns $17,500 of equity securities that it had originally intended to sell for a profit in the short term and so had classified the investment in its trading portfolio. Its intent has now changed, and it wishes to hold the securities for a considerably longer period, so it must shift the securities into the available-for-sale account. It had marked the securities to market one month previously, but now the securities have lost $350 of value. The company records the next entry to reclassify the security and recognize the additional loss:

	Debit	Credit
Investments—available for sale	$17,150	
Loss on equity securities	350	
Investments—held for trading		$17,500

EXAMPLE

TRANSFER FROM THE AVAILABLE-FOR-SALE PORTFOLIO TO THE TRADING PORTFOLIO

The Arabian Knights Security Company finds that it must liquidate $250,000 of its available-for-sale portfolio in the short term. This investment had previously been marked down to $250,000 from an initial investment value of $275,000, and its value has since risen by $12,000. The incremental gain must now be recognized in current income. The entry is:

	Debit	Credit
Investments—held for trading	$262,000	
Investments—available for sale		$250,000
Gain on security investments		12,000

What Is the Accounting for Investments in Debt Securities?

A debt security can be classified as held for trading or available for sale, or as held to maturity. The held-to-maturity portfolio is intended for any debt securities for which a company has the intent and ability to retain the security for its full term until maturity is reached. An investment held in the held-to-maturity portfolio is recorded at its historical cost, which is not changed at any time during the holding period, unless it is shifted into a different investment portfolio. The only two exceptions to this rule are:

1. The periodic amortization of any discount or premium from the face value of a debt instrument, depending on the initial purchase price; and
2. Clear evidence of a permanent reduction in the value of the investment.

EXAMPLE

The Arabian Knights Security Company purchases $82,000 of debt securities at face value. The company has both the intent and ability to hold the securities to maturity. Given its intentions, these securities are added to the corporate portfolio of held-to-maturity securities with this entry:

	Debit	Credit
Investment in debt securities—held to maturity	$82,000	
Cash		$82,000

The fair value of the investment subsequently declines by $11,000. There is no entry to be made, since the investment is recorded at its historical cost. However, the company receives additional information that the debt issuer has filed for bankruptcy and intends to repay debt holders at 50 cents on the dollar. Since management considers this to be a permanent reduction, a charge of $41,000 is recorded in current income with this entry:

	Debit	Credit
Loss on debt investment		$41,000
Investment in debt securities—held to maturity	$41,000	

The company subsequently learns that the debt issuer is instead able to pay 75 cents on the dollar. This increase in value of $20,500 is not recorded in a journal entry, since it is a recovery of value, but is instead recorded in a footnote accompanying the financial statements.

What Is the Accounting for Debt Securities among Portfolios?

The accounting for transfers among debt securities portfolios varies based on the portfolio from which the accounts are being shifted, with the basic principle being that transfers are recorded at the fair market value of the security on the date of the transfer. The treatment of gains or losses on all possible transfers is noted in Exhibit 2.1.

The offsetting entry for any gain or loss reported in the Other Comprehensive Income section of the income statement goes to a contra account, which is used to offset the investment account on the balance sheet, thereby revealing the extent of changes in the trading securities from their purchased cost.

"From" Portfolio	"To" Portfolio	Accounting Treatment
Trading	Available for Sale	No entry (assumes gains and losses have already been recorded)
Trading	Held to Maturity	No entry (assumes gains and losses have already been recorded)
Available for sale	Trading	Shift any previously recorded gain or loss shown in Other Comprehensive Income to operating income.
Available for sale	Held to maturity	Amortize to income over the remaining period to debt maturity any previously recorded gain or loss shown in Other Comprehensive Income, using the effective interest method.
Held to maturity	Trading	Record the unrealized gain or loss in operating income.
Held to maturity	Available for sale	Record the unrealized gain or loss in the Other Comprehensive Income section of the income statement.

Exhibit 2.1 ACCOUNTING TREATMENT OF DEBT TRANSFERS BETWEEN PORTFOLIOS

How Are Deferred Tax Effects Recognized for Changes in Investment Valuation?

A deferred tax benefit or tax liability should be recognized alongside the recognition of any change in the fair value of an investment listed in either a trading or available-for-sale portfolio or of a permanent decline in the value of a debt security being held to maturity. The tax impact varies by investment type, and is noted as:

- *Gains or losses on the trading portfolio.* The deferred tax effect is recognized in the income statement. If there is a loss in value, debit the Deferred Tax Benefit account and credit the Provision for Income Taxes account. If there is a gain in value, debit the Provision for Income Taxes account and credit the Deferred Tax Liability account.
- *Gains or losses on the available-for-sale portfolio.* The same treatment noted for gains or losses on the trading portfolio, except that taxes are noted in the Other Comprehensive Income section of the income statement.
- *Gains or losses on the held-to-maturity portfolio.* There is no tax recognition if changes in value are considered to be temporary in nature. If there is a permanent reduction in value, the treatment is identical to the treatment of losses in the trading portfolio, as just noted.

What Is the Accounting for Significant Equity Investments?

There are three ways to account for an investment:

1. Report the investment at its fair value
2. Report it under the "equity method"
3. Fully consolidate the results of the investee in the investing company's financial statements

The rules under which each of these methods is applied are noted in Exhibit 2.2.

The presence of "significant influence" over an investee is assumed if the investor owns at least 20% of its common stock. However, this is not the case if there is clear evidence of not having influence, such as being unable to obtain financial information from the investee, not being able to place a representative on its board of directors,

Investment Method	Proportion of Ownership	Notes
Fair Value	Less than 20% ownership or no significant influence over investee	Record gains or losses based on fair market value of shares held
Equity Method	20% to 50% ownership and significant influence over the investee	Record proportionate share of investee earnings, less dividends received
Consolidation	50%+ ownership of the investee	Fully consolidate results of the investor and investee

Exhibit 2.2   Accounting Treatment of Significant Equity Investments

clear opposition to the investor by the investee, loss of voting rights, or proof of a majority voting block that does not include the investor.

Income taxes are recognized only when dividends are received from an investee or the investment is liquidated. Nonetheless, deferred income taxes are recognized when a company records its share of investee income, and are then shifted from the Deferred Income Tax account to Income Taxes Payable when dividends are received.

As noted in Exhibit 2.2, the equity method of accounting requires one to record the investor's proportionate share of investee earnings, less any dividends received. However, what if the investee records such a large loss that the investor's share of the loss results in a negative investment? When this happens, the correct treatment is to limit the investment to zero and ignore subsequent losses. Resume use of the equity method only if subsequent investee earnings completely offset the losses that had previously been ignored. The main exception to this rule is when the investor has committed to fund investee operations or indemnifies other creditors or investors for losses incurred.

EXAMPLE
The Arabian Knights Security Company purchases 35% of the common stock of the Night Patrollers Security Company for $500,000. At the end of a year, Night Patrollers has earned $80,000 and issued $20,000 in dividends. Under the equity method, Arabian Knights reports a gain in its investment of $28,000 *(Continued)*

(*Continued*)

(35% investment × $80,000 in earnings), less dividends of $7,000 (35% investment × $20,000 in dividends) for a total investment change of $21,000. The two entries required to record these changes are:

	Debit	Credit
Investment in Night Patrollers	$28,000	
Equity in Night Patrollers		$28,000
Cash	$7,000	
Investment in Night Patrollers		$7,000

In addition, Arabian Knight's controller assumes that the investment will eventually be sold, which requires a full corporate tax rate of 34%. Accordingly, the next entry records a deferred income tax on the $28,000 share of Night Patrollers income, while the second entry records the shifting of a portion of this deferred tax to income taxes payable to reflect the company's short-term tax liability for the dividends received (assuming a 34% tax rate for dividend income):

	Debit	Credit
Income tax expense	$9,520	
Deferred taxes		$9,520
Deferred taxes	$2,380	
Taxes payable		$2,380

If a company *increases* its investment in an investee to the 20% to 50% range from a lesser figure, it must convert *to* the equity method of accounting on a retroactive basis. This means the investor must go back to the initial investment date and recalculate its investment using the equity method of accounting. The offset to any resulting adjustment in the investment account must then be charged to the Retained Earnings account as a prior period adjustment. This also requires restatement of prior financial statements in which the fair value method was used to record this investment.

What Is the Accounting for an Investment Amortization?

An investor may pay a premium over the book value of the investee's common stock. When this happens under the equity method, one should informally (i.e., without the use of journal entries) assign the difference in value to other assets and liabilities of the investee to the extent that the fair value of those assets differs from their net book value. Any changes in these assumed assets should be amortized, resulting in a periodic journal entry to reduce the value of the investor's recorded investment.

EXAMPLE

To continue with the last example, 35% of the book value of Night Patrollers Security Company was $350,000, as compared to the $500,000 paid by Arabian for 35% of Night Patrollers. Arabian's controller must assign this differential to the excess fair value of any Night Patrollers assets or liabilities over their book value. The only undervalued Night Patrollers asset category is its fixed assets, to which the controller can assign $30,000. The remaining unassigned $120,000 is designated as goodwill. Given the nature of the underlying assets, the $30,000 assigned to fixed assets should be amortized over five years, resulting in a monthly amortization charge of $500. The monthly journal entry is:

	Debit	Credit
Equity in Night Patrollers income	$500	
Investment in Night Patrollers		$500

What Is the Accounting for an Equity Method Investment Impairment?

Any unassigned excess value in an equity method investment is considered to be goodwill and is subject to annual impairment testing that may result in an additional reduction in the recorded level of investment. An impairment test requires a periodic comparison of the fair value of the investment to the current book value of the investment as recorded by the investor. If the fair value is less than the recorded book value, goodwill is reduced until the re-corded investment value matches the new fair value. If the amount of the reduction is greater than the informal goodwill associated with the transaction, the excess is used to proportionally reduce any amounts previously as-signed to the investee's assets. In effect, a large enough re-duction in the fair value of its investment will result in an immediate write-down of the recorded investment rather than a gradual reduction due to amortization.

EXAMPLE

To continue with the last example, Night Patrollers loses several large security contracts, resulting in a significant reduction in the value of the business. Arabian's controller estimates this loss in value to be $130,000, which requires her to eliminate the entire $120,000 goodwill portion of the initial investment as well as $10,000 that had been assigned to the fixed assets category. This latter reduction results in a de-crease in the monthly amortization charge of $166.66 ($10,000/60 months).

 ## When Is the Equity Method No Longer Used?

If a company *reduces* its investment in an investee to the point where its investment comprises less than 20% of the investee's common stock, it should discontinue use of the equity method of accounting and instead record the in-vestment at its fair value, most likely tracking it as part of the company's available-for-sale portfolio. When the transi-tion occurs from the equity method to the fair value method, no retroactive adjustment in the investment account is required — the investor simply begins using the ending in-vestment balance it had derived under the equity method.

What Are the Key Decisions for Recording Gains or Losses on Securities?

The flowchart in Exhibit 2.3 shows the decision tree for how gains and losses are handled for different types of securities portfolios. The decision flow begins in the upper

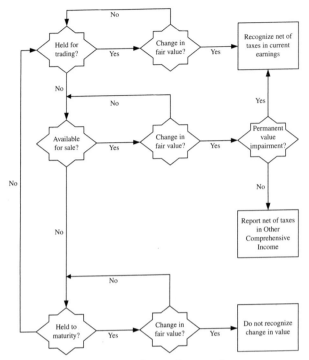

Exhibit 2.3   ACCOUNTING FOR GAINS OR LOSSES ON SECURITIES

left corner. For example, if a security is designated as available for sale and there is a change in its fair value, the decision tree moves to the right, asking if there is a permanent value impairment. If so, the proper treatment matches that of a loss for a held-for-trading security; if not, the proper treatment is listed as being reported in the Other Comprehensive Income section of the income statement.

CHAPTER 3

INVENTORY ACCOUNTING

 How Do I Account for Goods in Transit?

*I*nventory that is in transit to the buyer continues to be owned by the seller as long as that entity is responsible for the transportation costs. If the seller is only paying for transportation to a certain point, such as to a third-party shipper, its ownership stops at that point and is transferred to the buyer.

In reality, companies do not usually track goods in transit, preferring instead to not count them if they have either already left the facility (in the case of the seller) or have not yet arrived at the facility (in the case of the buyer). The reason for avoiding this task is the difficulty in determining the amount of goods in transit that belong to the company. This avoidance has minimal impact on the receiving company's record keeping, since a missing inventory item would have required both a debit to an inventory account and a credit to a liability account, which cancel each other out.

How Does Inventory Ownership Vary under Different Delivery Situations?

The transfer of ownership varies among the buyer, seller, and shipping company, depending on the terms of these types of shipments:

- If goods are shipped under a *cost, insurance, and freight (C&F)* contract, the buyer is paying for all delivery costs and so acquires title to the goods as soon as they leave the seller's location.
- If goods are shipped *free alongside (FAS)*, it is paying for delivery of the goods to the side of the ship that will transport the goods to the buyer. If so, it retains ownership of the goods until they are alongside the

ship, at which point the buyer acquires title to the goods.

○ If goods are shipped *free on board (FOB)* destination, transport costs are paid by the seller, and ownership will not pass to the buyer until the carrier delivers the goods to the buyer.

○ As indicated by the name, an *ex-ship* delivery means that the seller pays for a delivery until it has departed the ship, so it retains title to the goods until that point.

○ If goods are shipped *FOB shipping point,* transport costs are paid by the buyer, and ownership passes to the buyer as soon as the carrier takes possession of the delivery from the seller.

○ If goods are shipped *FOB to a specific point,* such as Nashville, the seller retains title until the goods reach Nashville, at which point ownership transfers to the buyer.

How Do I Account for Consigned Inventory?

Consigned inventory is any inventory shipped by a company to a reseller, while retaining ownership until the product is sold by the reseller. Until sold, the inventory remains on the books of the originating company and not on the books of the reseller. A common cause of inventory valuation problems is the improper recording of consignment inventory on the books of a reseller. Inventory that has been sold with a *right of return* receives treatment similar to consignment inventory if the amount of future inventory returns cannot be reasonably estimated. Until the probability of returns is unlikely, the inventory must remain on the books of the selling company, even though legal title to the goods has passed to the buyer.

EXAMPLE
A company has sold a large shipment of refrigerators to a new customer. Included in the sales agreement is a provision allowing the customer to return one-third of the refrigerators within the next 90 days. Since the company has no experience with this customer, it cannot record the full amount of the sale. Instead, it records that portion of the sale associated with the refrigerators for which there is no right of return and waits 90 days until the right of return has expired before recording the remainder of the sale.

Depreciation of factory equipment	Quality control and inspection
Factory administration expenses	Rent, facility and equipment
Indirect labor and production supervisory wages	Repair expenses
Indirect materials and supplies	Rework labor, scrap and spoilage
Maintenance, factory and production equipment	Taxes related to production assets
Officer salaries related to production	Uncapitalized tools and equipment
Production employees' benefits	Utilities

Exhibit 3.1 Costs to Allocate to Overhead

 ## What Overhead Do I Allocate to Inventory?

All costs can be assigned to inventory that are incurred to put goods in a salable condition. For raw materials, this is the purchase price, inbound transportation costs, insurance, and handling costs. If inventory is in the work-in-process or finished goods stages, an allocation of the overhead costs shown in Exhibit 3.1 must be added.

Allocation of overhead costs can be made by any reasonable measure but must be consistently applied across reporting periods. Common bases for overhead allocation are direct labor hours or machine hours used during the production of a product.

EXAMPLE

A company manufactures and sells Product A and Product B. Both require considerable machining to complete, so it is appropriate to allocate overhead costs to them based on total hours of standard machine time used. In March, Product A manufacturing required a total of 4,375 hours of machine time. During the same month, all units of Product B manufactured required 2,615 hours of machine time. Thus, 63% of the overhead cost pool was allocated to Product A and 37% to Product B. This example results in a reasonably accurate allocation of overhead to products, especially if the bulk of expenses in the overhead
(Continued)

(*Continued*)
pool relate to the machining equipment used to complete the products. However, if a significant proportion of expenses in the overhead cost pool could be reasonably assigned to some other allocation measure, these costs could be stored in a separate cost pool and allocated in a different manner. For example, if Product A was quite bulky and required 90% of the storage space in the warehouse, as opposed to 10% for Product B, 90% of the warehouse-related overhead costs could be reasonably allocated to Product A.

How Do I Account for the Lower of Cost or Market Rule?

A company is required to recognize an additional expense in its cost of goods sold in the current period for any of its inventory whose replacement cost (subject to certain restrictions) has declined below its carrying cost. If the market value of the inventory subsequently rises back to or above its original carrying cost, its recorded value cannot be increased back to the original carrying amount.

More specifically, the *lower of cost or market* (LCM) calculation means that the cost of inventory cannot be recorded higher than its replacement cost on the open market; the replacement cost is bounded at the high end by its eventual selling price, less costs of disposal. Nor can it be recorded lower than that price, less a normal profit percentage. The concept is best demonstrated with the four scenarios listed in the next example.

EXAMPLE

In the next table, the numbers in the first six columns are used to derive the upper and lower boundaries of the market values that will be used for the lower of cost or market calculation. By subtracting the completion and selling costs from each product's selling price, we establish the upper price boundary (in bold) of the market cost calculation. By subtracting the normal profit from the upper cost boundary of each product, we establish the lower price boundary.

Item	Selling Price	− Completion/ Selling Cost	= Upper Price Boundary	− Normal Profit	= Lower Price Boundary	Existing Inventory Cost	Replacement Cost[1]	Market Value[2]	LCM
A	$15.00	$4.00	$11.00	$2.20	$8.80	$8.00	$12.50	$11.00	$8.00
B	40.15	6.00	34.15	5.75	28.40	35.00	34.50	34.15	34.15
C	20.00	6.50	13.50	3.00	10.50	17.00	12.00	12.00	12.00
D	10.50	2.35	8.15	2.25	5.90	8.00	5.25	5.90	5.90

[1] The cost at which an inventory item could be purchased on the open market
[2] Replacement cost, bracketed by the upper and lower price boundaries

(Continued)

(*Continued*)

Using this information, the LCM calculation for each of the listed products is:

○ *Product A, replacement cost higher than existing inventory cost.* The market price cannot be higher than the upper boundary of $11.00, which is still higher than the existing inventory cost of $8.00. Thus, the LCM is the same as the existing inventory cost.

○ *Product B, replacement cost lower than existing inventory cost but higher than upper price boundary.* The replacement cost of $34.50 exceeds the upper price boundary of $34.15, so the market value is designated at $34.15. This is lower than the existing inventory cost, so the LCM becomes $34.15.

○ *Product C, replacement cost lower than existing inventory cost and within price boundaries.* The replacement cost of $12.00 is within the upper and lower price boundaries, and so is used as the market value. This is lower than the existing inventory cost of $17.00, so the LCM becomes $12.00.

○ *Product D, replacement cost lower than existing inventory cost but lower than lower price boundary.* The replacement cost of $5.25 is below the lower price boundary of $5.90, so the market value is designated as $5.90. This is lower than the existing inventory cost of $8.00, so the LCM becomes $5.90.

How Does the First-in, First-out Valuation Method Work?

The *first-in, first-out* (FIFO) valuation method assumes that the oldest parts in stock are always used first, which means that their associated costs are used first as well. The concept is best illustrated with the next example.

EXAMPLE

In the first row of the table shown in Exhibit 3.2, we create a single layer of inventory that results in 50 units of inventory, at a per-unit cost of $10.00. So far, the extended cost of the inventory is the same as we saw under the Last In, First Out, (LIFO), but that will change as we proceed to the second row of data. In this row, we have monthly inventory usage of

Part Number BK0043

Column 1	Column 2	Column 3	Column 4	Column 5	Column 6	Column 7	Column 8	Column 9
Date Purchased	Quantity Purchased	Cost per Unit	Monthly Usage	Net Inventory Remaining	Cost of 1st Inventory Layer	Cost of 2nd Inventory Layer	Cost of 3rd Inventory Layer	Extended Inventory Cost
05/03/10	500	$10.00	450	50	(50 × $10.00)	—	—	$500
06/04/10	1,000	$9.58	350	700	(700 × $9.58)	—	—	$6,706
07/11/10	250	$10.65	400	550	(300 × $9.58)	(250 × $10.65)	—	$5,537
08/01/10	475	$10.25	350	675	(200 × $10.65)	(475 × $10.25)	—	$6,999
08/30/10	375	$10.40	400	650	(275 × $10.40)	(375 × $10.40)	—	$6,760
09/09/10	850	$9.50	700	800	(800 × $9.50)	—	—	$7,600
12/12/10	700	$9.75	900	600	(600 × $9.75)	—	—	$5,850
02/08/11	650	$9.85	800	450	(450 × $9.85)	—	—	$4,433
05/07/11	200	$10.80	0	650	(450 × $9.85)	(200 × $10.80)	—	$6,593
09/23/11	600	$9.85	750	500	(500 × $9.85)	—	—	$4,925

Exhibit 3.2 Inventory Accounting—FIFO

(Continued)

(Continued)

350 units, which FIFO assumes will use the entire stock of 50 inventory units that were left over at the end of the preceding month, as well as 300 units that were purchased in the current month. This wipes out the first layer of inventory, leaving us with a single new layer that is composed of 700 units at a cost of $9.58 per unit. In the third row, there are 400 units of usage, which again comes from the first inventory layer, shrinking it down to just 300 units. However, since extra stock was purchased in the same period, we now have an extra inventory layer that is comprised of 250 units, at a cost of $10.65 per unit. Exhibit 3.2 proceeds using the same FIFO layering assumptions.

What Are the Advantages and Disadvantages of FIFO Valuation?

There are several factors to consider before implementing a FIFO costing system. They are:

- ○ *Fewer inventory layers.* The FIFO system generally results in fewer layers of inventory costs in the inventory database than does a last-in, first out (LIFO) system (as explained next), because a LIFO system will leave some layers of costs completely untouched for long time periods if inventory levels do not drop. Conversely, a FIFO system will continually clear out old layers of costs, so that multiple costing layers do not have a chance to accumulate.

- ○ *Reduces taxes payable in periods of declining costs.* Though it is very unusual to see declining inventory costs, it sometimes occurs in industries where there is either strong price competition among suppliers or else extremely high rates of innovation that in turn lead to cost reductions. In such cases, using the earliest costs first will result in the immediate recognition of the highest possible expense, which reduces the reported profit level and therefore reduces taxes payable.

- ○ *Shows higher profits in periods of rising costs.* Since it charges off the earliest costs first, any very recent increase in costs will be stored in inventory rather than being immediately recognized. This will result in higher levels of reported profits, though the attendant income tax liability will also be higher.

○ *Less risk of outdated costs in inventory.* Because old costs are used first in a FIFO system, there is no way for old and outdated costs that might eventually flow into the cost of goods sold to accumulate in inventory.

How Does the Last-in, First-out Valuation Method Work?

In a supermarket, the shelves are stocked several rows deep with products. A shopper will walk by and pick products from the front row. If the stocking person is lazy, he will then add products to the front row locations from which products were just taken rather than shifting the oldest products to the front row and putting new ones in the back. This concept of always taking the newest products first is called *last-in, first-out*, or LIFO. The concept is best illustrated with an example.

EXAMPLE

The Magic Pen Company has made 10 purchases, which are itemized in the table shown in Exhibit 3.3. The company has purchased 500 units of a product with part number BK0043 on May 3, 2010 (as noted in the first row of data) and uses 450 units during that month, leaving the company with 50 units. These 50 units were all purchased at a cost of $10.00 each, so they are itemized in Column 6 as the first layer of inventory costs for this product. In the next row of data, an additional 1,000 units were bought on June 4, 2010, of which only 350 units were used. This leaves an additional 650 units at a purchase price of $9.58, which are placed in the second inventory layer, as noted on Column 7. In the third row, there is a net decrease in the amount of inventory, so this reduction comes out of the second (or last) inventory layer in Column 7; the earliest layer, as described in Column 6, remains untouched, since it was the first layer of costs added and will not be used until all other inventory has been eliminated. Exhibit 3.3 continues through seven more transactions, at one point increasing to four layers of inventory costs.

Part Number BK0043

Column 1 Date Purchased	Column 2 Quantity Purchased	Column 3 Cost per Unit	Column 4 Monthly Usage	Column 5 Net Inventory Remaining	Column 6 Cost of 1st Inventory Layer	Column 7 Cost of 2nd Inventory Layer	Column 8 Cost of 3rd Inventory Layer	Column 9 Cost of 4th Inventory Layer	Column 10 Extended Inventory Cost
05/03/10	500	$10.00	450	50	(50 × $10.00)	—	—	—	$500
06/04/10	1,000	$9.58	350	700	(50 × $10.00)	(650 × $9.58)	—	—	$6,727
07/11/10	250	$10.65	400	550	(50 × $10.00)	(500 × $9.58)	—	—	$5,290
08/01/10	475	$10.25	350	675	(50 × $10.00)	(500 × $9.58)	(125 × $10.25)	—	$6,571
08/30/10	375	$10.40	400	650	(50 × $10.00)	(500 × $9.58)	(100 × $10.25)	—	$6,315
09/09/10	850	$9.50	700	800	(50 × $10.00)	(500 × $9.58)	(100 × $10.25)	(150 × $9.50)	$7,740
12/12/10	700	$9.75	900	600	(50 × $10.00)	(500 × $9.58)	(50 × $9.58)	—	$5,769
02/08/11	650	$9.85	800	450	(50 × $10.00)	(400 × $9.58)	—	—	$4,332
05/07/11	200	$10.80	0	650	(50 × $10.00)	(400 × $9.58)	(200 × $10.80)	—	$6,492
09/23/11	600	$9.85	750	500	(50 × $10.00)	(400 × $9.58)	(50 × $9.85)	—	$4,825

Exhibit 3.3 INVENTORY ACCOUNTING—LIFO

42

What Are the Advantages and Disadvantages of LIFO Valuation?

There are several factors to consider before implementing a LIFO costing system. They are:

○ *Many layers.* The LIFO cost flow approach can result in a large number of inventory layers, as shown in the exhibit. Though this is not important when a computerized accounting system is used that will automatically track a large number of such layers, it can be burdensome if the cost layers are manually tracked.

○ *Alters the inventory valuation.* If there are significant changes in product costs over time, the earliest inventory layers may contain costs that are wildly different from market conditions in the current period, which could result in the recognition of unusually high or low costs if these cost layers are ever accessed.

○ *Reduces taxes payable in periods of rising costs.* In an inflationary environment, costs that are charged off to the cost of goods sold as soon as they are incurred will result in a higher cost of goods sold and a lower level of profitability, which in turn results in a lower tax liability. This is the principle reason why LIFO is used by most companies.

○ *Requires consistent usage for all reporting.* Under IRS rules, if a company uses LIFO to value its inventory for tax reporting purposes, it must do the same for its external financial reports. The result of this rule is that a company cannot report lower earnings for tax purposes and higher earnings for all other purposes by using an alternative inventory valuation method. However, it is still possible to mention in a footnote what profits would have been if some other method had been used.

○ *Interferes with the implementation of just-in-time systems.* As just noted, clearing out the final cost layers of a LIFO system can result in unusual cost of goods sold figures. If these results will cause a significant skewing of reported profitability, company management may oppose the implementation of advanced manufacturing concepts, such as just-in-time, that reduce or eliminate inventory levels.

How Does the Dollar-Value LIFO Valuation Method Work?

This method computes a conversion price index for the year-end inventory in comparison to the base-year cost. This index is computed separately for each company business unit. The conversion price index can be computed with the *double-extension method*. Under this approach, the total extended cost of the inventory at both base year prices and the most recent prices are calculated. Then the total inventory cost at the most recent prices is divided by the total inventory cost at base year prices, resulting in a conversion price percentage, or index. The index represents the change in overall prices between the current year and the base year. This index must be computed and retained for each year in which the LIFO method is used.

Tax regulations require that any new item added to inventory, no matter how many years after the establishment of the base year, have a base-year cost included in the LIFO database for purposes of calculating the index. This base-year cost is supposed to be the one in existence at the time of the base year, which may require considerable research to determine or estimate. Only if it is impossible to determine a base-year cost can the current cost of a new inventory item be used as the base-year cost.

EXAMPLE

ABC Company carries a single item of inventory in stock. It has retained this year-end information about the item for the past four years:

Year	Ending Unit Quantity	Ending Current Price	Extended at Current Year-End Price
1	3,500	$32.00	$112,000
2	7,000	34.50	241,500
3	5,500	36.00	198,000
4	7,250	37.50	271,875

The first year is the base year upon which the double-extension index will be based in later years. In the second year, ABC extends the total year-end inventory by both the base-year price and the current-year price, as shown next.

Year-End Quantity	Base-Year Cost	Extended at Base-Year Cost	Ending Current Price	Extended at Ending Current Price
7,000	$32.00	$224,000	$34.50	$241,500

To arrive at the index between year 2 and the base year, ABC divides the extended ending current price of $241,500 by the extended base-year cost of $224,000, yielding an index of 107.8%.

The next step is to calculate the incremental amount of inventory added in year 2, determine its cost using base-year prices, and multiply this extended amount by our index of 107.8% to arrive at the cost of the incremental year 2 LIFO layer. The incremental amount of inventory added is the year-end quantity of 7,000 units, less the beginning balance of 3,500 units, which is 3,500 units. When multiplied by the base-year cost of $32.00, ABC arrives at an incremental increase in inventory of $112,000. Finally, ABC multiplies the $112,000 by the price index of 107.8% to determine that the cost of the year 2 LIFO layer is $120,736.

Thus, at the end of year 2, the total double-extension LIFO inventory valuation is the base-year valuation of $112,000 plus the year 2 layer's valuation of $120,736, totaling $232,736.

In year 3, the amount of ending inventory has declined from the previous year, so no new layering calculation is required. Instead, ABC assumes that the entire reduction of 1,500 units during that year was taken from the year 2 inventory layer. To calculate the amount of this reduction, ABC multiplies the remaining amount of the year 2 layer (5,500 units less the base year amount of 3,500 units, or 2,000 units) times the ending base year price of $32.00 and the year 2 index of 107.8%. This calculation results in a new year 2 layer of $68,992.

Thus, at the end of year 3, the total double-extension LIFO inventory valuation is the base layer of $112,000 plus the reduced year 2 layer of $68,992, totaling $180,992.

In year 4, there is an increase in inventory, so ABC calculates the presence of a new layer using the next table.

(*Continued*)

(*Continued*)

Year-End Quantity	Base-Year Cost	Extended at Base-Year Cost	Ending Current Price	Extended at Ending Current Price
7,250	$32.00	$232,000	$37.50	$271,875

Again, ABC divides the extended ending current price of $271,875 by the extended base-year cost of $232,000, yielding an index of 117.2%. To complete the calculation, ABC then multiplies the incremental increase in inventory over year three of 1,750 units, multiplies it by the base-year cost of $32.00/unit, and then multiplies the result by the new index of 117.2% to arrive at a year 4 LIFO layer of $65,632.

Thus, after four years of inventory layering calculations, the double-extension LIFO valuation consists of these three layers:

Layer Type	Layer Valuation	Layer Index
Base layer	$112,000	0.0%
Year 2 layer	68,992	107.8%
Year 4 layer	65,632	117.2%
Total	$246,624	—

How Does the Link-Chain Valuation Method Work?

This approach is designed to avoid the problem encountered during double-extension calculations, where one must determine the base-year cost of each new item added to inventory. However, tax regulations require that the link-chain method be used for tax reporting purposes only if it can be clearly demonstrated that all other dollar-value LIFO calculation methods are not applicable due to high rates of churn in the types of items included in inventory.

The *link-chain method* creates inventory layers by comparing year-end prices to prices at the beginning of each year, thereby avoiding the problems associated with comparisons to a base year that may be many years in the past. This results in a rolling cumulative index that is linked (hence the name) to the index derived in the preceding year. Tax regulations allow one to create the index using a representative sample of the total inventory valuation that must comprise at least one-half of the total inventory valuation. In brief, a link-chain calculation is derived by extending the cost of inventory at both beginning-of-year and end-of-year prices to arrive at a pricing index within the current year; this index is multiplied by the ongoing cumulative index from the previous year to arrive at a new cumulative index that is used to price out the new inventory layer for the most recent year.

EXAMPLE

This example assumes the same inventory information just used for the double-extension example. However, we have also noted the beginning inventory cost for each year and included the extended beginning inventory cost for each year, which facilitates calculations under the link-chain method.

Year	Ending Unit Quantity	Beginning-of-Year Cost/each	End-of-Year Cost/Each	Extended at Beginning-of-Year Price	Extended at End-of-Year Price
1	3,500	$—	$32.00	$—	$112,000
2	7,000	32.00	34.50	224,000	241,500
3	5,500	34.50	36.00	189,750	198,000
4	7,250	36.00	37.50	261,000	271,875

As was the case for the double-extension method, there is no index for year 1, which is the base year. In year 2, the index will be the extended year-end price of $241,500 divided by the extended beginning-of-year price of $224,000, or 107.8%. This is the same percentage calculated for year 2 under the double-extension method, because the beginning-of-year price is the same as the base price used under the double-extension method.

We then determine the value of the year 2 inventory layer by first dividing the extended year-end price of $241,500 by the cumulative index of 107.8% to arrive at an inventory valuation restated to the base-year cost of $224,026. We then subtract the year 1 base layer of $112,000 from the $224,026 to arrive at a new layer at the base-year cost of $112,026, which

(*Continued*)

(*Continued*)

we then multiply by the cumulative index of 107.8%
to bring it back to current-year prices. This results in a
year 2 inventory layer of $120,764. At this point, the
inventory layers are:

Layer Type	Base-Year Valuation	LIFO Layer Valuation	Cumulative Index
Base layer	$112,000	$112,000	0.0%
Year 2 layer	112,026	120,764	107.8%
Total	$224,026	$232,764	—

In year 3, the index will be the extended year-end
price of $198,000 divided by the extended beginning-
of-year price of $189,750, or 104.3%. Since this is the
first year in which the base year was not used to compile beginning-of-year costs, we must first derive the
cumulative index, which is calculated by multiplying
the preceding year's cumulative index of 107.8% by
the new year 3 index of 104.3%, resulting in a new
cumulative index of 112.4%. By dividing year 3's
extended year-end inventory of $198,000 by this
cumulative index, we arrive at inventory priced at
base-year costs of $176,157.

This is less than the amount recorded in year 2, so
there will be no inventory layer. Instead, we must
reduce the inventory layer recorded for year 2. To do
so, we subtract the base-year layer of $112,000 from
the $176,157 to arrive at a reduced year 2 layer of
$64,157 at base-year costs. We then multiply the
$64,157 by the cumulative index in year 2 of 107.8% to
arrive at an inventory valuation for the year 2 layer of
$69,161. At this point, the inventory layers and associ-
ated cumulative indexes are:

Layer Type	Base-Year Valuation	LIFO Layer Valuation	Cumulative Index
Base layer	$112,000	$112,000	0.0%
Year 2 layer	64,157	69,161	107.8%
Year 3 layer	—	—	112.4%
Total	$176,157	$181,161	—

In year 4, the index will be the extended year-end price of $271,875 divided by the extended beginning-of-year price of $261,000, or 104.2%. We then derive the new cumulative index by multiplying the preceding year's cumulative index of 112.4% by the year 4 index of 104.2%, resulting in a new cumulative index of 117.1%. By dividing year 4's extended year-end inventory of $271,875 by this cumulative index, we arrive at inventory priced at base-year costs of $232,173. We then subtract the preexisting base-year inventory valuation for all previous layers of $176,157 from this amount to arrive at the base-year valuation of the year 4 inventory layer, which is $56,016. Finally, we multiply the $56,016 by the cumulative index in year 4 of 117.1% to arrive at an inventory valuation for the year 4 layer of $62,575. At this point, the inventory layers and associated cumulative indexes are:

Layer Type	Base-Year Valuation	LIFO Layer Valuation	Cumulative Index
Base layer	$112,000	$112,000	0.0%
Year 2 layer	64,157	69,161	107.8%
Year 3 layer	—	—	112.4%
Year 4 layer	56,016	62,575	117.1%
Total	$232,173	$243,736	—

Compare the results of this calculation to those from the double-extension method. The indexes are nearly identical, as are the final LIFO layer valuations. The primary differences between the two methods is the avoidance of a base-year cost determination for any new items subsequently added to inventory, for which a current cost is used instead.

How Does the Weighted-Average Valuation Method Work?

The *weighted-average costing method* is a weighted average of the costs in inventory. The weighted average of all units in stock is determined, at which point *all* of the units in stock are accorded that weighted-average value. When parts are used from stock, they are all issued at the same weighted-average cost. If new units are added to stock, the cost of the additions are added to the weighted average of all existing items in stock, which will result in a new, slightly modified weighted average for *all* of the parts in inventory (both the old and new ones).

This system has no particular advantage in relation to income taxes, since it does not skew the recognition of income based on trends in either increasing or declining costs. This makes it a good choice for those organizations that do not want to deal with tax planning. It is also useful for very small inventory valuations, where there would not be any significant change in the reported level of income even if the LIFO or FIFO methods were to be used.

EXAMPLE

The table in Exhibit 3.4 illustrates the weighted-average calculation for inventory valuations, using a series of 10 purchases of inventory. There is a maximum of 1 purchase per month, with usage (reductions from stock) also occurring in most months. Each of the columns show how the average cost is calculated after each purchase and usage transaction.

We begin the illustration with the first row of calculations, which shows that we have purchased 500 units of item BK0043 on May 3, 2010. These units cost $10.00 per unit. During the month in which the units were purchased, 450 units were sent to production, leaving 50 units in stock. Since there has only been one purchase thus far, we can easily calculate, as shown in column 7, that the total inventory valuation is $500, by multiplying the unit cost of $10.00 (in column 3) by the number of units left in stock (in column 5). So far, we have a per-unit valuation of $10.00.

Next we proceed to the second row of the exhibit, where we have purchased another 1,000 units of BK0043 on June 4, 2010. This purchase was less expensive, since the purchasing volume was larger, so the per-unit cost for this purchase is only $9.58. Only 350 units are sent to production during the month, so we now have 700 units in stock, of which 650 are added from the most recent purchase. To determine the new weighted-average cost of the total inventory, we first determine the extended cost of this newest addition to the inventory. As noted in column 7, we arrive at $6,227 by multiplying the value in column 3 by the value in column 6. We then add this amount to

Part Number BK0043								
Column 1	Column 2	Column 3	Column 4	Column 5	Column 6	Column 7	Column 8	Column 9
Date Purchased	Quantity Purchased	Cost per Unit	Monthly Usage	Net Inventory Remaining	Net Change in Inventory During Period	Extended Cost of New Inventory Layer	Extended Inventory Cost	Average Inventory Cost/Unit
05/03/10	500	$10.00	450	50	50	$500	$500	$10.00
06/04/10	1,000	$9.58	350	700	650	$6,227	$6,727	$9.61
07/11/10	250	$10.65	400	550	−150	$0	$5,286	$9.61
08/01/10	475	$10.25	350	675	125	$1,281	$6,567	$9.73
08/30/10	375	$10.40	400	650	−25	$0	$6,324	$9.73
09/09/10	850	$9.50	700	800	150	$1,425	$7,749	$9.69
12/12/10	700	$9.75	900	600	−200	$0	$5,811	$9.69
02/08/11	650	$9.85	800	450	−150	$0	$4,359	$9.69
05/07/11	200	$10.80	0	650	200	$2,160	$6,519	$10.03
09/23/11	600	$9.85	750	500	−150	$0	$5,014	$10.03

Exhibit 3.4 INVENTORY ACCOUNTING—WEIGHTED AVERAGE

(Continued)

(*Continued*)

the existing total inventory valuation ($6,227 plus $500) to arrive at the new extended inventory cost of $6,727, as noted in column 8. Finally, we divide this new extended cost in column 8 by the total number of units now in stock, as shown in column 5, to arrive at our new per-unit cost of $9.61.

The third row reveals an additional inventory purchase of 250 units on July 11, 2010, but more units are sent to production during that month than were bought, so the total number of units in inventory drops to 550 (column 5). This inventory reduction requires no review of inventory layers, as was the case for the LIFO and FIFO calculations. Instead, we simply charge off the 150 unit reduction at the average per-unit cost of $9.61. As a result, the ending inventory valuation drops to $5,286, with the same per-unit cost of $9.61. Thus, reductions in inventory quantities under the average costing method require little calculation—just charge off the requisite number of units at the current average cost.

CHAPTER 4

FIXED ASSET ACCOUNTING

What Is Included in the Capitalized Cost of a Fixed Asset?

When a company purchases a fixed asset, it can include several associated expenses in the capitalized cost of the asset. These costs include the sales tax and ownership registration fees (if any). Also, the cost of all freight, insurance, and duties required to bring the asset to the company can be included in the capitalized cost. Further, the cost required to install the asset can be included. Installation costs include the cost to test and break in the asset, which can include the cost of test materials.

What Is the Price of a Purchased Fixed Asset?

If a fixed asset is acquired for nothing but cash, its recorded cost is the amount of cash paid. However, if the asset is acquired by taking on a payable, such as a stream of debt payments (or taking over the payments that were initially to be made by the seller of the asset), the present value of all future payments yet to be made must also be rolled into the recorded asset cost. If the stream of future payments contains no stated interest rate, one must be imputed based on market rates when making the present value calculation. If the amount of the payable is not clearly evident at the time of purchase, it is also admissible to record the asset at its fair market value.

If an asset is purchased with company stock, assign a value to the assets acquired based on the fair market value of either the stock or the assets, whichever is more easily determinable.

EXAMPLE

The St. Louis Motor Car Company issues 500 shares of its stock to acquire a sheet metal bender. This is a publicly held company, and on the day of the acquisition, its shares were trading for $13.25 each. Since this is an easily determinable value, the cost assigned to the equipment is $6,625 (500 shares times $13.25/share). A year later, the company has taken itself private and chooses to issue another 750 shares of its stock to acquire a router. In this case, the value of the shares is no longer so easily determined, so the company asks an appraiser to determine the router's fair value, which she sets at $12,000. In the first transaction, the journal entry was a debit of $6,625 to the fixed asset equipment account and a credit of $6,625 to the common stock account, while the second transaction was to the same accounts, but for $12,000 instead.

What Is the Price of a Fixed Asset Obtained through an Exchange?

If a company obtains an asset through an exchange involving a dissimilar asset, it should record the incoming asset at the fair market value of the asset for which it was exchanged. However, if this fair value is not readily apparent, the fair value of the incoming asset can be used instead. If no fair market value is readily obtainable for either asset, the net book value of the relinquished asset can be used.

EXAMPLE

The Dakota Motor Company swaps a file server for an overhead crane. Its file server has a book value of $12,000 (net of accumulated depreciation of $4,000), while the overhead crane has a fair value of $9,500. The company has no information about the fair value of its file server, so Dakota uses its net book value instead to establish a value for the swap. Dakota recognizes a loss of $2,500 on the transaction, as noted in the next entry.

	Debit	Credit
Factory equipment	$9,500	
Accumulated depreciation	4,000	
Loss on asset exchange	2,500	
Factory equipment		$16,000

What Is the Price of a Fixed Asset Obtained with a Trade-in?

A company may trade in an existing asset for a new one, along with an additional payment that covers the incremental additional cost of the new asset over that of the old one being traded away. The additional payment portion of this transaction is called the *boot*. When the boot comprises at least 25% of the exchange's fair value, both entities must record the transaction at the fair value of the assets involved. If the amount of boot is less than 25% of the transaction, the party receiving the boot can recognize a gain in proportion to the amount of boot received.

EXAMPLE

ASSET EXCHANGE WITH AT LEAST 25% BOOT

The Dakota Motor Company trades in a copier for a new one from the Fair Copy Company, paying an additional $9,000 as part of the deal. The fair value of the copier traded away is $2,000, while the fair value of the new copier being acquired is $11,000 (with a book value of $12,000, net of $3,500 in accumulated depreciation). The book value of the copier being traded away is $2,500, net of $5,000 in accumulated depreciation. Because Dakota has paid a combination of $9,000 in cash and $2,500 in the net book value of its existing copier ($11,500 in total) to acquire a new copier with a fair value of $11,000, it must recognize a loss of $500 on the transaction, as noted in the next entry.

	Debit	Credit
Office equipment (new asset)	$11,000	
Accumulated depreciation	5,000	
Loss on asset exchange	500	
Office equipment (asset traded away)		$7,500
Cash		9,000

(*Continued*)

On the other side of the transaction, Fair Copy is accepting a copier with a fair value of $2,000 and $9,000 in cash for a replacement copier with a fair value of $11,000, so its journal entry is:

	Debit	Credit
Cash	$9,000	
Office equipment (asset acquired)	2,000	
Accumulated depreciation	3,500	
Loss on sale of asset	1,000	
Office equipment (asset traded away)		$15,500

ASSET EXCHANGE WITH LESS THAN 25% BOOT

As was the case in the last example, the Dakota Motor Company trades in a copier for a new one, but now it pays $2,000 cash and trades in its old copier, with a fair value of $9,000 and a net book value of $9,500 after $5,000 of accumulated depreciation. Also, the fair value of the copier being traded away by Fair Copy remains at $11,000, but its net book value drops to $10,000 (still net of accumulated depreciation of $3,500). All other information remains the same. In this case, the proportion of boot paid is 18% ($2,000 cash, divided by total consideration paid of $2,000 cash plus the copier fair value of $9,000). As was the case before, Dakota has paid a total of $11,500 (from a different combination of $9,000 in cash and $2,500 in the net book value of its existing copier) to acquire a new copier with a fair value of $11,000, so it must recognize a loss of $500 on the transaction, as noted in the next entry.

	Debit	Credit
Office equipment (new asset)	$11,000	
Accumulated depreciation	5,000	
Loss on asset exchange	500	
Office equipment (asset traded away)		$14,500
Cash		2,000

The main difference is on the other side of the transaction, where Fair Copy is now accepting a copier with a fair value of $9,000 and $2,000 in cash in exchange for a copier with a book value of $10,000, so there is a potential gain of $1,000 on the deal. However, because it receives boot that is less than 25% of the transaction fair value, it recognizes a pro rata gain of $180, which is calculated as the 18% of the deal attributable to the cash payment, multiplied by the $1,000 gain. Fair Copy's journal entry to record the transaction is:

	Debit	Credit
Cash	$2,000	
Office equipment (asset acquired)	8,180	
Accumulated depreciation	3,500	
Office equipment (asset traded away)		$13,500
Gain on asset transfer		180

In this entry, Fair Copy can recognize only a small portion of the gain on the asset transfer, with the remaining portion of the gain being netted against the recorded cost of the acquired asset.

What Is the Price of a Group of Fixed Assets?

If a group of assets are acquired through a single purchase transaction, the cost should be allocated amongst the assets in the group based on their proportional share of their total fair market values. The fair market value may be difficult to ascertain in many instances, in which case an appraisal value or tax assessment value can be used. It may also be possible to use the present value of estimated cash flows for each asset as the basis for the allocation, though this measure can be subject to considerable variability in the foundation data and also requires a great deal of analysis to obtain.

EXAMPLE

The Dakota Motor Company acquires three machines for $80,000 as part of the Chapter 7 liquidation auction of a competitor. There is no ready market for the machines. Dakota hires an appraiser to determine their value. She judges machines A and B to be worth $42,000 and $18,000, respectively, but can find no basis of comparison for machine C and passes on an

(Continued)

(*Continued*)
appraisal for that item. Dakota's production manager thinks the net present value of cash flows arising from the use of machine C will be about $35,000. Based on this information, the next costs are allocated to the machines:

Machine Description	Value	Proportions	Allocated Costs
Machine A	$42,000	44%	$35,200
Machine B	18,000	23%	18,400
Machine C	35,000	33%	26,400
Totals	$95,000	100%	$80,000

What Is the Accounting for Improvements to Fixed Assets?

Once an asset is put into use, the majority of expenditures related to it must be charged to expense. If expenditures are for basic maintenance, not contributing to an asset's value or extending its usable life, they must be charged to expense. If expenditures are considerable in amount and increase the asset's value, they are charged to the asset capital account, though they will be depreciated only over the predetermined depreciation period. If expenditures are considerable in amount and increase the asset's usable life, they are charged directly to the accumulated depreciation account, effectively reducing the amount of depreciation expense incurred.

If an existing equipment installation is moved or rearranged, the cost of doing so is charged to expense if there is no measurable benefit in future periods. If there is a measurable benefit, the expenditure is capitalized and depreciated over the periods when the increased benefit is expected to occur.

If an asset must be replaced that is part of a larger piece of equipment, remove the cost and associated accumulated depreciation for the asset to be replaced from the accounting records and recognize any gain or loss on its disposal. If there is no record of the subsidiary asset's cost, ignore this step. In addition, the cost of the replacement asset should be capitalized and depreciated over the remaining term of the larger piece of equipment.

An example of current-period expenditures is routine machine maintenance, such as the replacement of worn-out parts. This expenditure will not change the ability of an asset to perform in a future period and so should be charged to expense within the current period. If repairs are effected in order to repair damage to an asset, this is also a current-period expense. Also, even if an expenditure can be proven to impact future periods, it may still be charged to expense if it is too small to meet the corporate capitalization limit. If a repair cost can be proven to have an impact covering more than one accounting period, but not many additional periods into the future, a company can spread the cost over a few months or all months of a single year by recording the expense in an allowance account that is gradually charged off over the course of the year. In this last case, there may be an ongoing expense accrual throughout the year that will be charged off, even in the absence of any major expenses in the early part of the year—the intention being that the company knows that expenses will be incurred later in the year, and chooses to smooth out its expense recognition by recognizing some of the expense prior to it actually being incurred.

If a company incurs costs to avoid or mitigate environmental contamination, these costs must generally be charged to expense in the current period. The only case in which capitalization is an alternative is when the costs incurred can be demonstrated to reduce or prevent future environmental contamination as well as improve the underlying asset. If so, the asset life associated with these costs should be the period over which environmental contamination is expected to be reduced.

A decision tree that addresses these issues for fixed asset improvements is shown in Exhibit 4.1.

How Is Interest Associated with a Fixed Asset Capitalized?

When a company is constructing assets for its own use or as separately identifiable projects intended for sale, it should capitalize as part of the project cost all associated interest expenses. Capitalized interest expenses are calculated based on the interest rate of the debt used to construct the asset or (if there was no new debt) at the weighted-average interest rate the company pays on its other debt. Interest is not capitalized when its addition

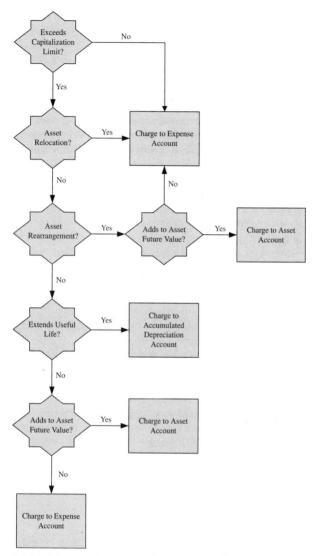

Exhibit 4.1 ASSET IMPROVEMENT CAPITALIZATION OR EXPENSE DECISION

would result in no material change in the cost of the resulting asset, or when the construction period is quite short, or when there is no prospect of completing a project.

The interest rate is multiplied by the average capital expenditures incurred to construct the targeted asset. The amount of interest expense capitalized is limited to an amount less than or equal to the total amount of interest expense actually incurred by the company during the period of asset construction.

	EXAMPLE

The Carolina Astronautics Corporation (CAC) is constructing a new launch pad for its suborbital rocket launching business. It pays a contractor $5,000,000 up front and $2,500,000 after the project completion six months later. At the beginning of the project, it issued $15,000,000 in bonds at 9% interest to finance the project as well as other capital needs. The calculation of interest expense to be capitalized is shown next.

Investment Amount	Months to Be Capitalized	Interest Rate	Interest to Be Capitalized
$5,000,000	6	9%/12	$225,000
2,500,000	0	—	0
		Total	$225,000

There is no interest expense to be capitalized on the final payment of $2,500,000, since it was incurred at the very end of the construction period. CAC accrued $675,000 in total interest expenses during the period when the launch pad was built ($15,000,000 × 9%/12 × 6 months). Since the total expense incurred by the company greatly exceeds the amount of interest to be capitalized for the launch pad, there is no need to reduce the amount of capitalized interest to the level of actual interest expense incurred. Accordingly, CAC's controller makes the next journal entry to record the capitalization of interest.

	Debit	Credit
Assets (Launch Pad)	$22,500	
Interest expense		$22,500

What Is the Accounting for a Fixed Asset Disposition?

When a company disposes of a fixed asset, it should completely eliminate all record of it from the fixed asset and related accumulated depreciation accounts. In addition, it should recognize a gain or loss on the difference between the net book value of the asset and the price at which it was sold.

> ### EXAMPLE
>
> Company ABC is selling a machine that was origi-
> nally purchased for $10,000 and against which $9,000
> of depreciation has been recorded. The sale price of
> the used machine is $1,500. The proper journal entry
> is to credit the fixed asset account for $10,000 (thereby
> removing the machine from the fixed asset journal),
> debit the accumulated depreciation account for $9,000
> (thereby removing all related depreciation from the
> accumulated depreciation account), debit the cash
> account for $1,500 (to reflect the receipt of cash from
> the asset sale), and credit the Gain on Sale of Assets
> account for $500.

What Is the Accounting for an Asset Retirement Obligation?

There may be identifiable costs associated with an asset
disposition that are required by a legal agreement,
known as an *asset retirement obligation* (ARO). For example, a building lease may require the lessee to remove
all equipment by the termination date of the lease; the
cost of this obligation should be recognized at the time
the lease is signed. As another example, the passage of
legislation requiring the cleanup of hazardous waste
sites would require the recognition of these costs as
soon as the legislation is passed.

The amount of ARO recorded is the range of cash
flows associated with asset disposition that would be
charged by a third party, summarized by their probability
weightings. This amount is then discounted at the company's credit-adjusted risk-free interest rate. The risk-free
interest rate can be obtained from the rates at which zero-
coupon United States Treasury instruments are selling.

If there are upward adjustments to the amount of
the ARO in subsequent periods, these adjustments are
accounted for in the same manner, with the present value
for each one being derived from the credit-adjusted risk-
free rate at the time of the transaction. These incremental
transactions are recorded separately in the fixed asset register, though their depreciation periods and methods will
all match that of the underlying asset. If a reduction of the
ARO occurs in any period, this amount should be recognized as a gain in the current period, with the amount
being offset pro rata against all layers of ARO recorded in
the fixed asset register.

When an ARO situation arises, the amount of the ARO is added to the fixed asset register for the related asset, with the offset to a liability account that will eventually be depleted when the costs associated with the retirement obligation are actually incurred. The amount of the ARO added to the fixed asset is depreciated under the same method used for the related asset. In subsequent periods, one must also make an entry to accretion expense to reflect ongoing increases in the present value of the ARO, which naturally occurs as the date of the ARO event comes closer to the present date.

EXAMPLE

The Ever-Firm Tire Company installs a tire molding machine in a leased facility. The lease expires in three years, and the company has a legal obligation to remove the machine at that time. The controller polls local equipment removal companies and obtains estimates of $40,000 and $60,000 of what it would cost to remove the machine. She suspects the lower estimate to be inaccurate and so assigns probabilities of 25% and 75% to the two transactions, resulting in the next probability-adjusted estimate.

Cash Flow Estimate	Assigned Probability	Probability-Adjusted Cash Flow
$40,000	25%	$10,000
60,000	75%	45,000
	100%	$55,000

She assumes that inflation will average 4% in each of the next three years and so adjusts the $55,000 amount upward by $6,868 to $61,868 to reflect this estimate. Finally, she estimates the company's credit-adjusted risk-free rate to be 8%, based on the implicit interest rate in its last lease, and uses the 8% figure to arrive at a discount rate of 0.7938. After multiplying this discount rate by the inflation- and probability-adjusted ARO cost of $61,868, she arrives at $49,111 as the figure to add to the machinery asset account as a debit and the asset retirement obligation account as a credit.

In the three following years, she must also make entries to increase the asset retirement obligation account by the amount of increase in the present value of the ARO, which is calculated as:

(Continued)

(Continued)

Year	Beginning ARO	Inflation Multiplier	Annual Accretion	Ending ARO
1	$49,111	8%	$3,929	$53,041
2	53,041	8%	4,243	57,285
3	57,285	8%	4,583	61,868

After three years of accretion entries, the balance in the ARO liability account matches the original inflation- and probability-adjusted estimate of the amount of cash flows required to settle the ARO obligation.

 ## What Is the Accounting for Donated Assets?

If an asset is donated to a company, the receiving company can record the asset at its fair market value, which can be derived from market rates on similar assets, an appraisal, or the net present value of its estimated cash flows.

When a company donates an asset to another entity, it must recognize the fair value of the asset donated, which is netted against its net book value. The difference between the asset's fair value and its net book value is recognized as either a gain or loss.

EXAMPLE

The Nero Fiddle Company has donated to the local orchestra a portable violin repair workbench from its manufacturing department. The workbench was originally purchased for $15,000, and $6,000 of depreciation has since been charged against it. The workbench can be purchased on the eBay auction site for $8,500, which establishes its fair market value. The company uses the next journal entry to record the transaction.

	Debit	Credit
Charitable donations	$8,500	
Accumulated depreciation	6,000	
Loss on property donation	500	
Machinery asset account		$15,000

What Is the Accounting for Construction in Progress?

If a company constructs its own fixed assets, it should capitalize all direct labor, materials, and overhead costs that are clearly associated with the construction project. In addition, charge to the capital account those fixed overhead costs considered to have "discernible future benefits" related to the project. From a practical perspective, this makes it unlikely that a significant amount of fixed overhead costs should be charged to a capital project.

If a company constructs its own assets, it should compile all costs associated with it into the *construction-in-progress* (CIP) account. There should be a separate account or journal for each project that is currently under way, so there is no risk of commingling expenses among multiple projects. The costs that can be included in the CIP account include all costs normally associated with the purchase of a fixed asset as well as the direct materials and direct labor used to construct the asset. In addition, all overhead costs that are reasonably apportioned to the project may be charged to it as well as the depreciation expense associated with any other assets that are used during the construction process.

One may also charge to the CIP account the interest cost of any funds that have been loaned to the company for the express purpose of completing the project. If this approach is used, either use the interest rate associated with a specific loan that was procured to fund the project or the weighted-average rate for a number of company loans, all of which are being used for this purpose. The amount of interest charged in any period should be based on the cumulative amount of expenditures thus far incurred for the project. The amount of interest charged to the project should not exceed the amount of interest actually incurred for all associated loans through the same time period.

Once the project has been completed, all costs should be carried over from the CIP account into one of the established fixed asset accounts, where the new asset is recorded on a summary basis. All of the detail-level costs should be stored for future review. The asset should be depreciated beginning on the day when it is officially completed. Under no circumstances should depreciation begin prior to this point.

What Is the Accounting for Land?

Land cannot be depreciated, so companies tend to avoid charging expenses to this account on the grounds that they cannot recognize taxable depreciation expenses. Nonetheless, those costs reasonably associated with the procurement of land, such as real estate commissions, title examination fees, escrow fees, and accrued property taxes paid by the purchaser, should all be charged to the fixed asset account for land. This should also include the cost of an option to purchase land. In addition, all subsequent costs associated with the improvement of the land, such as draining, clearing, and grading, should be added to the land account. The cost of interest that is associated with the development of land should also be capitalized. Property taxes incurred during the land development process should also be charged to the asset account but should be charged to current expenses once the development process has been completed.

What Is the Accounting for Leasehold Improvements?

When a lessee makes improvements to a property that is being leased from another entity, it can still capitalize the cost of the improvements, but the time period over which these costs can be amortized must be limited to the lesser of the useful life of the improvements or the length of the lease.

If the lease has an extension option that would allow the lessee to increase the time period over which it can potentially lease the property, the total period over which the leasehold improvements can be depreciated must still be limited to the initial lease term, on the grounds that there is no certainty that the lessee will accept the lease extension option. This limitation is waived for depreciation purposes only if there is either a bargain renewal option or extensive penalties in the lease contract that would make it highly likely that the lessee would renew the lease.

How Is an Asset's Depreciation Basis Calculated?

The basis used for an asset when conducting a depreciation calculation should be its capitalized cost less any salvage value that the company expects to receive at the time when the asset is expected to be taken out of active use.

The salvage value can be difficult to determine, for several reasons.

○ *Removal costs.* There may be a removal cost associated with the asset, which will reduce the net salvage value that will be realized. If the equipment is especially large or involves environmental hazards, the removal cost may exceed the salvage value. In this latter instance, the salvage value may be negative, in which case it should be ignored for depreciation purposes.

○ *Obsolescence.* Asset obsolescence is so rapid in some industries that a reasonable appraisal of salvage value at the time an asset is put into service may require drastic revision shortly thereafter.

○ *No market.* There may be no ready market for the sale of used assets.

○ *Appraisal cost.* The cost of conducting an appraisal in order to determine a net salvage value may be excessive in relation to the cost of the equipment being appraised.

Consequently, it may be necessary to make regular revisions to a salvage value estimate in order to reflect the ongoing realities of asset resale values.

In the case of low-cost assets, it is rarely worth the effort to derive salvage values for depreciation purposes; as a result, these items are typically fully depreciated on the assumption that they have no salvage value.

What Are the General Depreciation Concepts?

Depreciation is designed to spread an asset's cost over its entire useful service life. Its *service life* is the period over which it is worn out for any reason, at the end of which it is no longer usable, or not usable without extensive overhaul. Its useful life can also be considered terminated at the point when it no longer has a sufficient productive capacity for ongoing company production needs, rendering it essentially obsolete.

Anything can be depreciated that has a business purpose, has a productive life of more than one year, gradually wears out over time, and whose cost exceeds the corporate capitalization limit. Since land does not wear out, it cannot be depreciated.

If an asset is present but is temporarily idle, its depreciation should be continued using the existing assumptions for the usable life of the asset. Only if it is permanently idled should the accountant review the need to recognize impairment of the asset.

An asset is rarely purchased or sold precisely on the first or last day of the fiscal year, which brings up the issue of how depreciation is to be calculated in these first and last partial years of use. One option is to record a full year of depreciation in the year of acquisition and no depreciation in the year of sale. Another option is to record a half-year of depreciation in the first year and a half-year of depreciation in the last year. One can also prorate the depreciation more precisely, making it accurate to within the nearest month (or even the nearest day) of when an acquisition or sale transaction occurs.

How Is Straight-Line Depreciation Calculated?

The *straight-line depreciation method* is the simplest method available and is the most popular one when a company has no need to recognize depreciation costs at an accelerated rate. It is also used for all amortization calculations.

The straight-line method is calculated by subtracting an asset's expected salvage value from its capitalized cost and then dividing this amount by the estimated life of the asset.

EXAMPLE

A candy wrapper machine has a cost of $40,000 and an expected salvage value of $8,000. It is expected to be in service for eight years. Given these assumptions, its annual depreciation expense is:

$= (\text{Cost} - \text{salvage value})/\text{number of years in service}$
$= (\$40,000 - \$8,000)/8 \text{ years}$
$= \$32,000/8 \text{ years}$
$= \$4,000 \text{ depreciation per year}$

How Is Double-Declining Balance Depreciation Calculated?

The *double-declining balance* (DDB) method is the most aggressive depreciation method for recognizing the bulk of the expense toward the beginning of an asset's useful

life. To calculate it, determine the straight-line depreciation for an asset for its first year. Then double this amount,
which yields the depreciation for the first year. Then subtract the first-year depreciation from the asset cost (using
no salvage value deduction), and run the same calculation
again for the next year. Continue to use this methodology
for the useful life of the asset.

EXAMPLE

A dry cleaning machine costing $20,000 is estimated
to have a useful life of six years. Under the straight-
line method, it would have depreciation of $3,333 per
year. Consequently, the first year of depreciation under the 200% DDB method would be double that
amount, or $6,667. The calculation for all six years of
depreciation is noted in the next table.

Year	Beginning Cost Basis	Straight-Line Depreciation	200% DDB Depreciation	Ending Cost Basis
1	$24,000	$3,333	$6,667	$17,333
2	17,333	2,889	5,778	11,555
3	11,555	1,926	3,852	7,703
4	7,703	1,284	2,568	5,135
5	5,135	856	1,712	3,423
6	3,423	571	1,142	2,281

Note in the example that there is still some cost left at
the end of the sixth year that has not been depreciated.
This is usually handled by converting over from the DDB
method to the straight-line method in the year in which
the straight-line method would result in a higher amount
of depreciation; the straight-line method is used until all
of the available depreciation has been recognized.

  **How Is Sum-of-the-Years' Digits
Depreciation Calculated?**

This depreciation method recognizes the bulk of all depreciation within the first few years of an asset's depreciable
period but does not do so quite as rapidly as the double-
declining balance method. Its calculation can be surmised
from its name. For the first year of depreciation, add up
the number of years over which an asset is scheduled to

be depreciated and divide this into the total number of years remaining. The resulting percentage is used as the depreciation rate. In succeeding years, simply divide the reduced number of years left into the same total number of years remaining.

EXAMPLE

A punch press costing $24,000 is scheduled to be depreciated over five years. The sum of the years' digits is 15 (Year 1 + Year 2 + Year 3 + Year 4 + Year 5). The depreciation calculation in each of the five years is:

Year 1 = (5/15) × $24,000 = $8,000
Year 2 = (4/15) × $24,000 = $6,400
Year 3 = (3/15) × $24,000 = $4,800
Year 4 = (2/15) × $24,000 = $3,200
Year 5 = (1/15) × $24,000 = $1,600
$24,000

 ## How Is Units-of-Production Depreciation Calculated?

The *units-of-production depreciation method* can result in the most accurate matching of actual asset usage to the related amount of depreciation that is recognized in the accounting records. Its use is limited to those assets to which some estimate of production can be attached.

To calculate it, first estimate the total number of units of production that are likely to result from the use of an asset. Then divide the total capitalized asset cost (less salvage value, if this is known) by the total estimated production to arrive at the depreciation cost per unit of production. Then derive the depreciation recognized by multiplying the number of units of actual production during the period by the depreciation cost per unit. If there is a significant divergence of actual production activity from the original estimate, the depreciation cost per unit of production can be altered from time to time to reflect the realities of actual production volumes.

EXAMPLE

An oil derrick is constructed at a cost of $350,000. It is expected to be used in the extraction of 1,000,000 barrels of oil, which results in an anticipated depreciation rate of $0.35 per barrel. During the first month, 23,500 barrels of oil are extracted. Under this method, the resulting depreciation cost is:

$$= \text{(cost per unit of production)} \times \text{(number of units of production)}$$
$$= (\$0.35 \text{ per barrel}) \times (23,500 \text{ barrels})$$
$$= \$8,225$$

This calculation can also be used with service hours as its basis rather than units of production. When used in this manner, the method can be applied to a larger number of assets for which production volumes would not otherwise be available.

What Is the Accounting for Asset Impairment?

A company is allowed to write down its remaining investment in an asset if it can be proven that the asset is impaired. Impairment can be proven if an asset's net book value is greater than the sum of the undiscounted cash flows (including proceeds from its sale) expected to be generated by it in the future. Having an asset's net book value be greater than its fair value is not a valid reason for an asset write-down, since the asset may still have considerable utility within the company, no matter what its market value may be.

There is no requirement for the periodic testing of asset impairment. Instead, it should be done if there is a major drop in asset usage or downgrading of its physical condition, or if government regulations or business conditions will likely result in a major drop in usage. For example, if new government regulations are imposed that are likely to significantly reduce a company's ability to use the asset, such as may be the case for a coal-fired electricity-generating facility that is subject to pollution controls, an asset impairment test would be necessary. The test can also be conducted if there are major cost overruns during the construction of an asset or if there is a history or future expectation of operating losses associated with an asset. An expectation of early asset disposition can also trigger the test.

To calculate an impairment loss, determine an asset's fair value, either from market quotes or by determining the expected present value of its future cash flows. Then write off the difference between its net book value and its fair value. This action may also result in a change in the method or duration of depreciation. For example, if an asset impairment write-down is made because an asset's life is expected to be shortened by five years, the period over which its associated depreciation will be calculated should also be reduced by five years. If asset impairment is being calculated for a group of assets (such as an entire assembly line or production facility), the amount of the asset impairment is allocated to the assets within the group based on their proportional net book values (though not below the separately identifiable fair value of any asset within the group).

If an asset is no longer in use and there is no prospect for it to be used at any point in the future, it must be written down to its expected salvage value. Since there will then be no remaining asset value to depreciate, all depreciation stops at the time of the write-down.

What Is the Accounting for Intangible Assets?

When an intangible asset is purchased, it should be capitalized on the company books at the amount of cash for which it was paid. If some other asset was used in exchange for the intangible, the cost should be set at the fair market value of the asset given up. A third alternative for costing is the present value of any liability that is assumed in exchange for the intangible asset. It is also possible to create an intangible asset internally (such as the creation of a customer list), as long as the detail for all costs incurred in the creation of the intangible asset is adequately tracked and summarized.

If an intangible asset has an indefinite life, as demonstrated by clearly traceable cash flows well into the future, it is not amortized. Instead, it is subject to an annual impairment test, resulting in the recognition of an impairment loss if its net book value exceeds its fair value. If an intangible asset in this category were to no longer have a demonstrably indefinite life, it would convert to a normal amortization schedule based on its newly defined economic life.

If any intangible asset's usefulness is declining or evidently impaired, its remaining value should be written down to no lower than the present value of its remaining future cash flows.

When a company acquires another company or its assets, any excess of the purchase price over the fair value of tangible assets should be allocated to intangible assets to the greatest degree possible. Examples of such assets are customer lists, patents, trademarks, and brand names. When some value is assigned to these intangible assets, they will then be amortized over a reasonable time period. If the excess purchase price cannot be fully allocated to intangible assets, the remainder is added to the goodwill account.

EXAMPLE

INTANGIBLE AMORTIZATION

Mr. Mel Smith purchases cab license #512 from the city of St. Paul for $20,000. The license term is for five years, after which he can renew it with no anticipated difficulties. The cash flows from the cab license can reasonably be shown to extend into the indefinite future, so there is no amortization requirement. However, the city council changes the renewal process to a lottery where the odds of obtaining a renewal are poor. Mr. Smith must now assume that the economic life of his cab license will end in five years, so he initiates amortization to coincide with the license renewal date.

INTANGIBLE ASSET PURCHASE

An acquirer spends $1 million more to purchase a competitor than its book value. The acquirer decides to assign $400,000 of this excess amount to the patent formerly owned by the competitor, which it then amortizes over the remaining life of the patent. If the acquirer assigns the remaining $600,000 to a customer list asset, and the customer loss rate is 20% per year, it can reasonably amortize the $600,000 over five years to match the gradual reduction in value of the customer list asset.

CHAPTER 5

DEBT ACCOUNTING

When Is Debt Categorized as Short Term or Long Term?

*I*t is generally not allowable to reclassify a debt that is coming due in the short term as a long-term liability on the grounds that it is about to be refinanced as a long-term debt. This treatment is allowable only if a company has the intention to refinance the debt on a long-term basis rather than simply rolling over the debt into another short-term debt instrument that will, in turn, become due and payable in the next accounting year. Also, there must be firm evidence of this rollover into a long-term debt instrument, such as the presence of a debt agreement or an actual conversion to long-term debt subsequent to the balance sheet date.

If a debt can be called by the creditor, it must be classified as a current liability. However, if the period during which the creditor can call the debt is at some point subsequent to one year, it may still be classified as a long-term debt. Also, if the call option applies only if the company defaults on some performance measure related to the debt, the debt needs to be classified as a current liability only if the company cannot cure the performance measure within whatever period is specified under the terms of the debt. Further, if a debt agreement contains a call provision that is likely to be activated under the circumstances present as of the balance sheet date, the debt should be classified as a current liability; conversely, if the probability of the call provision being invoked is remote, the debt does not have to be so classified. Finally, if only a portion of the debt can be called, only that portion need be classified as a current liability.

How Are Bonds Sold at a Discount or Premium Recorded?

When bonds are initially sold, the entry is a debit to cash and a credit to bonds payable. However, this occurs only when the price paid by investors exactly matches the face amount of the bond. A more common occurrence is when the market interest rate varies somewhat from the stated interest rate on the bond, so investors pay a different price in order to achieve an effective interest rate matching the market rate. For example, if the market rate was 8% and the stated rate was 7%, investors would pay less than the face amount of the bond so that the 7% interest they later receive will equate to an 8% interest rate on their reduced investment. Alternatively, if the rates were reversed, with a 7% market rate and 8% stated rate, investors would pay more for the bond, thereby driving down the stated interest rate to match the market rate. If the bonds are sold at a discount, the entry will include a debit to a discount on bonds payable account. For example, if $10,000 of bonds are sold at a discount of $1,500, the entry would be:

	Debit	Credit
Cash	$8,500	
Discount on bonds payable	1,500	
Bonds payable		$10,000

If the same transaction were to occur, except that a premium on sale of the bonds occurs, the entry would be:

	Debit	Credit
Cash	$11,500	
Premium on bonds payable		$1,500
Bonds payable		10,000

EXAMPLE

The Arabian Knights Security Company issues $1,000,000 of bonds at a stated rate of 8% in a market where similar issuances are being bought at 11%. The bonds pay interest once a year and are to be paid off in 10 years. Investors purchase these bonds at a discount in order to earn an effective yield on their investment of 11%.

The discount calculation requires one to determine the present value of 10 interest payments at 11% interest as well as the present value of $1,000,000 discounted at 11% for 10 years. The result is:

Present value of 10 payments of $80,000 =	$80,000 × 5.8892	=	$471,136
Present value of $1,000,000 =	$1,000,000 × .3522	=	$352,200
			$823,336
	Less: stated bond price		1,000,000
	Discount on bond		$176,664

In this example, the entry would be a debit to Cash for $823,336, a credit to Bonds Payable for $1,000,000, and a debit to Discount on Bonds Payable for $176,664. If the calculation had resulted in a premium (which would have occurred only if the market rate of interest was less than the stated interest rate on the bonds), a credit to Premium on Bonds Payable would be in order.

 ## What Is the Effective Interest Method?

The amount of a discount or premium should be gradually written off to the interest expense account over the life of the bond. The only acceptable method for writing off these amounts is through the *effective interest method*, which allows one to charge off the difference between the market and stated rate of interest to the existing discount or premium account, gradually reducing the balance in the discount or premium account over the life of the bond. If interest payment dates do not coincide with the end of financial reporting periods, a journal entry must be made to show the amount of interest expense and related discount or premium amortization that would have occurred during the days following the last interest payment date and the end of the reporting period.

EXAMPLE
To continue with the preceding example, the interest method holds that, in the first year of interest payments, the Arabian Knights Security Company's *(Continued)*

(Continued)
controller would determine that the market interest expense for the first year would be $90,567 (bond stated price of $1,000,000 minus discount of $176,664, multiplied by the market interest rate of 11%). The resulting journal entry would be:

	Debit	Credit
Interest expense	$90,567	
Discount on bonds payable		$10,567
Cash		$80,000

The reason why only $80,000 is listed as a reduction in cash is that the company only has an obligation to pay an 8% interest rate on the $1,000,000 face value of the bonds, which is $80,000. The difference is netted against the existing Discount on Bonds Payable account. The next table shows the calculation of the discount to be charged to expense each year for the full 10-year period of the bond, where the annual amortization of the discount is added back to the bond present value, eventually resulting in a bond present value of $1,000,000 by the time principal payment is due, while the discount has dropped to zero.

Year	Beginning Bond Present Value[4]	Unamortized Discount	Interest Expense[1]	Cash Payment[2]	Credit to Discount[3]
1	$ 823,336	$176,664	$ 90,567	$80,000	$10,567
2	$ 833,903	$166,097	$ 91,729	$80,000	$11,729
3	$ 845,632	$154,368	$ 93,020	$80,000	$13,020
4	$ 858,652	$141,348	$ 94,452	$80,000	$14,452
5	$ 873,104	$126,896	$ 96,041	$80,000	$16,041
6	$ 889,145	$110,855	$ 97,806	$80,000	$17,806
7	$ 906,951	$ 93,049	$ 99,765	$80,000	$19,765
8	$ 926,716	$ 73,284	$101,939	$80,000	$21,939
9	$ 948,655	$ 51,346	$104,352	$80,000	$24,352
10	$ 973,007	$ 26,994	$107,031	$80,000	$26,994
	$1,000,000	$ 0			

[1]Bond present value multiplied by the market rate of 11%
[2]Required cash payment of 8% stated rate multiplied by face value of $1,000,000
[3]Interest expense reduced by cash payment
[4]Beginning present value of the bond plus annual reduction in the discount

How Is Debt Issued with No Stated Interest Rate Recorded?

If a company issues debt that has no stated rate of interest, the controller must create an interest rate for it that approximates the rate that the company would likely obtain, given its credit rating, on the open market on the date when the debt was issued. The controller uses this rate to discount the face amount of the debt down to its present value and records the difference between this present value and the loan's face value as the loan balance.

EXAMPLE

A company issues debt with a face amount of $1,000,000, payable in five years and at no stated interest rate. The market rate for interest at the time of issuance is 9%, so the discount factor to be applied to the debt is 0.6499. This gives the debt a present value of $649,900. The difference between the face amount of $1,000,000 and the present value of $649,900 is recorded as a discount on the note, as shown in the next entry.

	Debit	Credit
Cash	$649,900	
Discount on note payable	350,100	
Notes payable		$1,000,000

How Are Debt Issuance Costs Recorded?

The costs associated with issuing bonds include the legal costs of creating the bond documents, printing the bond certificates, and (especially) the underwriting costs of the investment banker. Since these costs are directly associated with the procurement of funds that the company can be expected to use for a number of years (until the bonds are paid off), the related bond issuance costs should be recorded as an asset and then written off on a straight-line basis over the period during which the bonds are expected to be used by the company. This entry is a debit to a bond issuance asset account and a credit to cash. However, if the bonds associated with these costs are subsequently paid off earlier than anticipated, one can reasonably argue that the associated remaining bond issuance costs should be charged to expense at the same time.

How Is a Debt Issuance with Attached Rights Recorded?

An issuing company can grant additional benefits to the other party, such as exclusive distribution rights on its products, discounts on product sales, and so on—the range of possibilities is endless. In these cases, one should consider the difference between the present value and face value of the debt to be the value of the additional consideration. When this occurs, the difference is debited to the Discount on Note Payable account and is amortized using the effective interest method. The offsetting credit can be to a variety of accounts, depending on the nature of the transaction. The credited account is typically written off either ratably (if the attached benefit is equally spread over many accounting periods) or in conjunction with specific events (such as the shipment of discounted products to the holder of the debt). Though less common, it is also possible to issue debt at an above-market rate in order to obtain additional benefits from the debt holder. In this case, the entry is reversed, with a credit to the Premium on Note Payable account and the offsetting debit to a number of possible accounts related to the specific consideration given.

EXAMPLE

The Arabian Knights Security Company has issued a new note for $2,500,000 at 4% interest to a customer, the Alaskan Pipeline Company. Under the terms of the five-year note, Alaskan obtains a 20% discount on all security services it purchases from Arabian during the term of the note. The market rate for similar debt was 9% on the date the loan documents were signed.

The present value of the note at the 9% market rate of interest over a five-year term is $1,624,750, while the present value of the note at its stated rate of 4% is $2,054,750. The difference between the two present value figures is $430,000, which is the value of the attached right to discounted security services granted to Alaskan. Arabian should make this entry to record the loan:

	Debit	Credit
Cash	$2,500,000	
Discount on note payable	430,000	
Note payable		$2,500,000
Unearned revenue		430,000

The unearned revenue of $430,000 either can be recognized incrementally as part of each invoice billed to Alaskan, or it can be recognized ratably over the term of the debt. Since Arabian does not know the exact amount of the security services that will be contracted for by Alaskan during the term of the five-year note, the better approach is to recognize the unearned revenue ratably over the note term. The first month's entry would be shown next, where the amount recognized is 1/60th of the beginning balance of unearned revenue:

	Debit	Credit
Unearned revenue	$7,166.67	
Services revenue		$7,166.67

How Is a Debt Issuance for Property Recorded?

When a note is issued in exchange for some type of property, the stated interest rate on the note is used to value the debt for reporting purposes unless the rate is not considered to be "fair." If it is not fair, the transaction should be recorded at the fair market value of either the property or the note, whichever can be more clearly determined.

EXAMPLE

The Arabian Knights Security Company exchanges a $50,000 note for a set of motion detection equipment from the Eye Spy Company. The equipment is custom-built for Arabian, so there is no way to assign a fair market value to it. The note has a stated interest rate of 3% and is payable in three years. The 3% rate appears to be quite low, especially since Arabian just secured similar financing from a local lender at a 7% interest rate. The 3% rate can thus be considered not fair for the purposes of valuing the debt, so Arabian's controller elects to use the 7% rate instead.

(Continued)

(*Continued*)

The discount rate for debt due in three years at 7% interest is 0.8163. After multiplying the $50,000 face value of the note by 0.8163, the controller arrives at a net present value for the debt of $40,815, which is recorded in the next entry as the value of the motion detection equipment, along with a discount that shall be amortized to interest expense over the life of the loan.

	Debit	Credit
Motion detection equipment	$40,815	
Discount on notes payable	9,185	
Notes payable		$50,000

How Is a Debt Extinguishment Recorded?

A company may find it advisable to repurchase its bonds prior to their maturity date, perhaps because market interest rates have dropped so far below the stated rate on the bonds that the company can profitably refinance at a lower interest rate. The resulting transaction should recognize any gain or loss on the transaction as well as recognize the transactional cost of the retirement and any proportion of the outstanding discount, premium, or bond issuance costs relating to the original bond issuance.

EXAMPLE

To return to the earlier example, if the Arabian Knights Security Company were to buy back $200,000 of its $1,000,000 bond issuance at a premium of 5%, and does so with $125,000 of the original bond discount still on its books, it would record a loss of $10,000 on the bond retirement ($200,000 × 5%) while also recognizing 1/5 of the remaining discount, which is $25,000 ($125,000 × 1/5). The entry would be:

	Debit	Credit
Bonds payable	$200,000	
Loss on bond retirement	10,000	
Discount on bonds payable		$25,000
Cash		185,000

How Is a Temporary or Permanent Bond Default Recorded?

If the issuing company finds itself in the position of being unable to pay either interest or principal to its bond holders, there are two directions the controller can take in reflecting the problem in the accounting records. In the first case, the company may be in default only temporarily and is attempting to work out a payment solution with the bond holders. Under this scenario, the amortization of discounts or premiums, as well as of bond issuance costs and interest expense, should continue as they have in the past. However, if there is no chance of payment, the amortization of discounts or premiums, as well as of bond issuance costs, should be accelerated, being recognized in full in the current period. This action is taken on the grounds that the underlying accounting transaction that specified the period over which the amortizations occurred has now disappeared, requiring the controller to recognize all remaining expenses.

How Is a Restructured Bond Obligation Recorded?

If the issuing company has not defaulted on a debt but rather has restructured its terms, the controller must determine the present value of the new stream of cash flows and compare it to the original carrying value of the debt arrangement. In the likely event that the new present value of the debt is less than the original present value, the difference should be recognized in the current period as a gain.

Alternatively, if the present value of the restructured debt agreement is *more* than the carrying value of the original agreement, a loss is *not* recognized on the difference; instead, the effective interest rate on the new stream of debt payments is reduced to the point where the resulting present value of the restructured debt matches the carrying value of the original agreement. This will result in a reduced amount of interest expense being accrued for all future periods during which the debt is outstanding.

How Is an Asset Transfer to Eliminate Debt Recorded?

A company may be unable to pay its bond holders and so gives them other company assets in exchange for the interest or principal payments owed to them. When this occurs, the issuing company first records a gain or loss on the initial revaluation of the asset being transferred to its fair market value. Next it records a gain or loss on the transaction if there is a difference between the carrying value of the debt being paid off and the fair market value of the asset being transferred to the bond holder.

EXAMPLE

The Arabian Knights Security Company is unable to pay off its loan from a local lender. The lender agrees to cancel the debt, with a remaining face value of $35,000 in exchange for a company truck having a book value of $26,000 and a fair market value of $29,000. There is also $2,500 of accrued but unpaid interest expense associated with the debt. Arabian's controller first revalues the truck to its fair market value and then records a gain on the debt settlement transaction. The entries are:

	Debit	Credit
Vehicles	$3,000	
Gain on asset transfer		$3,000
Note payable	$35,000	
Interest payable	2,500	
Vehicles		$29,000
Gain on debt settlement		8,500

How Is Convertible Debt Recorded?

A *convertible bond* contains a feature allowing the holder to turn in the bond in exchange for stock when a preset strike price for the stock is reached, sometimes after a specific date. This involves a specific conversion price per share, which is typically set at a point that makes the transaction uneconomical unless the share price rises at some point in the future.

To account for this transaction under the *book value method*, the principal amount of the bond is moved to an Equity account, with a portion being allocated to the capital account at par value and the remainder going to the Additional Paid-in Capital account. A portion of the discount or premium associated with the bond issuance is also retired, based on the proportion of bonds converted to equity. If the *market value method* is used instead, the conversion price is based on the number of shares issued to former bond holders, multiplied by the market price of the shares on the conversion date. This will likely create a gain or loss as compared to the book value of the converted bonds.

EXAMPLE

BOOK VALUE METHOD

A bond holder owns $50,000 of bonds and wishes to convert them to 1,000 shares of company stock that has a par value of $5. The total amount of the premium associated with the original bond issuance was $42,000, and the amount of bonds to be converted to stock represents 18% of the total amount of bonds outstanding. In this case, the amount of premium to be recognized will be $7,560 ($42,000 × 18%), while the amount of funds shifted to the Capital Stock at Par Value account will be $5,000 (1,000 shares × $5). The entry is:

	Debit	Credit
Bonds payable	$50,000	
Premium on bonds payable	7,560	
Capital stock at par value		$5,000
Additional paid-in capital		52,560

MARKET VALUE METHOD

Use the same assumptions as the last example, except that the fair market value of the shares acquired by the former bond holder is $5.50 each. This creates a loss on the bond conversion of $5,000, which is added to the Additional Paid-in Capital account. The entry is:

	Debit	Credit
Bonds payable	$50,000	
Loss on bond conversion	5,000	
Premium on bonds payable	7,560	
Capital stock at par value		$5,000
Additional paid-in capital		57,560

How Is Debt Issued with Stock Warrants Recorded?

A company may attach warrants to its bonds in order to sell the bonds to investors more easily. A *warrant* gives an investor the right to buy a specific number of shares of company stock at a set price for a given time interval. To account for the presence of a warrant, the controller must determine its value if it were sold separately from the bond, determine the proportion of the total bond price to allocate to it, and then credit this proportional amount into the Additional Paid-in Capital account.

EXAMPLE

A bond/warrant combination is purchased by an investor for $1,100. The investment banker handling the transaction estimates that the value of the warrant is $150, while the bond (with a face value of $1,000) begins trading at $975. Accordingly, the value the accountant assigns to the warrant is $146.67, which is calculated as:

$$\frac{\text{Warrant value}}{\text{Bond value} + \text{Warrant value}} \times \text{Purchase price}$$

$$= \text{Price assigned to warrant}$$

$$\frac{\$150}{\$975 + \$150} \times \$1,100 = \$146.67$$

The controller then credits the $146.67 assigned to the warrant value to the Additional Paid-in Capital account, since this is a form of equity funding, rather than debt funding, for which the investor has paid. The Discount on Bonds Payable represents the difference between the $1,000 face value of the bond and its assigned value of $953.33. The journal entry is:

	Debit	Credit
Cash	$1,100.00	
Discount on bonds payable	46.67	
Bonds payable		$1,000.00
Additional paid-in capital		146.67

CHAPTER 6

STOCKHOLDERS' EQUITY

What Is Par Value?

Most types of stock contain a *par value*, which is a minimum price below which the stock cannot be sold. The original intent for using par value was to ensure that a residual amount of funding was contributed to the company and could not be removed from it until dissolution of the corporate entity. In reality, most common stock now has a par value that is so low (typically anywhere from a penny to a dollar) that its original intent no longer works.

If an investor purchases a share of stock at a price greater than its par value, the difference is credited to an Additional Paid-in Capital account. For example, if an investor buys one share of common stock at a price of $82, and the stock's par value is $1, the entry would be:

	Debit	Credit
Cash	$82	
Common stock—par value		$1
Common stock—additional paid-in capital		81

How Is Stock Valued that Is Issued for Property or Services?

If a company accepts property or services in exchange for stock, the amount listed on the books as the value of stock issued should be based on the fair market value of the property or services received. If this cannot easily be determined, the current market price of the shares issued should be used. If neither is available, the value assigned by the board of directors at the time of issuance is assumed to be the fair market value.

 ## What Are the Characteristics of Preferred Stock?

Preferred stock is stock that has few (or none) of the rights conferred upon common stock but that offers a variety of incentives, such as guaranteed dividend payments and preferential distributions over common stock, to convince investors to buy it. The dividends can also be preconfigured to increase to a higher level at a later date, which is called *increasing rate preferred stock*.

The dividends provided for in a preferred stock agreement can be distributed only after the approval of the board of directors, and so may be withheld. If the preferred stock has a cumulative provision, any dividends not paid to the holders of preferred shares in preceding years must be paid prior to dividend payments for any other types of shares. Also, some preferred stock will give its owners voting rights in the event of one or more missed dividend payments.

Many companies issue preferred stock with a call feature stating the price at which the company will buy back the shares.

What Is Convertible Preferred Stock?

Preferred stock may be converted by the shareholder into common stock at a preset ratio, if the preferred stock agreement specifies that this option is available. If this conversion occurs, the controller must reduce the Par Value and Additional Paid-in Capital accounts for the preferred stock by the amount at which the preferred stock was purchased and then shift these funds into the same common stock funds.

EXAMPLE

If a shareholder of preferred stock was to convert one share of the Grinch Toy Removal Company's preferred stock into five shares of its common stock, the journal entry would be as shown next, on the assumption that the preferred stock was bought for $145, that the par value of the preferred stock is $50, and the par value of the common stock is $1:

	Debit	Credit
Preferred stock—par value	$50	
Preferred stock—additional paid-in capital	95	
Common stock—par value		$5
Common stock—additional paid-in capital		140

In the journal entry, the par value account for the common stock reflects the purchase of five shares, since the par value of five individual shares (i.e., $5) has been recorded, with the remaining excess funds from the preferred stock being recorded in the Additional Paid-in Capital account. However, if the par value of the common stock were to be greater than the entire purchase price of the preferred stock, the journal entry changes to bring in extra funds from the Retained Aarnings account in order to make up the difference. If this were to occur with the previous assumptions, except with a common stock par value of $40, the journal entry is:

	Debit	Credit
Preferred stock—par value	$50	
Preferred stock—additional paid-in capital	95	
Retained earnings	55	
Common stock—par value		$200

 ## What Is a Stock Split?

A *stock split* involves the issuance of a multiple of the current number of shares outstanding to current shareholders. For example, a one-for-two split of shares when there are currently 125,000 shares outstanding will result in a new amount outstanding of 250,000. This is done to reduce the market price on a per-share basis. In addition, by dropping the price into a lower range, it can have the effect of making it more affordable to small investors, who may then bid up the price to a point where the split stock is cumulatively more valuable than the unsplit stock.

A stock split is typically accompanied by a proportional reduction in the par value of the stock. For example, if a share with a par value of $20 were to be split on a two-for-one basis, the par value of the split stock would be $10 per share. This transaction requires no entry on a company's books. However, if the split occurs without a change in the par value, funds must be shifted from the Additional Paid-in Capital account to the Par Value account.

A *reverse split* is used if a company wishes to proportionally increase the market price of its stock. For example, if a company's common stock sells for $2.35 per share and management wishes to see the price trade above the $20 price point, it can conduct a 10-for-1 reverse split, which will raise the market price to $23.50 per share while reducing the number of outstanding shares by 90%. In this case, the par value per share would be increased proportionally, so that no funds were ever removed from the Par Value account.

EXAMPLE

If 250,000 shares were to be split on a one-for-three basis, creating a new pool of 750,000 shares, and the existing par value per share of $2 was not changed, the controller would have to transfer $1,000,000 (the number of newly created shares times the par value of $2) from the Additional Paid-in Capital account to the Par Value account to ensure that the legally mandated amount of par value per share was stored there.

What Is a Stock Subscription?

Stock subscriptions allow investors or employees to pay a company a consistent amount over time and receive shares of the company's stock in exchange. When such an arrangement occurs, a receivable is set up for the full amount expected, with an offset to a Common Stock Subscription account and the Additional Paid-in Capital account (for the par value of the subscribed shares). When the cash is collected and the stock is issued, the funds are deducted from these accounts and shifted to the Standard Common Stock account.

EXAMPLE

EXAMPLE OF A STOCK SUBSCRIPTION

If the Slo-Mo Molasses Company sets up a stock subscription system for its employees and they choose to purchase 10,000 shares of common stock with a par value of $1 for a total of $50,000, the entry would be:

	Debit	Credit
Stock subscriptions receivable	$50,000	
Common stock subscribed		$40,000
Additional paid-in capital		10,000

When the $50,000 cash payment is received, the Stock Subscriptions Receivable account will be offset, while funds stored in the Common Stock Subscribed account are shifted to the Common Stock account, as noted in the next entry:

	Debit	Credit
Cash	$50,000	
Stock subscriptions receivable		$50,000
Common stock subscribed	$50,000	
Common stock		$50,000

What Is Retained Earnings?

Retained earnings is that portion of equity not encompassed by the various Par Value or Additional Paid-in Capital accounts. It is increased by profits and decreased by distributions to shareholders and several types of stock transactions.

Retained earnings can be impacted if the controller makes a prior period adjustment that results from an error in the prior financial statements; the offset to this adjustment will be the Retained Earnings account and will appear as an adjustment to the opening balance in the Retained Earnings account. A financial statement error would be one that involved a mathematical error or the incorrect application of accounting rules to accounting entries. A change in *accounting estimate* is not an accounting error and so should not be charged against retained earnings.

Retained earnings can be restricted through the terms of lending agreements. For example, a lender may require the company to restrict some portion of its retained earnings through the term of the loan, thereby giving the lender some assurance that funds will be available to pay off the loan. Such a restriction would keep the company from issuing dividends in amounts that cut into the restricted retained earnings.

What Is a Stock Warrant?

A *stock warrant* is a legal document giving the holder the right to buy a company's shares at a specific price, and usually for a specific time period, after which it becomes invalid. It is used as a form of compensation instead of cash for services performed by other entities to the company and may also be attached to debt instruments in order to make them appear more attractive to buyers.

If the warrant attached to a debt instrument cannot be detached and sold separately from the debt, it should not be separately accounted for. However, if it can be sold separately by the debt holder, the fair market value of each item (the warrant and the debt instrument) should be determined, and the controller should apportion the price at which the combined items were sold among the two, based on their fair market values.

EXAMPLE
If the fair market value of a warrant is $63.50 and the fair market value of a bond to which it was attached is $950, and the price at which the two items were sold is $1,005, an entry should be made to an Additional Paid-in Capital Account for $62.97 to account for the warrants, while the remaining $942.03 is accounted for as debt. The apportionment of the actual sale price of $1,005 to warrants is calculated as shown next.

$$\frac{\text{Fair market value of warrant}}{\text{Fair market value of warrant} + \text{Fair market value of bond}}$$
$$\times \text{Price of combined instruments}$$

or

$$\frac{\$63.50}{(\$63.50 + \$950.00)} \times \$1,005 = \$62.97$$

If a warrant expires, the funds are shifted from the Outstanding Warrants account to an Additional Paid-in capital account. To continue with the last example, this would require the next entry.

	Debit	Credit
Additional paid-in capital—Warrants	$62.97	
Additional paid-in capital—Expired Warrants		$62.97

If a warrant is subsequently used to purchase a share of stock, the value allocated to the warrant in the accounting records should be shifted to the Common Stock accounts. To use the preceding example, if the warrant valued at $62.97 is used to purchase a share of common stock at a price of $10.00, and the common stock has a par value of $25, the Par Value account is credited with $25 (since it is mandatory that the par value be recorded) and the remainder of the funds are recorded in the Additional Paid-in Capital account. The entry is:

	Debit	Credit
Cash	$10.00	
Additional Paid-In Capital — Warrants	62.97	
Common stock—par value		$25.00
Common stock—additional paid-in capital		47.97

What Are the Key Dates Associated with Dividends?

When the board of directors votes to issue dividends, this is the *declaration date*. At this time, by the board's action, the company has incurred a liability to issue a dividend. Unless the dividend is a stock dividend, the controller must record a dividend payable at this time and debit the Retained Earnings account to indicate the eventual source of the dividend payment.

The dividend will be paid as of a *record date*. This date is of considerable importance to shareholders, since the entity holding a share on that date will be entitled to receive the dividend. If a share is sold the day before the record date, the old shareholder forgoes the dividend and the new one receives it. As of the payment date, the company issues dividends, thereby debiting the Dividends Payable account and crediting the Cash account (or the account of whatever asset is distributed as a dividend).

What Is a Property Dividend?

A company may choose to issue a *property dividend* to its shareholders. Under this scenario, the assets being distributed must be recorded at their fair market value, which usually triggers the recognition of either a gain or loss in the current income statement.

EXAMPLE

The Burly Book Binders Company declares a property dividend for its shareholders of a rare set of books, which have a fair market value of $500 each. The 75 shareholders receive one book each, which represents a total fair market value of $37,500. The books were originally obtained by the company at a cost of $200 each, or $15,000 in total. Consequently, a gain of $22,500 ($37,500 minus $15,000) must be recognized. To do so, the controller debits the Retained Earnings account for $37,500, credits the Gain on Property Disposal account for $22,500, and credits its Dividends Payable account for $15,000. Once the books are distributed to the shareholders, the controller debits the Dividends Payable account for $15,000 and credits the Inventory account for $15,000 in order to eliminate the dividend liability and reflect the reduction in book inventory.

What Is a Stock Dividend?

A *stock dividend* allows a company to shift funds out of the Retained Earnings account and into the Par Value and Additional Paid-in Capital accounts, which reduces the amount of funding that the Internal Revenue Service would see when reviewing the company for an excessive amount of retained earnings (which can be taxed). These distributions are also not taxable to the recipient. If the amount of a stock dividend represents less than one-quarter of the total number of shares currently outstanding, this is considered to be a distribution that will not greatly impact the price of existing shares through dilution; accordingly, the controller records the fair market value of these shares in the Par Value and Additional Paid-in Capital accounts and takes the offsetting funds out of the Retained Earnings account.

EXAMPLE

If the Bobber Fishing Equipment Company wishes to issue a stock dividend of 10,000 shares and their fair market value is $32 per share, with a par value of $1, the entry would be:

	Debit	Credit
Retained earnings	$320,000	
Common stock—par value		$32,000
Additional paid-in capital		288,000

If more than one-quarter of the total amount of outstanding shares is to be distributed through a stock dividend, we assume that the value of the shares will be watered down through such a large distribution. In this case, funds are shifted from retained earnings only to cover the amount of the par value for the shares to be distributed.

EXAMPLE

Using the preceding example (and assuming that 10,000 shares were more than 25% of the total outstanding), the entry would change to:

	Debit	Credit
Retained earnings	$32,000	
Common stock—par value		$32,000

If there are not sufficient funds in the Retained Earnings account to make these entries, the number of shares issued through the stock dividend must be reduced. However, given the small size of the par values that many companies have elected to use for their stock, the amount of retained earnings required may actually be less for a very large stock dividend than for a small one, since only the par value of the stock must be covered in the event of a large distribution.

What Is a Liquidating Dividend?

A *liquidating dividend* is used to return capital to investors; thus, it is not strictly a dividend, which is intended to be a distribution of earnings. This transaction is impacted by the laws of the state of incorporation for each organization; the general entry in most cases is to credit cash and debit the Additional Paid-in Capital account.

What Is Treasury Stock?

If the board of directors elects to have the company buy back shares from shareholders, the stock that is brought in-house is called *treasury stock*. A corporation's purchase of its own stock is normally accounted for under the *cost method*. Under this approach, the cost at which shares are bought back is listed in a Treasury Stock account. When the shares are subsequently sold again, any sale amounts exceeding the repurchase cost are credited to the Additional Paid-in Capital account, while any shortfalls are first charged to any remaining additional paid-in capital remaining from previous treasury stock transactions and then to retained earnings if there is no additional paid-in capital of this type remaining. For example, if a company chooses to buy back 500 shares at $60 per share, the transaction would be:

	Debit	Credit
Treasury stock	$30,000	
Cash		$30,000

If management later decides to permanently retire treasury stock that was originally recorded under the cost method, it backs out the original par value and additional paid-in capital associated with the initial stock sale and charges any remaining difference to the Retained Earnings account. To continue with the previous example, if the 500 shares had a par value of $1 each, had originally been sold for $25,000. and all were to be retired, the entry would be:

	Debit	Credit
Common stock—par value	$500	
Additional paid-in capital	24,500	
Retained earnings	5,000	
Treasury stock		$30,000

If instead the company subsequently chooses to sell the shares back to investors at a price of $80 per share, the transaction is:

	Debit	Credit
Cash	$40,000	
Treasury stock		$30,000
Additional paid-in capital		10,000

If treasury stock is subsequently sold for more than it was originally purchased, the excess amount may also be recorded in an Additional Paid-in Capital account that is specifically used for treasury stock transactions.

 ## What Is the Constructive Retirement Method?

When there is no intention of ever reselling treasury stock, it is accounted for at the point of purchase from shareholders under the *constructive retirement method*. Under this approach, the stock is assumed to be retired, and so the original Common Stock and Additional Paid-in Capital accounts will be reversed, with any loss on the purchase being charged to the Retained Earnings account and any gain being credited to the Additional Paid-in Capital account. For example, if a company were to buy back 500 shares at $60 per share and the original issuance price was $52 (par value of $1), the transaction would be:

	Debit	Credit
Common stock—par value	$500	
Additional paid-in capital	25,500	
Retained earnings	4,000	
Cash		$30,000

 ## What Is a Stock Option?

An *option* is an agreement between a company and another entity (frequently an employee), that allows the entity to purchase shares in the company at a specific price within a specified date range. The assumption is that the options will only be exercised if the fixed purchase price is lower than the market price, so that the buyer can sell the stock on the open market for a profit. Options are accounted for under either the *intrinsic value method* or the *fair value method*.

How Is a Stock Option Recorded under the Intrinsic Value Method?

If stock options are issued at a strike price that is the same as the current market price, there is no journal entry to record when the intrinsic value method is used. However, if the strike price at the time of the issuance is lower than the market price, the difference must be recorded in a Deferred Compensation account.

The same rule applies if there is a guaranteed minimum to the value of the stock option grants. In this situation, one must recognize as compensation expense over the service period of the options the amount of the guaranteed minimum valuation.

If the term of the options granted were to be extended, one must compare the difference between the market price and the exercise price of the options on the extension date and recognize compensation expense at that time if the exercise price is lower than the market price.

EXAMPLE

If 5,000 options are issued at a price of $25 each to the president of the Long Walk Shoe Company on a date when the market price is $40, Long Walk's controller must charge a Deferred Compensation account for $75,000 ($40 market price minus $25 option price, times 5,000 options) with this entry:

	Debit	Credit
Deferred compensation expense	$75,000	
Options—additional paid-in capital		$75,000

The options cannot be exercised for a period of three years from the date of grant, so the controller regularly charges off the deferred compensation account to expense over the next three years. For example, in the first year, the controller would charge one-third of the deferred compensation to expense with this entry:

	Debit	Credit
Compensation expense	$25,000	
Deferred compensation expense		$25,000

If Long Walk's president elects to use all of the stock options to buy stock at the end of the three-year period, and the par value of the stock is $1, the entry would be:

	Debit	Credit
Cash	$125,000	
Options—additional paid-in capital	75,000	
Common stock—par value		$5,000
Common stock—additional paid-in capital		195,000

Alternatively, if Long Walk's president were to leave the company at the end of the second year without having used any of the options to purchase stock, the compensation expense recognized thus far would have to be reversed, as would the deferred compensation associated with the options that would have vested in year 3. The entry is:

	Debit	Credit
Options—additional paid-in capital	$75,000	
Deferred compensation expense		$25,000
Compensation expense		50,000

If, during the period between the option grant date and the purchase of stock with the options, the market price of the stock were to vary from the $40 price at which the deferred compensation liability was initially recorded, the controller would not be required to make any entry, since subsequent changes in the stock price are beyond the control of the company and so should not be recorded as a change in the Deferred Compensation account.

How Is a Stock Option Recorded under the Fair Value Method?

Under the *fair value method*, compensation expense must be recognized for options granted, even if there is no difference between the current market price of the stock and the price at which the recipient can purchase the stock under the terms of the option. A compensation expense arises because the holder of an option does not actually pay for any stock until the date when the option is exercised and so can earn interest by investing the money elsewhere until that time. This ability to invest elsewhere has a value and is measured by using the risk-free interest rate (usually derived from the current interest rate on U.S. Government securities). The present value of these interest earnings is based on the expected term of the option (i.e., the time period extending to the point when one would reasonably expect them to be used) and is reduced by the present value of any stream of dividend payments that the stock might be expected to yield during the interval between the present time and the point when the stock is expected to be purchased, since this is income forgone by the buyer.

The prospective volatility of the stock is also factored into the equation. If a stock has a history of considerable volatility, an option holder can wait to exercise his options until the stock price spikes, which creates more value to the option holder than if the underlying shares had minimal volatility. The difference between the discounted price of the stock and the exercise price is then recognized as compensation expense.

The calculations required to determine the present value of options are complex and typically require the use of a computer program. Consequently, the next example is greatly simplified and does not account for stock price volatility at all.

EXAMPLE

If the current interest rate on 90-day treasury bills is 7% (assumed to be the risk-free interest rate), the expectation for purchase of stock is three years in the future, and the option price of the stock is $25, its present value is $20.41 ($25 times 0.8163). The difference between $25 and $20.41 is $4.59, which must be recognized as compensation expense.

How Do Option Expirations Impact Compensation Expense?

The use of present value calculations under the fair value method means that financial estimates are being used to determine the most likely scenario that will eventually occur. One of the key estimates to consider is that not all stock options will be exercised—some may lapse due to employees leaving the company, for example. One should include these estimates when calculating the total amount of accrued compensation expense, so that actual results do not depart significantly from the initial estimates. However, despite the best possible estimates, the controller will find that actual option use will inevitably vary from original estimates. When these estimates change, one should account for them in the current period as a change of accounting estimate. However, if estimates are not changed and the controller simply waits to see how many options actually are exercised, any variances from the accounting estimate will be made on the date when options either lapse or are exercised. Either of these methods is acceptable and eventually will result in the same compensation expense.

What Happens When an Option Expires?

A major difference between the intrinsic value and fair value methods is their varying treatment of vested options that expire unexercised. Under the intrinsic value method, any related compensation expense is reversed, whereas the fair value method requires that the compensation expense remain. Depending on the circumstances, this can result in a significant difference in expenses recognized.

What Happens if the Company Buys Options from the Option Holder?

If a company elects to cancel options by purchasing them from an option holder, and the price paid is higher than the value of the options as calculated under the fair value method, the difference is fully recognized as compensation expense at once, since any vesting period has been accelerated to the payment date.

How Is the Option Vesting Period Recognized?

The compensation expense should be recognized ratably over the vesting period. If there is "cliff vesting," where all options fully vest only after a set time period has passed, the calculation is simple enough— ratably spread the expense over the entire vesting period.

EXAMPLE

The Arabian Knights Security Company issues 9,000 options to its president. The compensation expense associated with the options is $50,000. The option plan calls for cliff vesting after three years, so the company's controller records a monthly charge to compensation expense of $1,388.89 ($50,000 divided by 36 months).

The situation becomes more complex if the vesting schedule calls for vesting of portions of the option grant at set intervals. When this happens, the compensation expense associated with each block of vested options is recognized ratably over the period leading up to the vesting. For example, the compensation associated with a block of options that vest in one year must be recognized as expense entirely within that year, while the compensation associated with a block of options that vest in two years must be recognized as expense over the two years leading up to the vesting date. The net impact of this approach is significantly higher compensation expense recognition in the early years of an option plan that allows incremental vesting over multiple years.

EXAMPLE

Assume the same information as the last example, except that the president's options vest in equal proportions at the end of years 1, 2, and 3. The next table shows that 61% of the total compensation expense recognition is now shifted into the first year of the vesting period.

	Year 1 Vesting	Year 2 Vesting	Year 3 Vesting
1st 3,000 options	100%		
2nd 3,000 options	50%	50%	
3rd 3,000 options	33%	33%	33%
Percent of total	61%	28%	11%
Expense recognition	$30,500	$14,000	$5,500

What Are Stock Appreciation Rights?

Sometimes the management team chooses not to issue stock options to employees, perhaps because employees do not have the funds to purchase shares or because no stock is available for an option plan. If so, an alternative is the *stock appreciation right* (SAR). Under this approach, the company essentially grants an employee a fake stock option and issues compensation to the employee at a future date if the price of company stock has risen from the date of grant to the date at which the compensation is calculated. The amount of compensation paid is the difference between the two stock prices.

How Do I Account for Stock Appreciation Rights?

To account for stock appreciation rights, the controller must determine the amount of any change in company stock during the reporting period and charge the amount to an accrued compensation expense account. If there is a decline in the stock price, the accrued expense account can be reduced. If an employee cancels the SAR agreement (perhaps by leaving the company), the entire amount of accrued compensation expense related to that individual should be reversed in the current period.

If the company pays the recipients of SAR compensation in stock, it usually grants shares on the payment date based on the number of shares at their fair market value that will eliminate the amount of the accrued compensation expense. The journal entry required is a debit to the Accrued Compensation Liability account and a credit to the Stock Rights Outstanding account.

If a service period is required before a SAR can be exercised, the amount of the compensation expense should be recognized ratably over the service period.

EXAMPLE

The Big Fat Pen Company decides to grant 2,500 SARs to its chief pen designer. The stock price at the grant date is $10. After one year, the stock price has increased to $12. After the second year, the stock price has dropped to $11. After the third year, the price increases to $15, at which point the chief pen designer chooses to cash in his SARs and receive payment. The related transactions would be:

(Continued)

(*Continued*)

End of Year 1:	Debit	Credit
Compensation expense ($2 net gain × 2,500 shares)	$5,000	
SAR liability		$5,000
End of Year 2:	$2,500	
SAR liability		
Compensation expense ($1 net loss × 2,500 shares)		$2,500
End of Year 3:	$10,000	
Compensation expense ($4 net gain × 2,500 shares)		
SAR liability		$10,000
SAR liability (payment of employee)	$12,500	
Cash		$12,500

How Does an Employee Stock Ownership Plan Work?

An *employee stock ownership plan* (ESOP) is one where employees receive additional compensation in the form of stock that is purchased by the ESOP from the corporation. Since the company usually has a legal obligation to provide shares or contributions to the ESOP (which are then used to buy its stock), the ESOP should be considered an extension of the company for accounting purposes. This means that if the ESOP obligates itself to a bank loan in order to buy shares from the company, the company should record this liability on its books even if the company is not a guarantor of the loan. The entry would be a debit to cash and a credit to loans payable. However, a loan from the company to the ESOP does not require an accounting entry, since the company is essentially making a loan to itself.

In addition, if the company has obligated itself to a series of future contributions of stock or cash to the ESOP, it should recognize this obligation by recording a journal entry that debits the full amount of the obligation to an Unearned ESOP Shares account (this is reported as a contra-equity account) and crediting the Common Stock account.

When the company makes a contribution to the plan, the funds are usually shifted to the lender that issued a loan to pay for the initial purchase of stock. Accordingly, the Note Payable and Related Interest Expense accounts are both debited, while a second entry also debits a Compensation Expense account and credits the Additional Paid-in Capital and Unearned ESOP Shares accounts to reflect the coincident allocation of shares to ESOP participants.

If the sponsoring company declares a dividend, compensation expense must be recognized for all shares in the ESOP that have *not* been allocated to ESOP participants rather than the usual charge to retained earnings. This tends to be a disincentive for the board of directors to declare a dividend, since the declaration immediately triggers an expense recognition.

EXAMPLE

The Arabian Knights Security Company establishes an ESOP for its employees. The ESOP arranges for a bank loan of $100,000 and uses it to purchase 10,000 shares of no par value stock. The entry is:

	Debit	Credit
Cash	$100,000	
Notes payable		$100,000
Unearned ESOP shares	$100,000	
Common stock		$100,000

Arabian then contributes $10,000 to the plan, which is used to pay down both the principal and interest components of the debt. The entry is:

	Debit	Credit
Interest expense	$2,000	
Notes payable	8,000	
Cash		$10,000

The ESOP plan requires an allocation of shares to plan participants at the end of each calendar year. For the current year, 2,000 shares are allocated. On the date of allocation, the fair market value of the shares is $13. Since the fair value is $3 higher than the original share purchase price of $10, the difference is credited to the Additional Paid-in Capital account. The entry is:

(Continued)

(Continued)

	Debit	Credit
Compensation expense	$26,000	
Additional paid-in capital		$6,000
Unearned ESOP shares		20,000

Arabian then declares a dividend of $0.50 per share. The dividend applied to the 8,000 remaining unallocated shares is charged to a compensation expense account, while the dividend applied to the 2,000 allocated shares is charged to the Retained Earnings account. The entry is:

	Debit	Credit
Retained earnings	$8,000	
Compensation expense	2,000	
Dividend payable		$10,000

CHAPTER 7

LEASE ACCOUNTING

 What Is the Accounting for an Operating Lease by the Lessee?

A typical lease is recorded by the lessee as an operating lease. The lessee accounts for an operating lease by charging lease payments directly to expense. There is no balance sheet recognition of the leased asset at all. If the schedule of lease payments varies in terms of either timing or amount, the lessee should consistently charge the same rental amount to expense in each period, which may result in some variation between the lease payment made and the recorded expense. However, if there is a demonstrable change in the asset being leased that justifies a change in the lease payment being made, there is no need to use straight-line recognition of the expense.

EXAMPLE

The Alabama Botox Clinics (ABC) Company has leased a group of operating room equipment under a five-year operating lease arrangement. The monthly lease cost is $1,000 for the first 30 months and $1,500 for the second 30 months. There is no change in the equipment being leased at any time during the lease period. The correct accounting is to charge the average monthly lease rate of $1,250 to expense during every month of the lease. For the first 30 months, the monthly entry will be:

	Debit	Credit
Equipment rent expense	$1,250	
Accounts payable		$1,000
Accrued lease liability		250

(Continued)

(*Continued*)
During the final 30 months, the monthly entry will be:

	Debit	Credit
Equipment rent expense	$1,250	
Accrued lease liability	250	
Accounts payable		$1,500

What Is the Accounting for a Capital Lease by the Lessee?

The lessee must record a lease as a capital lease if the lease agreement contains any one of these clauses:

- ○ A bargain purchase option, whereby the lessee can purchase the asset from the lessor at the end of the lease term at a price substantially lower than its expected residual value at that time.
- ○ Transfer of asset ownership to the lessee at the end of the lease term.
- ○ A lease term so long that it equals or exceeds 75% of the asset's anticipated economic life.
- ○ The present value of the minimum lease payments is at least 90% of the asset's fair value.

The lessee accounts for a capital lease by recording as an asset the lower of its fair value or the present value of its minimum (i.e., excluding taxes and executory costs) lease payments (less the present value of any guaranteed residual asset value). When calculating the present value of minimum lease payments, use the lesser of the lessee's incremental borrowing rate or the implicit rate used by the lessor. The time period used for the present value calculation should include not only the initial lease term, but also additional periods where nonrenewal will result in a penalty to the lessee, or where lease renewal is at the option of the lessor.

If the lessee treats a leased asset as a capital lease because the lease agreement results in an actual or likely transfer of ownership to the lessee by the end of the lease term, it is depreciated over the full expected life of the asset. However, if a leased asset is being treated as a capital lease when the lessor is still likely to retain ownership of the asset after the end of the lease term, it is depreciated only for the period of the lease.

EXAMPLE

The Arkansas Barrel Company (ABC) leases a wood-working machine under a five-year lease that has a one-year extension clause at the option of the lessor as well as a guaranteed residual value of $15,000. ABC's incremental borrowing rate is 7%. The machine is estimated to have a life of seven years, a current fair value of $90,000, and a residual value (*not* the guaranteed residual value) of $5,000. Annual lease payments are $16,000.

The first step in accounting for this lease is to determine if it is a capital or operating lease. If it is a capital lease, one must calculate its present value, use the effective interest method to determine the allocation of payments between interest expense and reduction of the lease obligation, and determine the depreciation schedule for the asset. Later, there will be a closeout journal entry to record the lease termination. The five steps are:

1. *Determine the lease type.* The woodworking machine is considered to have a life of seven years; since the lease period (including the extra year at the option of the lessor) covers more than 75% of the machine's useful life, the lease is designated a capital lease.
2. *Calculate asset present value.* The machine's present value is a combination of the present value of the $15,000 residual payment due in six years and the present value of annual payments of $16,000 per year for six years. Using the company incremental borrowing rate of 7%, the present value multiplier for $1 due in six years is 0.6663; when multiplied by the guaranteed residual value of $15,000, this results in a present value of $9,995. Using the same interest rate, the present value multiplier for an ordinary annuity of $1 for six years is 4.7665; when multiplied by the annual lease payments of $16,000, this results in a present value of $76,264. After combining the two present values, we arrive at a total lease present value of $86,259. The initial journal entry to record the lease is:

	Debit	Credit
Leased equipment	$86,259	
Lease liability		$86,259

(*Continued*)

(*Continued*)

3. *Allocate payments between interest expense and reduction of lease liability.* ABC's controller then uses the effective interest method to allocate the annual lease payments between the lease's interest expense and reductions in the lease obligation. The interest calculation is based on the beginning balance of the lease obligation. The calculation for each year of the lease is:

Year	Annual Payment	Interest Expense	Reduction in Lease Obligation	Remaining Lease Obligation
0				$86,259
1	$16,000	$6,038	$9,962	76,297
2	16,000	5,341	10,659	65,638
3	16,000	4,595	11,405	54,233
4	16,000	3,796	12,204	42,029
5	16,000	2,942	13,058	28,991
6	16,000	2,009	13,991	15,000

4. *Create depreciation schedule.* Though the asset has an estimated life of seven years, the lease term is for only six years, after which the asset is expected to be returned to the lessor. Accordingly, the asset will be depreciated only over the lease term of six years. Also, the amount of depreciation will only cover the asset's present value of $86,259 *minus* the residual value of $5,000. Therefore, the annual depreciation will be $13,543 (($86,259 present value – $5,000 residual value)/6 years lease term).

5. *Record lease termination.* Once the lease is completed, a journal entry must record the removal of the asset and its related depreciation from the fixed assets register as well as the payment to the lessor of the difference between the $15,000 guaranteed residual value and the actual $5,000 residual value, or $10,000. That entry is:

	Debit	Credit
Lease liability	$15,000	
Accumulated depreciation	81,259	
Cash		$10,000
Leased equipment		86,259

How Does the Lessor Account for an Operating Lease?

If the lessor treats a lease as an *operating lease*, it records any payments received from the lessee as rent revenue. As was the case for the lessee, if there is an unjustified change in the lease rate over the lease term, the average revenue amount should be recognized on a straight-line basis in each reporting period. Any assets being leased are recorded in a separate Investment in Leased Property account in the fixed assets portion of the balance sheet and are depreciated in accordance with standard company policy for similar assets. If the lessor extends incentives (such as a month of no lease payments) or incurs costs associated with the lease (such as legal fees), they should be recognized over the lease term.

How Does the Lessor Account for a Sales-Type Lease?

If the lessor treats a lease as a *sales-type lease* (where the lessor earns both a profit and interest income on the transaction), the initial transaction bears some similarity to a standard sale transaction, except that there is an unearned interest component to the entry. A description of the required entry is contained in the next table, which shows all debits and credits.

Debit	Credit	Explanation
Lease receivable		The sum of all minimum lease payments, minus executory costs, plus the actual residual value
Cost of goods sold		The asset cost, plus initial direct costs, minus the present value* of the actual residual value
	Revenue	The present value* of all minimum lease payments
	Leased asset	The book value of the asset
	Accounts payable	Any initial direct costs associated with the lease
	Unearned interest	The lease receivable, minus the present value* of both the minimum lease payments and actual residual value

*The present value multiplier is based on the lease term and implicit interest rate.

Once payments are received, an entry is needed to record the receipt of cash and corresponding reduction in the lease receivable as well as a second entry to recognize a portion of the unearned interest as interest revenue, based on the effective interest method.

At least annually during the lease term, the lessor should record any permanent reductions in the estimated residual value of the leased asset. It cannot record any increases in the estimated residual value.

When the asset is returned to the lessor at the end of the lease term, a closing entry eliminates the lease receivable associated with the actual residual value, with an offsetting debit to the fixed asset account.

EXAMPLE

The Albany Boat Company (ABC) has issued a seven-year lease to the Adventure Yachting Company (AYC) on a boat for its yacht rental business. The boat cost ABC $450,000 to build and should have a residual value of $75,000 at the end of the lease. Annual lease payments are $77,000. ABC's implicit interest rate is 8%. The present value multiplier for an ordinary annuity of $1 for seven years at 8% interest is 5.2064. The present value multiplier for $1 due in seven years at 8% interest is 0.5835. We construct the initial journal entry with these calculations:

○ *Lease receivable.* This is the sum of all minimum lease payments, which is $539,000 ($77,000/year × 7 years), plus the actual residual value of $75,000, for a total lease receivable of $614,000.

○ *Cost of goods sold.* This is the asset cost of $450,000, minus the present value of the residual value, which is $43,763 ($75,000 residual value × present value multiplier of 0.5835).

○ *Revenue.* This is the present value of all minimum lease payments, or $400,893 ($77,000/year × present value multiplier of 5.2064).

○ *Inventory.* ABC's book value for the yacht is $450,000, which is used to record a reduction in its inventory account.

○ *Unearned interest.* This is the lease receivable of $614,000, minus the present value of the minimum lease payments of $400,893, minus the present value of the residual value of $43,763, which yields $169,344.

Based on these calculations, the initial journal entry is:

	Debit	Credit
Lease receivable	$614,000	
Cost of goods sold	406,237	
Revenue		$400,893
Boat asset		450,000
Unearned interest		169,344

The next step in the example is to determine the allocation of lease payments between interest income and reduction of the lease principle, which is accomplished through the next effective interest table.

Year	Annual Payment	Interest Revenue	Reduction in Lease Obligation	Remaining Lease Obligation
0				$444,656
1	$77,000	$35,572	$41,428	403,228
2	77,000	32,258	44,742	358,486
3	77,000	28,679	48,321	310,165
4	77,000	24,813	52,187	257,978
5	77,000	20,638	56,362	201,616
6	77,000	16,129	60,871	140,745
7	77,000	11,255	65,745	75,000

The interest expense shown in the effective interest table can be used to record the allocation of each lease payment between interest revenue and principal reduction. For example, the entries recorded for Year 4 of the lease are:

	Debit	Credit
Cash	$77,000	
Lease receivable		$77,000
Unearned interest	$24,813	
Interest revenue		$24,813

Once the lease expires and the boat is returned to ABC, the final entry to close out the lease transaction is:

(Continued)

(*Continued*)

	Debit	Credit
Boat asset	$75,000	
Lease receivable		$75,000

How Does the Lessor Account for a Direct Financing Lease?

If the lessor treats a lease as a *direct financing lease*, it will recognize interest income only from the transaction; there will be no additional profit from the implicit sale of the underlying asset to the lessee. This treatment arises when the lessor purchases an asset specifically to lease it to the lessee. The other difference between a direct financing lease and a sales-type lease is that any direct costs incurred when a lease is originated must be amortized over the life of the lease, which reduces the implicit interest rate used to allocate lease payments between interest revenue and a reduction of the lease principal.

A description of the required entry is contained in the next table, which shows all debits and credits.

Debit	Credit	Explanation
Lease receivable		The sum of all minimum lease payments, plus the actual residual value
	Leased asset	The book value of the asset
	Unearned interest	The lease receivable minus the asset book value

At least annually during the lease term, the lessor should record any permanent reductions in the estimated residual value of the leased asset. It cannot record any increases in the estimated residual value.

EXAMPLE

The Albany Leasing Company (ALC) purchases a boat from a third party for $700,000 and intend to lease it to the Adventure Yachting Company for six years at an annual lease rate of $140,093. The boat should have a residual value of $120,000 at the end of the lease term. Also, there is $18,000 of initial direct costs associated with the lease. ALC's implicit interest rate is 9%. The present value multiplier for an ordinary annuity of $1 for six years at 9% interest is 4.4859. The present value multiplier for $1 due in six years at 9% interest is 0.5963. We construct the initial journal entry with the next calculations:

○ *Lease receivable.* This is the sum of all minimum lease payments, which is $840,558 ($140,093/year × 6 years), plus the residual value of $120,000, for a total lease receivable of $960,558.
○ *Leased asset.* This is the asset cost of $700,000.
○ *Unearned interest.* This is the lease receivable of $942,558, minus the asset book value of $700,000, which yields $260,558.

Based on these calculations, the initial journal entry is:

	Debit	Credit
Lease receivable	$960,558	
Initial direct costs	18,000	
Leased asset		$700,000
Unearned interest		260,558
Cash		18,000

Next, ALC's controller must determine the implicit interest rate associated with the transaction. Though ALC intended the rate to be 9%, the controller must add to the lease receivable the initial direct costs of $18,000, resulting in a final gross investment of $978,558 and a net investment (net of unearned interest income of $260,558) of $718,000. The determination of the implicit interest rate with this additional information is derived most easily through an electronic spreadsheet. For example, the IRR function in Microsoft Excel automatically creates the new implicit interest rate, which is 8.2215%.

With the revised implicit interest rate completed, the next step in the example is to determine the allocation of lease payments between interest income, a reduction of initial direct costs, and a reduction of the lease principal, which is accomplished through the next effective interest table.

(Continued)

(*Continued*)

Year	Annual Payment	Unearned Interest Reduction	Interest Revenue	Reduction of Initial Direct Costs	Reduction in Lease Obligation	Remaining Lease Obligation (1)	Remaining Lease Obligation (2)
0						$718,000	$700,000
1	$140,093	$63,000	$59,031	$3,969	$81,062	636,938	622,907
2	140,093	56,062	52,366	3,696	87,727	549,211	538,876
3	140,093	48,499	45,154	3,345	94,939	454,271	447,281
4	140,093	40,255	37,348	2,907	102,745	351,526	347,444
5	140,093	31,270	28,901	2,369	111,192	240,334	238,621
6	140,093	21,476	19,759	1,717	120,334	120,000	120,000*
	Totals	$260,558*		$18,000*			

*Rounded

The calculations used in the table are shown next.:

○ *Annual payment.* The annual cash payment due to the lessor.
○ *Unearned interest reduction.* The original implicit interest rate of 9% multiplied by the beginning balance in the Remaining Lease Obligation (2) column, which does not include the initial direct lease cost. The total at the bottom of the column equals the unearned interest liability that will be eliminated over the course of the lease.
○ *Interest revenue.* The revised implicit interest rate of 8.2215% multiplied by the beginning balance in the Remaining Lease Obligation (1) column, which includes the initial direct lease costs.
○ *Reduction of initial direct costs.* The amount in the Unearned Interest Reduction column minus the amount in the Interest Revenue column, which is used to reduce the balance of the initial direct costs incurred. The total at the bottom of the column equals the initial direct costs incurred at the beginning of the lease.
○ *Reduction in lease obligation.* The Annual Payment minus the Interest Revenue.
○ *Remaining lease obligation (1).* The beginning lease obligation (including initial direct costs) less the principal portion of the annual payment.
○ *Remaining lease obligation (2).* The beginning lease obligation, not including initial direct costs, less the principal portion of the annual payment.

Based on the calculations in the effective interest table, the journal entry at the end of the first year would show the receipt of cash and a reduction in the lease receivable. Another entry would reduce the unearned interest balance while offsetting the initial direct costs and recognizing interest revenue. The first-year entries are:

	Debit	Credit
Cash	$140,093	
Lease receivable		$140,093
Unearned interest	$63,000	
Interest revenue		$59,031
Initial direct costs		3,969

What Is the Accounting for a Lease Termination?

On the date that a lessee notifies the lessor that it intends to terminate a lease, the lessee must recognize a liability for the fair value of the termination costs, which include any continuing lease payments, less prepaid rent, plus deferred rent, minus the amount of any sublease payments. Changes in these estimates are recorded immediately in the income statement.

If the lessor has recorded a lease as a sales-type or direct financing lease, it records the underlying leased asset at the lower of its current net book value, present value, or original cost, with any resulting adjustment being recorded in current earnings. At the time of termination notice, the lessor records a receivable in the amount of any termination payments yet to be made, with an offsetting credit to a deferred rent liability account. The lessor then recognizes any remaining rental payments on a straight-line basis over the revised period during which the payments are to be received.

What Is the Accounting for a Lease Extension by the Lessee?

If a lessee extends an operating lease and the extension is also classified as an operating lease, the lessee continues to treat the extension in the same manner it has used for the existing lease. If the lease extension requires payment amounts differing from those required under the initial agreement but the asset received does not change, the lessee should consistently charge the same rental amount to expense in each period, which may result in some variation between the lease payment made and the recorded expense.

If a lessee extends an existing capital lease but the lease structure now requires the extension to be recorded as an operating lease, the lessee writes off the existing asset as well as all associated accumulated depreciation and recognizes either a gain or loss on the transaction. Payments made under the lease extension are handled in accordance with the rules of a standard operating lease.

If a lessee extends an existing capital lease and the structure of the extension agreement requires the lease to continue to be recorded as a capital lease, the lessee changes the asset valuation and related lease liability by the difference between the present value of the new series of future minimum lease payments and the existing balance. The present value calculation must use the interest rate used for the same calculation at the inception of the original lease.

What Is the Accounting for a Lease Extension by the Lessor?

When a *lease extension* occurs and the lessor classifies the extension as a direct financing lease, the lease receivable and estimated residual value (downward only) are adjusted to match the new lease terms, with any adjustment going to unearned income. When a lease extension occurs and the lessor classifies an existing direct financing or sales-type lease as an operating lease, the lessor writes off the remaining lease investment and instead records the asset at the lower of its current net book value, original cost, or present value. The change in value from the original net investment is recorded against income in the period when the lease extension date occurs.

What Is the Accounting for a Sublease?

A *sublease* arises when leased property is leased by the original lessee to a third party. When this happens, the original lessee accounts for the sublease as if it were the original lessor. This means that it can account for the lease as an operating, a direct sales, or a sales-type lease. The original lessee continues to account for its ongoing lease payments to the original lessor as though the sublease did not exist.

What Is the Accounting for a Sale-Leaseback Transaction?

A *sale-leaseback transaction* arises when a property owner sells the property to another entity, which leases the property back to the original owner. If the transaction results in a loss, the lessee recognizes it fully in the current period.

If the present value of the rental payments is at least 90% of the property's fair value, the lessee is considered to have retained substantially all rights to use the property. Under this scenario, there are two ways to account for the transaction:

1. If the lease qualifies as a capital lease, the lessee accounts for it as such and recognizes any profits on

the initial property sale over the lease term in proportion to the asset amortization schedule.
2. If the lease qualifies as an operating lease, the lessee accounts for it as such and recognizes any profits on the initial property sale over the lease term in proportion to the lease payments.

If the present value of the rental payments is less than 10% of the property's fair value, the lessee should recognize all gains from the transaction fully in the current period. If the rental payments under the transaction appear unreasonable based on market prices at the time of lease inception, the payments are adjusted to make them "reasonable." The difference between the adjusted and existing lease rates is amortized over the life of the asset (if a capital lease) or the life of the lease (if an operating lease).

If the present value of the rental payments is more than 10% but less than 90% of the property's fair value, any excess profit on the asset sale can be recognized by the lessee on the sale date. If the lease is treated as a capital lease, excess profit is calculated as the difference between the asset sale price and the recorded value of the leased asset. If the lease is treated as an operating lease, excess profit is calculated as the difference between the asset sale price and the present value of the minimum lease payments, using the lower of the lessor's implicit lease rate or the lessee's incremental borrowing rate.

CHAPTER 8

FOREIGN CURRENCY ACCOUNTING

What Is the Goal of Foreign Currency Accounting?

*T*he key consideration when making foreign currency translations is that when the conversion is complete, we have an accurate translation of accounting performance in a foreign currency into precisely the same performance in U.S. dollars. In other words, a foreign subsidiary whose financial statements have specific current ratios, gross margins, and net profits will see the same results when translated into a report presentation in U.S. dollars.

The current rate method and the remeasurement method are the two techniques used to translate the financial results of a foreign entity's operations into the currency of its corporate parent.

How Does the Current Rate Method Convert Foreign Currency Transactions into U.S. Dollars?

The *current rate translation method* is used when a currency besides the U.S. dollar is determined to be the primary currency used by a subsidiary. This approach is usually selected when a subsidiary's operations are not integrated into those of its U.S.-based parent, if its financing is primarily in that of the local currency, or if the subsidiary conducts most of its transactions in the local currency.

However, one cannot use this method if the country in which the subsidiary is located suffers from a high rate of inflation, which is defined as a cumulative rate of 100% or more over the most recent three years. In this case, the remeasurement method must be used. If the local economy is considered to no longer be inflationary, the reporting method may be changed back to the current rate method; when this happens, the accounting staff must convert the financial statements of the impacted subsidiary back into the local currency using the exchange rate on the date when the determination is made.

To complete the current rate translation method, the first step is to determine the functional currency of the subsidiary. This should be the currency in which the bulk of its transactions and financing is used. Next, convert all of the subsidiary's transactions to this functional currency. Then convert all assets and liabilities of the subsidiary to U.S. dollars at the current rate of exchange as of the date of the financial statements. These conversion rules apply:

- ○ Revenues and expenses that have occurred throughout the current fiscal year are converted at a weighted-average rate of exchange for the entire year. A preferable approach is to convert them at the exchange rates in effect on the dates when they occurred, but this is considered too labor-intensive to be practical in most situations.
- ○ Stockholder's equity is converted at the historical rate of exchange. However, changes to retained earnings within the current reporting period are recorded at the weighted-average rate of exchange for the year, since they are derived from revenues and expenses that were also recorded at the weighted-average rate of exchange.
- ○ Dividends declared during the year are recorded at the exchange rate on the date of declaration.
- ○ Any resulting translation adjustments should be stored in the equity section of the corporate parent's consolidated balance sheet. This account is cumulative, so separately report in the footnotes to the financial statements the change in the translation adjustments account as a result of activities in the reporting period.

EXAMPLE

A division of the Oregon Clock Company is located in Mexico. This division maintains its books in pesos, borrows pesos from a local bank, and conducts the majority of its operations within Mexico. Accordingly, its functional currency is the peso, which requires the parent's accounting staff to record the division's results using the current rate method.

The peso exchange rate at the beginning of the year is assumed to be .08 to the dollar, while the rate at the end of the year is assumed to be .10 to the dollar. For the purposes of this example, the blended full-year rate of exchange for the peso is assumed to be .09 to the dollar. The Mexican division's balance sheet is shown in Exhibit 8.1, while its income statement is shown in Exhibit 8.2. Note that the net income figure derived from Exhibit 8.2 is incorporated into the retained earnings statement at the bottom of the exhibit and is incorporated from there into the retained earnings line item in Exhibit 8.1. For simplicity, the beginning retained earnings figure in Exhibit 8.2 is assumed to be zero, implying that the company is in its first year of existence.

	Pesos	Exchange Rate	U.S. Dollars
Assets			
Cash	427	.08	34
Accounts Receivable	1,500	.08	120
Inventory	2,078	.08	166
Fixed Assets	3,790	.08	303
Total Assets	7,795		623
Liabilities & Equity			
Accounts Payable	1,003	.08	80
Notes Payable	4,250	.08	340
Common Stock	2,100	.10	210
Additional Paid-in Capital	428	.10	43
Retained Earnings	14	Note 1	0
Translation Adjustments	—	—	−50
Total Liabilities & Equity	7,795		623

Note 1: As noted in the income statement

Exhibit 8.1 BALANCE SHEET CONVERSION UNDER THE CURRENT RATE METHOD

	Pesos	Exchange Rate	U.S. Dollars
Revenue	6,750	.09	608
Expenses	6,736	.09	607
Net Income	14		1
Beginning Retained Earnings	0		0
Add: Net Income	14	.09	0
Ending Retained Earnings	14		0

Exhibit 8.2 INCOME STATEMENT CONVERSION UNDER THE CURRENT RATE METHOD

How Does the Remeasurement Method Convert Foreign Currency Transactions into U.S. Dollars?

The *remeasurement method* is used when the U.S. dollar is designated as the primary currency in which transactions are recorded at a foreign location. Another clear indicator of when this method is used is when the subsidiary has close operational integration with its U.S. parent or when most of its financing, sales, and expenses are denominated in dollars.

Under this method, we translate not only cash but also any transactions that will be settled in cash (mostly accounts receivable and payable, as well as loans) at the current exchange rate as of the date of the financial statements. All other assets and liabilities (such as inventory, prepaid items, fixed assets, trademarks, goodwill, and equity) will be settled at the historical exchange rate on the date when these transactions occurred.

There are a few cases where the income statement is impacted by the items on the balance sheet that have been translated using historical interest rates. For example, the cost of goods sold will be impacted when inventory that has been translated at a historical exchange rate is liquidated. When this happens, the inventory valuation at the historical exchange rate is charged through the income statement. The same approach is used for the depreciation of fixed assets and the amortization of intangible items.

Other income statement items primarily involve transactions that arise throughout the reporting year of the subsidiary. For these items, it would be too labor-intensive to determine the exact exchange rate for each item at the time it occurred. Instead, determine the weighted-average exchange rate for the entire reporting period, and apply this average to the income statement items that have occurred during that period.

EXAMPLE

A simplified example of a corporate subsidiary's (located in Mexico) balance sheet is shown in Exhibit 8.3. The peso exchange rate at the beginning of the year is assumed to be .08 to the dollar, while the rate at the end of the year is assumed to be .10 to the dollar. The primary difference in calculation from the current rate method shown earlier in Exhibit 8.1 is that the exchange rate for the inventory and fixed assets accounts have changed from the year-end rate to the rate at which they are assumed to have been originated at an earlier date. Also, there is no translation adjustment account in the equity section, as was the case under the current rate method.

An abbreviated income statement is also shown in Exhibit 8.4. For the purposes of this exhibit, the blended full-year rate of exchange for the peso is assumed to be .09 to the dollar. Note that the net income figure derived from Exhibit 8.4 is incorporated into the retained earnings statement at the bottom of Exhibit 8.4, and is incorporated from there into the retained earnings line item in Exhibit 8.3.

	Pesos	Exchange Rate	U.S. Dollars
Assets			
Cash	427	.08	34
Accounts Receivable	1,500	.08	120
Inventory	2,078	.10	208
Fixed Assets	3,790	.10	379
Total Assets	7,795		741
Liabilities & Equity			
Accounts Payable	1,003	.08	80
Notes Payable	4,250	.08	340
Common Stock	2,100	.10	210
Additional Paid-in Capital	428	.10	43
Retained Earnings	14	Note 1	68
Total Liabilities & Equity	7,795		741

Note 1: As noted in the income statement

Exhibit 8.3 BALANCE SHEET CONVERSION UNDER THE REMEASUREMENT METHOD

	Pesos	Exchange Rate	U.S. Dollars
Revenue	6,750	.09	608
Goodwill Amortization	500	.08	40
Other Expenses	6,236	.09	561
Remeasurement Gain	—		61
Net Income	14		68
Beginning Retained Earnings	0		0
Add: Net Income	14		68
Ending Retained Earnings	14		68

Exhibit 8.4 INCOME STATEMENT CONVERSION UNDER THE REMEASUREMENT METHOD

What Conversion Method Is Used for Occasional Foreign Currency Transactions?

If a company participates in only an occasional sales trans-action in which it pays or accepts payment in a foreign currency, it can record the initial sale and related account receivable based on the spot exchange rate on the date when the transaction is initially completed. From that point forward, the amount of the recorded sale will not change—only the related receivable will be altered based on the spot exchange rate as of the date of the balance sheet on which it is reported, adjusting it up or down to reflect the existence of a potential gain or loss at the time of the eventual collection of the receivable. The final gain or loss will be recorded when the receivable is settled, using the spot rate on that date.

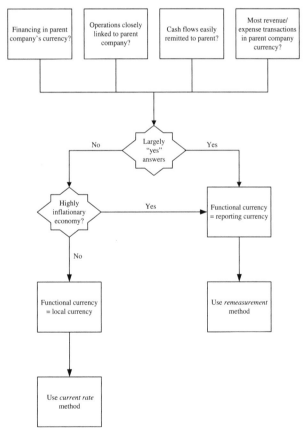

Exhibit 8.5   Decision Tree for Foreign Currency Translation Methods

How Do I Decide Which Conversion Method to Use?

The decision tree shown in Exhibit 8.5 can be used to determine whether to use the current rate method or remeasurement method when translating the financial statements of a foreign subsidiary into the currency of the corporate parent.

What Is the Accounting for Foreign Currency Translation Adjustments?

The gains and losses resulting from various translation adjustments are treated in different ways, with some initially being stored in the balance sheet and others being recorded at once in the income statement. Here are the key rules to remember:

○ If a company is directly engaged in foreign exchange transactions that are denominated in foreign currencies, any translation adjustments to U.S. dollars that result in gains or losses should be immediately recognized in the income statement. The company can continue to make these adjustments for changes between the last reporting date and the date of the current financial statements, and may continue to do so until the underlying transactions have been concluded.

EXAMPLE

The Louisiana Backhoe Company (LBC) sells backhoes to a variety of countries in the European Union, all of which are paid for in euros. It sold $200,000 of backhoes to Germany on March 15. The receivable was still outstanding on March 31, which was the date of the quarterly financial statements. As of that date, the exchange rate of the euro has dropped by 1%, so LBC has an unrecognized loss of $2,000. It records this as a loss on foreign currency transactions and credits its accounts receivable account to reduce the amount of its receivable asset. When payment on the receivable is made to LBC on April 15, the exchange rate has returned to its level on the sale date of March 15. LBC must now record a gain on its books of $2,000 to offset the loss it had previously recorded.

○ Do not report gains or losses on transactions of a long-term nature when accounted for by the equity method. These transactions are defined as those with no settlement date planned in the foreseeable future. Instead, include these transactions in the standard translation procedure used to translate the financial statements of a subsidiary into the currency of its corporate parent.

○ If a foreign entity has multiple distinct operations, it is possible that some have different functional currencies. If so, regularly review their operations to determine the correct functional currency to use, and translate their financial results accordingly. However, if the results of a selected operation on the financial reports of a foreign entity are insignificant, there is no requirement to break out its financial statements using a different functional currency.

○ If there has been a material change in an exchange rate in which a company's obligations or subsidiary results are enumerated, and the change has occurred subsequent to the date of financial statements that are being included in a company's audited results, the change and its impact on the financial statements should be itemized in a footnote that accompanies the audited results.

What Exchange Rates Are Used for Conversion Calculations?

There can be some confusion regarding the precise exchange rate to be used when conducting foreign currency translations. Here are some guidelines.

○ If there is no published foreign exchange rate available on the specific date when a transaction occurred that requires translation, use the rate for the date that most immediately follows the date of the transaction.

○ If the date of a financial statement that is to be converted from a foreign currency is different from the date of the financial statements into which they are to be converted into U.S. dollars, use the date of the foreign currency financial statements as the date for which the proper exchange rate shall be used as the basis for translation.

○ If there is more than one published exchange rate available that can be used as the basis for a translation, use the rate that could have been used as the basis for the exchange of funds which could then be used to remit dividends to shareholders. Alternatively, use the rate at which a settlement of the entire related transaction could have been completed.

How Is Foreign Exchange Handled in Intercompany Transactions?

When the results of a parent company and its subsidiaries are combined for financial statement reporting purposes, the gains or losses resulting from intercompany foreign exchange transactions must be reported in the consolidated statements. This happens when the parent has a receivable denominated in the currency of the subsidiary, or vice versa, and a change in the exchange rate results in a gain or loss. Thus, even though the intercompany transaction is purged from the consolidated financial statement, the associated gain or loss must still be reported.

EXAMPLE

The Seely Furniture Company owns a sawmill in Canada that supplies all of its wood raw materials. The subsidiary holds receivables from the corporate parent that is denominated in U.S. dollars. During the year, there has been a steady increase in the value of the dollar, resulting in a conversion into more Canadian dollars than was the case when each receivable was originally created. By the end of the year, the subsidiary has recorded a gain on currency transactions of $42,000 Canadian dollars. Accordingly, the Seely corporate parent records the gain on its books, denominated in U.S. dollars. Because the year-end exchange rate between the two currencies was $0.73 Canadian per U.S. dollar, the subsidiary's gain is recorded as a gain in U.S. dollars of $30,660 ($42,000 Canadian × 0.73 exchange rate) on the books of the parent.

PART II

ACCOUNTING MANAGEMENT

CHAPTER 9

CLOSING THE BOOKS

What Types of Closes Are There?

*T*he *standard close* is the typical closing process, involving extended wait times to ensure that all transactions are fully complete before financial statements are produced. The *fast close* is an acceleration of the standard closing process, resulting in approximately the same financial reporting package being issued (possibly somewhat reduced in size). The focus of this approach is a careful examination of the closing process to strip out wait times, consolidate tasks, eliminate unnecessary functions, add transaction best practices, and selectively apply automation where necessary.

The *soft close* is less labor-intensive than a standard close, because it does not generate as much information. It is designed solely for internal corporate use, so its end product is only those management reports needed to run operations. It typically does not include overhead allocations and many accruals. The *virtual close* involves the use of a largely automated accounting system, one that can produce required financial information at any time, on demand. It requires essentially error-free transactions.

What Problems Contribute to a Delayed Close?

Some or a combination of these issues can prolong the closing process:

○ *Management perfectionism.* The controller waits for all accounting situations to resolve themselves, so that the reported results are more likely to be perfectly correct.
○ *Lack of procedures.* There is no checklist for ensuring that all closing steps are completed.

○ *Multiple accounting software packages.* Each subsidiary compiles accounting information in a different system, which is manually transferred to the corporate system.

○ *Excessive decentralization.* Subsidiary-level results must be completed before being forwarded to the corporate staff for consolidation.

○ *Low-quality data.* Transactional errors must be corrected before the financial statements are issued.

○ *Varying charts of accounts.* Subsidiaries use different charts of accounts, so their results must be remapped into the corporate system.

○ *Multiple report formats.* Different managers receive different financial statement formats, which require additional report assembly work.

○ *Public reporting.* If financials must be converted into annual Form 10-K or quarterly Form 10-Q reports, auditors, attorneys, and the audit committee will be also involved.

How Does Activity Acceleration Improve the Close?

A large number of closing activities should be shifted into the month prior to the closing date. The listed items should be considered for this treatment.

○ *Review subledger accounts.* A continuing review will uncover transactional errors that can be fixed well before the end of the month.

○ *Reconcile bank accounts.* Reconciling cash records to bank balances every day leaves very little bank reconciliation work to complete at month-end.

○ *Update reserves.* The reserves for inventory obsolescence, bad debts, and sales returns can usually be updated prior to the end of the month.

○ *Review lower of cost or market (LCM).* Schedule LCM reviews prior to month-end, in order to process any necessary write-downs in advance of the close.

○ *Bill recurring invoices.* Print any recurring invoices for the following month in advance, assuming that billable amounts can be predicted.

○ *Review rebillable expenses.* Some employee expenses are rebilled to customers; if so, review the expenses early, to see if they are appropriate for rebilling.

○ *Review preliminary billable hours.* There are usually some errors in the employee records for billable hours, so review the time records in advance and correct them as necessary.

○ *Accrue interest expense.* Unless significant changes in debt levels are expected near the month-end, predict debt balances and accrue the related interest expense.

○ *Accrue unpaid wages.* Use a centralized timekeeping system and an estimate of overtime hours worked to accrue hourly wages payable just prior to the closing date.

○ *Reconcile asset and liability accounts.* Review the detail for all asset and liability accounts just prior to the close, when there is more time for a thoughtful review of these accounts. Any last-minute changes to these accounts can be reviewed in the following month.

○ *Calculate depreciation.* Calculate and record deprecation just prior to the close; for late asset changes, record a catch-up entry in the following month.

○ *Review financial statements for errors.* Print the financial statements a day or two in advance, looking for obvious errors, and correct them before the close begins.

○ *Complete supporting reports in advance.* If there are reports that accompany the financial statements, complete them to the extent possible before period-end.

How Do Reporting Changes Improve the Close?

The next possibilities can reduce the effort required to create and deliver the financial statements.

○ *Post the financial statements.* It can take time to physically print the financial reporting package and deliver it to recipients, so consider posting it in PDF format on a company intranet site and notifying recipients of the post.

○ *Standardize reports.* Some managers want different contents to their financial reporting packages. Instead, issue the same core package to all recipients, and follow up later with additional reports, as needed.

○ *Eliminate cost reporting.* Cost reports take a long time to complete, so issue them separately from the financial statements.

○ *Eliminate metrics.* Metrics calculations require additional time to complete, so issue them after the financial statements have been delivered.

How Can Journal Entry Optimization Improve the Close?

Proper management of journal entries and the chart of accounts can lead to significant improvements in the closing process. Here are the key factors to consider.

○ *Eliminate immaterial entries.* Many entries have an immaterial impact on the results shown in the financial statements, so do not waste time recording them.

○ *Standardize journal entries.* If journal entries are repeated in the same format every month, create a journal entry template and use it every month, thereby reducing labor and avoiding data entry errors.

○ *Use recurring entries.* If an entry is in the exact same amount every month and is recorded against the same accounts, set it up in the accounting system to be recurring, so that no additional entry labor is required.

○ *Restrict data entry.* Only one person who is expert at data entry should record journal entries. This reduces errors and also prevents duplicate entries from being made.

○ *Standardize the chart of accounts.* All subsidiaries should use the same version of the chart of accounts, with no exceptions. This prevents the need for mapping to the corporate chart of accounts.

How Can I Improve the Inventory Close?

The next factors are of great assistance in completing the inventory portion of the close, since they are instrumental in creating inventory records with a high degree of accuracy.

○ *Create inventory tracking system.* Create an inventory database in which the quantity of each item is shown as well as the location where it is located.

○ *Implement cycle counting.* The warehouse staff should count a small portion of the inventory every day, on a rolling basis, and reconcile the results to the inventory database.

○ *Reduce the inventory.* Use the techniques listed in Chapter 12, *Inventory Management*, to reduce the total number of stock-keeping units in the warehouse.

○ *Eliminate obsolete inventory.* Use the dispositioning methods noted in Chapter 12 to flush out all inventory designated as obsolete.

The first two points are needed to improve inventory record accuracy, while the last two points are needed to reduce the total number of records that must be maintained.

How Can I Improve the Payroll Close?

The central issue in improving the closing speed of the payroll function is to automate the entire function to the greatest extent possible. Here are specific areas that can benefit the most from automation.

- ○ *Computerize timekeeping.* Install computerized time clocks that summarize time postings into a central database and flag possibly incorrect information for further review.
- ○ *Grant system access to managers and employees.* Managers and employees can directly update information in the payroll system, thereby reducing the risk of data entry errors by the payroll staff.
- ○ *Automate pay calculations.* Either use an off-the-shelf accounting system that calculates pay, or outsource this task.
- ○ *Automate commission calculations.* Streamline the methodology for calculating commissions to the point where the computer system can generate the commissions with a simple report.
- ○ *Automate payments.* Use direct deposit or pay cards, so that the pay system automatically issues payments to employees.

These steps essentially automate the payroll process from beginning to end, so that the payroll staff only has to monitor the system for errors. It greatly expedites the payroll close.

How Can I Improve the Payables Close?

The essential parts of the payables function that impact the closing process are the sheer volume of transactions and the risk of delayed supplier invoices. The next points can improve the process.

- ○ *Record invoices upon receipt.* Do not route invoices outside the payables department for approvals and *then* record them, which increases the risk of lost invoices. Do the reverse, so that all invoices are recorded promptly upon receipt.

○ *Use procurement cards.* Procurement cards can be used to absorb much of the small-invoice volume that burdens the payables staff, making it easier to enter and reconcile all other information during the close.

○ *Accrue missing invoices.* Maintain a standard check-list of supplier invoices for which the company knows the approximate amount and which typically arrive late. If one of these invoices has not arrived by the closing date, accrue the related expense.

○ *Encourage electronic submissions.* Create a Web site that suppliers can use to enter their invoices straight into the company's accounting system. An electronic data interchange (EDI) system provides the same level of connectivity. Either approach eliminates manual date entry.

○ *Automate expense reporting.* Have employees enter their expenses directly into the accounting system or through the system of a third party.

 ## What Is Included in a Closing Checklist?

The next table includes the essential activities normally used in a close.

Prior to Month-End	During Core Closing Period
Review subledger transactions	Ensure inventory cutoff
Complete a daily bank reconciliation	Complete employee time records
Review uncashed checks	Count and value inventory
Update obsolete inventory reserve	Enter late supplier invoices
Determine lower of cost or market	Complete month-end invoicing
Calculate overhead allocation bases	Accrue revenue for unbilled jobs
Bill recurring invoices	Accrue commissions
Review rebillable expenses	Accrue royalties
Update bad debt reserve	Convert results to reporting currency
Review billable hours	Map division results to corporate books
Accrue interest expense	Eliminate intercompany transactions
Accrue unpaid wages	Review preliminary financial statements
Accrue unused vacation time	Adjust errors

Prior to Month-End	During Core Closing Period
Accrue travel expenses	Finalize and issue financial statements
Reconcile asset and liability accounts	**Deferred Activities**
Calculate depreciation	Defer mailing of invoices
Review financial statements for errors	Calculate closing metrics
Complete reports in advance	Update closing procedures

What Extra Closing Steps Are Needed by a Public Company?

A publicly held company must complete the next additional steps, which greatly delay the completion of its closing process.

- ○ *Construct the Securities and Exchange Commission (SEC) filing.* This is either the annual Form 10-K or quarterly Form 10-Q, which are described further in Chapter 22, *SEC Filings.* These forms incorporate the financial statements into a great deal of additional information about the company.
- ○ *Auditor review or audit.* Outside auditors must either audit the financial statements in the Form 10-K or review the same information in the Form 10-Q.
- ○ *Legal review.* The company's securities attorneys review the form to ensure that all legal requirements have been complied with.
- ○ *Officer certification.* The company's chief executive officer and chief financial officer must certify that the information contained within the report presents fairly, in all material respects, the company's financial condition and results of operations.
- ○ *Audit committee approval.* This committee must review and approve the 10-K and 10-Q filings.
- ○ *EDGARize.* The 10-K or 10-Q must be converted into a format acceptable to the SEC's EDGAR filing system and must be submitted to that system.

CHAPTER 10

CASH MANAGEMENT

 What Types of Float Are Associated with a Check Payment?

When a company issues a check, its bank balance will remain unchanged for several days, due to four different kinds of float.

1. There is a delay while the payment is delivered through the postal service, which is the *mail float*.
2. The supplier must deposit the check at its bank; the time between when the supplier receives the check and deposits it is the *processing float*.
3. The time between when the check is deposited and when it is available to the recipient is the *availability float*. Availability float is generally no longer than two days.
4. The time between when the check is deposited and when it is charged to the payer's account is the *presentation float*.

The same process works in reverse when a company receives a payment from a customer. In this case, the company receives a payment and records the receipt in its own records but must wait multiple days before the cash is credited to its bank account. This *availability float* works against the company, because it does not immediately have use of the funds noted on the check.

The combination of the floats associated with these inbound and outbound check payments is the *net float*.

The check process flow, with float periods included, is shown in Exhibit 10.1.

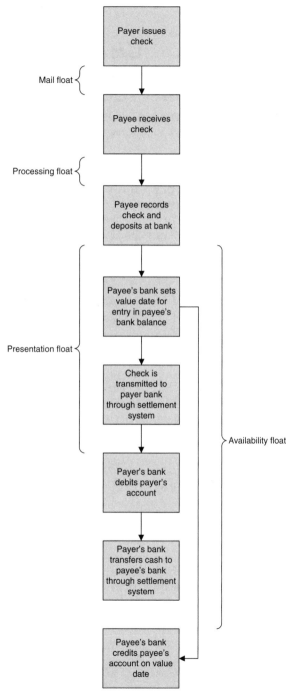

Exhibit 10.1 Check Process Flow

What Is Value Dating?

When a bank receives a deposit of checks from a payee, it will credit the payee's account with the funds represented by the checks. However, the bank has not really received the cash yet, since it must still collect the funds from the bank of the paying party. Until the bank collects the funds, it is at risk of having a negative cash flow situation if the payee uses the cash it has just received.

To avoid this risk, the bank posts the amount of the deposit with a *value date* that is one or more days later than the book date. This value date is the presumed date of receipt of the cash by the bank. Once the value date is reached, the payee has use of the funds. The value date may also be categorized by a bank as one-day float, two-plus-day float, or some similar term.

Some banks take advantage of their customers and extend the value dating out beyond the point when they have actually received the cash. This gives a bank use of the funds for an additional period of time, at the expense of its customers.

What Is a Lockbox?

A company can have its bank receive and process checks on its behalf, which is termed a *lockbox* service. The bank assigns a mailbox address to the company, which forwards this information to its customers. The customers mail their checks to the lockbox, where the bank opens the envelopes, scans all checks and accompanying documents, deposits the checks, and makes the scans available to the company through a Web site. By using a lockbox, a company can eliminate some of the float involved in check processing and eliminate some check-processing labor. This also means that checks are no longer processed through the company's location, which greatly reduces the amount of cash controls that it needs.

What Is Remote Deposit Capture?

Remote deposit capture allows a company to avoid the physical movement of received checks to its bank. Instead, the company uses a special scanner and scanning software to create an electronic image of each check, which it then transmits to the bank. The bank accepts the online image, posts it to the company's account, and assigns funds availability based on a predetermined schedule.

The key benefit of remote deposit capture is the complete elimination of the transportation float that arises when shifting checks from the company to the bank. Another benefit is that a company no longer needs a bank that is physically located near the company location. Instead, it can consolidate its banking relationships and use just a single provider that may be located anywhere in the country.

Why Is Cash Concentration Useful?

Aggregating cash from multiple accounts into a single one is useful for these reasons:

- *Elimination of idle cash.* Cash idling in a multitude of accounts can be aggregated into interest-earning investments.
- *Improved investment returns.* If cash can be aggregated, it is easier to allocate the cash into short-term, low-yield investments and higher-yield, longer-term investments. The overall results should be an improved return on investment.
- *More cost-effective oversight of accounts.* When an automated sweeping arrangement is used to concentrate cash, there is no need to manually review subsidiary account balances. This can yield a significant reduction in labor costs.
- *Internal funding of debit balances.* Where a company is grappling with ongoing debit balance problems in multiple accounts, the avoidance of high-cost bank overdraft charges alone may be a sufficient incentive to use cash concentration.

What Strategies Are Available for Cash Concentration?

A company having multiple locations can pursue a variety of cash concentration strategies, which tend to bring larger benefits with greater centralization. The four strategies are presented in increasing order of centralization.

1. *Complete decentralization.* Every subsidiary or branch office with its own bank account manages its own cash position. This is fine if balances are small, so that there is little synergy to be gained by concentrating cash in a single account.
2. *Centralized payments, decentralized liquidity management.* A company can implement a centralized

payment factory that handles all payables for all company subsidiaries but issues payments from local accounts. This improves the overall planning for cash outflows but does not improve the management of excess cash balances, for which local managers are still responsible.

3. *Centralized liquidity management, decentralized payments.* The corporate staff centralizes cash into a concentration account and has responsibility for investments. However, local managers are still responsible for disbursements.

4. *All functions centralized.* The corporate staff pools all cash into a concentration account, invests it, and manages disbursements. This is an excellent structure for optimizing investment income and also gives corporate headquarters considerable control over the accounts payable portion of the company's working capital. Larger companies usually follow this strategy.

What Is Physical Sweeping?

When a company sets up a *zero-balance account*, its bank automatically moves (sweeps) cash from that account into a concentration account, usually within the same bank. The cash balance in the zero-balance account (as the name implies) is reduced to zero whenever a sweep occurs. If the account has a debit balance at the time of the sweep, money is shifted from the concentration account back into the account having the debit balance. An example is shown in Exhibit 10.2.

In the example, two of three subsidiary accounts initially contain credit (positive) balances, and Account C contains a debit (negative) balance. In the first stage of the sweep transaction, the cash in the two accounts having credit balances are swept into the concentration account. In the next stage of the sweep, sufficient funds are transferred from the concentration account to offset the debit balance in Account C. At the end of the sweep, there are no credit or debit balances in the zero-balance accounts.

It is also possible to use *constant balancing* to maintain a predetermined minimum balance in a subsidiary account, which involves sweeping only those cash levels above the minimum balance and reverse sweeping cash into the subsidiary account if the balance drops below the minimum balance.

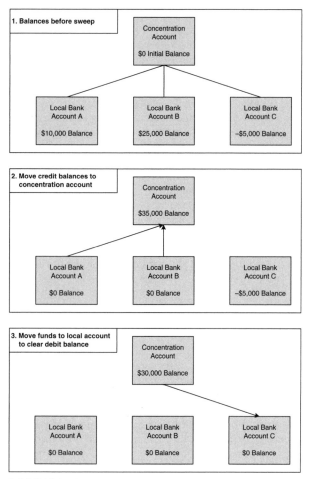

Exhibit 10.2 Zero-Balance Sweep Transaction

When Do Sweeps Occur?

In most sweeping transactions, the sweeps occur on an *intraday* basis, which means that balances are transferred to the concentration account before the end of the day. Consequently, some cash may be left behind in subsidiary accounts rather than being centralized. This occurs when cash arrives in an account after execution of the daily sweep. The cash will remain in the subsidiary account overnight and will be included in the following day's sweep. If a bank can accomplish true *end-of-day* sweeps, no cash will be left behind in local accounts. If a company is not dealing with such a bank, a proactive approach to depositing checks before cut-off times is the best way to avoid unused cash.

When Are Intercompany Loans Linked to Cash Sweeps?

A company may need to record an intercompany loan from the subsidiary to the corporate parent in the amount of the cash transferred through the cash concentration process. Here are several reasons for doing so:

○ *Subsidiary-level financial reporting requirements.* A subsidiary may have an outstanding loan, for which a bank requires the periodic production of a balance sheet. Since account sweeping shifts cash away from a subsidiary's balance sheet, detailed sweep tracking is needed to put the cash back on the subsidiary's balance sheet for reporting purposes. This can be done by recording an intercompany loan from the subsidiary to the corporate parent in exchange for any swept cash.

○ *Interest income allocation.* A company may elect to allocate the interest earned at the concentration account level back to the subsidiaries whose accounts contributed cash to the concentration account. Some countries require that this interest allocation be done, to keep a company from locating the concentration account in a low-tax jurisdiction, where the tax on interest income is minimized.

○ *Interest expense allocation.* Some tax jurisdictions may require the parent company to record interest expense on intercompany loans associated with the transfer of cash in a physical sweeping arrangement. If so, the company must track the intercompany loan balances outstanding per day; these balances are then used as the principal for the calculation of interest expense.

What Is Notional Pooling?

Notional pooling is a mechanism for calculating interest on the combined credit and debit balances of accounts that a corporate parent chooses to cluster together, without actually transferring any funds. Once a company earns interest on the funds in a notional account, interest income is usually allocated back to each of the accounts comprising the pool.

This approach allows each subsidiary company to take advantage of a single, centralized liquidity position while still retaining daily cash management privileges. Also, since the approach avoids the use of cash transfers to a central pooling account, there is no need to create or monitor intercompany loans.

Where global notional pooling is offered (usually where all participating accounts are held within a single bank), the pool offsets credit and debit balances on a multicurrency basis without the need to engage in any foreign exchange transactions. An additional benefit of global notional pooling lies in the area of intercompany cash flows; for example, if there are charges for administrative services, the transaction can be accomplished with no net movement of cash.

What Is a Bank Overlay Structure?

Companies operating on an international scale frequently have trouble reconciling the need for efficient cash concentration operations with the use of local banking partners with which they may have long-standing relationships and valuable business contacts. The solution is the *bank overlay structure*.

A bank overlay structure consists of two layers. The lower layer is comprised of all in-country banks that are used for local cash transaction requirements. The higher layer is a group of networked regional banks, or even a single global bank, that maintains a separate bank account for each country or legal entity of the corporate structure. Cash balances in the lower layer of banks are zero-balanced into the corresponding accounts in the higher layer of banks on a daily basis (where possible, subject to cash flow restrictions). These sweeps are accomplished with manual transfers, SWIFT messages from the networked banks to the local banks, or standing authorizations to the local banks. The concept is shown in Exhibit 10.3. This approach allows funds to be consolidated on either a regional or global basis for centralized cash management.

What Short-Term Investment Options Are Available?

There are a number of short-term investment options available. Here are the most common ones that have low

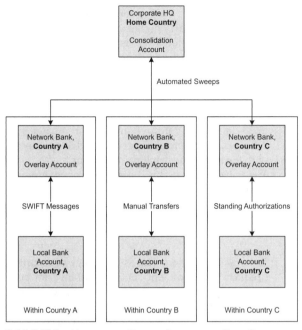

Exhibit 10.3 Multicountry Physical Sweeping with Bank Overlay Structure

risk levels, short maturity dates, and high levels of marketability.

- ○ *Bankers' acceptances.* Banks sometimes guarantee (or *accept*) corporate debt, usually when they issue a loan to a corporate customer and then sell the debt to investors. Because of the bank guarantee, these loans are viewed as obligations of the bank.
- ○ *Bonds near maturity dates.* A corporate bond may not mature for many years, but one can always purchase a bond that is close to its maturity date. There tends to be a minimal risk of loss (or gain) on the principal amount of this investment, since there is a low risk that interest rates will change so much in the short time period left before the maturity date of the bond that it will impact its value.
- ○ *Certificate of deposit.* These certificates are essentially term bank deposits, typically having durations of up to two years. They usually pay a fixed interest rate upon maturity, though some variable rate CDs are available. There is up to $100,000 of Federal Deposit Insurance Corporation (FDIC) insurance coverage of this investment.

○ *Commercial paper.* Larger corporations issue short-term notes that carry higher yields than government debt issuances offer. There is also an active secondary market for them, so there is usually no problem with liquidity. Commercial paper is generally not secured; however, staying with the commercial paper issued by blue-chip organizations minimizes the risk of default. Most commercial paper matures in 30 days or less; it rarely matures in greater than 270 days. Commercial paper is issued at a discount, with the face value being paid at maturity.

○ *Money market fund.* This is a package of government instruments, usually comprised of Treasury bills, notes, and bonds, that is assembled by a fund management company. The investment is highly liquid, with many investors putting in funds for as little as a day.

○ *Repurchase agreement.* This is a package of securities (frequently government debt) that an investor buys from a financial institution, under the agreement that the institution will buy it back at a specific price on a specific date. It is most commonly used for the overnight investment of excess cash from a company's cash concentration account, which can be handled automatically by the company's primary bank. The typical interest rate earned on this investment is equal to or less than the money market rate.

○ *U.S. Treasury issuances.* The United States government issues a variety of notes with maturity dates that range from less than a year (U.S. Treasury certificates) through several years (notes) to more than five years (bonds). There is a strong secondary market for these issuances, so they can be liquidated in short order. U.S. government debts of all types are considered to be risk-free and so have lower yields than other forms of investment.

What Investment Strategies Are Used for Short-Term Investments?

The next strategies can be used to invest excess cash, presented in order from the most passive to the most active strategies.

○ *Earnings credit strategy.* Do nothing and leave idle balances in the corporate bank accounts. As a result, the bank uses the earnings from these idle balances to offset its service fees. If a company has minimal cash balances, leaving the cash alone is a reasonable investment approach.

○ *Matching strategy.* Match the maturity date of an investment to the cash flow availability dates listed on the cash forecast. For example, ABC Company's cash forecast indicates that $80,000 will be available for investment immediately but must be used in two months for a capital project. The controller can invest the funds in a two-month instrument, such that its maturity date is just prior to when the funds will be needed. This approach is more concerned with short-term liquidity than return on investment.

○ *Laddering strategy.* Create a set of investments that have a series of consecutive maturity dates. For example, ABC Company's cash forecast indicates that $150,000 of excess cash will be available for the foreseeable future, and its investment policy forbids any investments having a duration of greater than three months. In order to keep the investment liquid while still taking advantage of the higher interest rates available through longer-term investments, the controller breaks the available cash into thirds and invests $50,000 in a one-month instrument, another $50,000 in a two-month instrument, and the final $50,000 in a three-month instrument. As each investment matures, the controller reinvests it into a three-month instrument. By doing so, ABC always has $50,000 of the invested amount coming due within one month or less. This method offers improves liquidity while still taking advantage of longer-term interest rates.

○ *Tranched cash flow strategy.* Determine what cash is available for short-, medium-, and long-term investment and then adopt different investment criteria for each of these investment tranches. The short-term tranche has low returns but high liquidity. The medium-term tranche includes cash that may be required for use within the next 3 to 12 months, and usually only for highly predictable events. Given the more predictable nature of these cash flows, longer-term maturities with somewhat higher returns can be used. The long-term tranche includes cash for which there is no planned operational use and which can be safely invested for at least a year at higher rates of return.

CHAPTER 11

RECEIVABLES MANAGEMENT

How Do I Create and Maintain a Credit Policy?

A cause of confusion not only within the credit department but also between the credit and sales departments is the lack of consistency in dealing with customer credit issues. Establishment of a credit policy helps resolve these issues. The policy should clearly state the mission and goals of the credit department, exactly which positions are responsible for the most critical credit and collection tasks, what formula shall be used for assigning credit levels, and what steps shall be followed in the collection process. Further comments are:

○ *Mission.* The mission statement should outline the general concept of how the credit department does business: Does it provide a loose credit policy to maximize sales, or work toward high-quality receivables (implying reduced sales), or manage credit at some point in between? A loose credit policy might result in this mission: "The credit department shall offer credit to all customers except those where the risk of loss is probable."

○ *Goals.* Goals describe the performance measurements against which the credit staff will be judged. For example: "The department goals are to operate with no more than one collections person per 1,000 customers while attaining a bad debt percentage no higher than 2% of sales and annual days sales outstanding of no higher than 42 days."

○ *Responsibilities.* This is the most critical part of the policy. It should state who has final authority over the granting of credit and the assignment of credit hold status. Normally the credit manager has this authority, but the policy can also state the order volume level at which someone else, such as the chief financial officer (CFO) or treasurer, can be called on to render final judgment.

○ *Credit level assignment.* The policy should state the sources of information to be used in the calculation of a credit limit, such as credit reports or financial statements, and can also include the minimum credit level automatically extended to all customers as well as the criteria used to grant larger limits.

○ *Collections methodology.* The policy can itemize what collection steps shall be followed, such as initial calls, customer visits, e-mails, notification of the sales staff, credit holds, and forwarding to a collection agency.

○ *Terms of sale.* If there are few product lines in a single industry, it is useful to clearly state a standard payment term, such as a 1% discount if paid in 10 days; otherwise full payment is expected in 30 days. An override policy can be included, noting a sign-off by the controller or CFO. By doing so, the sales staff will be less inclined to attempt to gain better terms on behalf of customers.

The credit policy should change to meet economic conditions. To do so, schedule a periodic review of the credit policy. To prepare for the meeting, assemble a list of leading indicators for the industry, tracked on a trend line, that show where the business cycle is most likely to be heading. This information is most relevant for the company's industry rather than the economy as a whole, since the conditions within some industries can vary substantially from the general economy.

How Do I Obtain Financial Information about Customers?

A credit report is a good source of information about prospective customers. The largest purveyor of these reports is Dun & Bradstreet (www.dnb.com), followed by Equifax (www.equifax.com). Report prices range from $40 to $125 for reports with varying amounts of information, with reduced pricing if one agrees to purchase a monthly subscription. Low-cost reports include only basic customer information, such as corporate names, locations, ownership, and corporate history, while the more expensive reports include a variety of financial and payment information. Equifax reports present information more graphically, but the two report providers issue essentially the same information. Both companies provide credit reports over the Internet.

It is substantially easier to obtain financial information about publicly held customers. By going to the www.sec.gov Web site, one can easily call up all of the most recent financial filings submitted by these entities. The best source of information is the 10-Q report, which details and discusses a company's quarterly results. Though a shorter report than the annual 10-K report, it contains much more current information and so is of more use to the credit department.

How Does a Credit-Granting System Work?

Credit-granting systems are customized by company and depend greatly on industry conditions, product margins, and the willingness of management to extend credit. An example of a credit-granting system follows, using a simple yes/no decision matrix that is based on a few key credit issues.

1. Is the initial order less than $1,000? If so, grant credit without review.
2. Is the initial order more than $1,000 but less than $10,000? Require a completed credit application. Grant a credit limit of 10% of the customer's net worth.
3. Is the initial order more than $10,000? Require a completed credit application and financial statements. If a profitable customer, grant a credit limit of 10% of the customer's net worth. Reduce the credit limit by 10% for every percent of customer loss reported.
4. Does an existing customer's order exceed its credit limit by less than 20% and there is no history of payment problems? If so, grant the increase.
5. Does an existing customer order exceed its credit limit by more than 20% or is there a history of payment problems? If so, forward to the credit manager for review. Use the same credit granting process listed in step 3.
6. Does an existing customer have any invoices at least 60 days past due? If so, freeze all orders.

While this approach does not completely eliminate variability from the credit-granting process, it sets up clear decision points governing what actions to take for the majority of situations, leaving only the more difficult customer accounts for additional review.

What Payment Terms Should I Offer to Customers?

The baseline payment terms that a company should consider offering to its customers are the standard terms offered in the industry, which may range from immediate payment to 60-day terms. The key issue is to give the appearance of offering competitive terms, so that prospective customers will not be turned away. However, it is quite acceptable to modify these baseline terms considerably if a customer appears to present a credit risk. Here are some alternatives.

- *Shorten the terms of sale.* For example, a customer may plan to place 10 orders for $3,000 each within the company's standard 30-day terms period, resulting in a required credit line of $30,000. Reducing payment terms to 15 days would mean that the customer should be able to purchase the same quantity of goods from the company on a credit line of just $15,000. This approach works only if a customer is placing many small orders rather than one large one, the orders are evenly spaced out, and the customer's own cash receipts cycle allows it to pay on such short terms.

- *Offer a lease.* A lease allows customers to make a series of smaller payments over time. Though the company could offer this service itself and earn extra interest income on the sale, this still leaves the risk of collection with the company. An alternative is to engage the services of an outside leasing firm, so the company receives payment from the lessor as soon as payment is authorized by the customer, thereby eliminating the collection risk in the shortest possible time frame. Of course, a lease is a viable alternative only when the company is selling a fixed asset that the customer intends to retain.

- *Obtain a personal guarantee.* The personal guarantee makes collection easier, since the signer knows that he or she is responsible for the amount of the receivable and will make sure that this invoice is paid before other unsecured invoices.

- *Obtain credit insurance.* This is a guarantee by an insurance company against customer nonpayment. Credit insurance is available for domestic credit, export credit, and coverage of custom products prior to delivery, in case customers cancel orders. If the insurance company considers a customer to be high risk, it will likely grant no insurance at all.

When Should I Review Customer Credit Levels?

If a customer only places small orders, there may be no need for a credit application. However, there should be a minimum order level above which a credit application is required. If a customer has not placed an order recently, its financial situation may have changed considerably, rendering its previously assigned credit level no longer valid. A solution is to require customers to complete a new credit application after a preset interval has passed, such as two years. However, if there are so many customers that this would be a burden for the credit staff, stratify the customer list by order volume over the past year, and review the credit of only that 20% of the list comprising 80% of the order volume. This approach drastically reduces the amount of credit analysis work while still ensuring a high level of review on those accounts that could have a serious bad debt impact on the company.

If a customer misses a payment due date by a predetermined number of days, skips payments, stops taking early-payment discounts, or issues a "not sufficient funds" check, these actions should also trigger a request to fill out a new credit application. Finally, a new application should be required if a customer consistently places orders above its original order limit.

How Can I Adjust the Invoice Content and Layout to Improve Collections?

Most invoices contain nearly all of the information customers need to make a payment, but the layout may be so poor that they must hunt for the information. In other cases, adding information will reduce payment problems. Here are some invoice layout changes that can help improve collections.

○ *Clearly state contact information.* Contact information should be delineated by a box and possibly noted in bold or colored print, so customers know whom to call if they have an issue. If the billing staff is large, it may not be practical to put a specific contact name on the invoice, but at least list a central contact phone number.

○ *Clearly state credit card contact information.* This information should be for the person who is specifically trained to handle credit card payments. Also, list on the invoice the types of credit cards accepted by the company, which may prevent customers from making unnecessary calls if they do not have the right types of cards.

○ *State the discount cutoff date.* Customers tend to misinterpret discount payment terms in their favor. To avoid this, clearly state the invoice payment date on the invoice, preferably in bold and located in a box.

○ *Reduce clutter.* Strip out information that is not needed by the customer, and clarify the labeling of the remaining items.

○ *Include proof of receipt.* If customers demand proof of receipt, extract receipt information from the Web site of an overnight delivery service and paste it directly into the invoice.

How Can I Adjust Billing Delivery to Improve Collections?

Ensuring that the correct person receives a company's invoice may be the key to timely payment. Here are several methods for improving invoice delivery.

○ *Issue invoices in PDF format.* Consider printing invoices in Adobe PDF format, which creates an electronic version of the invoice. Then e-mail the resulting invoice to the customer. The PDF format is built into many accounting systems, or can be bought separately from Adobe Corporation.

○ *Bill early.* If the company knows the exact amount of a customer billing prior to the date when it is normally sent, send it early. By doing so, the invoice has more time to be routed through the receiving organization, passing through the mail room, accounting staff, authorized signatory, and back to the accounts payable staff for payment. This makes it much more likely that the invoice will be paid on time.

○ *Split large invoices.* When an accounting department issues an invoice containing a large number of line items, it is more likely that the recipient will have an issue with one or more of the line items and will hold payment on the entire invoice while those line items are resolved. To avoid this problem, split apart large invoices into separate ones, with each invoice containing just one line item. By doing so, it is more likely that some invoices will be paid at once while other ones over which there are issues will be delayed.

○ *Match invoice delivery to payment dates.* Some customers with extremely large payment volumes create payments only on certain days of the month in order to yield the greatest level of efficiency in processing what may be thousands of checks. If a company does not send an invoice early enough to be included in the next check-processing run, it may have to wait a number of additional weeks before the next check run occurs, resulting in a late payment. The solution is to ask customers when they process checks and make sure that the company issues invoices well in advance of these dates in order to be paid as early as possible.

Should I Offer Early Payment Discounts?

Only a company having severe cash flow problems should offer early payment discounts to its customers. The problem is that the effective interest rate the company is offering to its customers is extremely high. For example, allowing customers to take a 2% discount if they pay in 10 days, versus the usual 30, means that the company is offering a 2% discount in order to obtain cash 20 days earlier than normal. The annualized interest rate of 2% for 20 days is about 36%. All but the most debt-burdened companies can borrow funds at rates far lower than that.

Furthermore, many customers will not pay within the 10-day discount period but will still take the discount. This can lead to a great deal of difficulty in obtaining payment of the withheld discount. In addition, the collection staff may have difficulty in applying the cash to open receivables if it is not clear on which invoice a customer is paying a discounted amount.

How Do I Optimize Customer Contacts?

The prime calling hours for most business customers are in the early to midmorning hours, before they have been called away for meetings or other activities. If customers are concentrated in a single time zone, this can mean that the time period available for calls is extremely short. Also, if the customer base spans multiple time zones, a collections staff based in one time zone may be making calls to customers that are outside the customers' prime calling hours, resulting in few completed calls. Consequently, set up a collections workday that is built around prime calling hours. For example, if the collections staff is based on the West Coast but most of its customer contacts are on the East Coast, its workday should begin very early in order to make up for the three-hour time difference.

The typical list of overdue invoices is so long that the existing collections staff cannot contact all customers about all invoices on a sufficiently frequent basis. A solution is to utilize collection call stratification. The concept behind this approach is to split up, or stratify, the overdue receivables and concentrate the bulk of the collection staff's time on the largest invoices. By doing so, a company can realize improved cash flow by collecting the largest dollar amounts sooner. The downside is that smaller invoices will receive less attention and therefore take longer to collect. For example, a collections staff can be required to contact customers about all high-dollar invoices once every three days, whereas low-dollar contacts can be limited to once every two weeks.

If customers are assigned to the collection staff based on their names or geographic locations, it is likely that difficult collection problems will be given to junior or ineffective collection staff, resulting in late payments. A solution is to assign the best collection staff to the most difficult customers. By doing so, the company orients its collection resources in the most targeted manner to achieve the highest possible collection percentage.

How Do I Manage Collection Information?

A poorly organized collections group is one that does not know which customers to call, what customers said during previous calls, and how frequently contacts should be made in the future. These problems can be overcome by using a collection call database. The basic concept of such a database is to keep a record of all contacts with the customer as well as when to contact the customer next and what other actions to take.

Several commercially available collection call databases are available. The typical database product is linked to a company's legacy accounting system by customized interfaces. A key feature it offers is the assignment of each customer to a specific collections person, so that each person can call up a subset of the overdue invoices for which he or she is responsible. Within this subset, the software will also categorize accounts in different sort sequences, such as placing those at the top that have missed their promised payment dates. Also, the software will present all of the contact information related to each customer, including the promises made by customers, open issues, and contact information. The system will also allow the user to enter information for a fax and then route it directly to the recipient without requiring the collections person to ever leave his or her chair. It can also be linked to an auto-dialer, so the collections staff spends less time attempting to establish connections with overdue customers. To further increase the efficiency of the collections staff, it will even determine the time zone in which each customer is located and prioritize the recommended list of calls, so that only those customers in time zones that are currently in the midst of standard business hours will be called.

How Do I Handle Payment Deductions?

An aggravating problem with deductions is how they are passed from person to person within the company without ever reaching resolution. Here are several possible solutions.

- ○ *Assign responsibility.* Make a single person responsible for the deductions of a small group of customers and monitor the status of each open deduction on a daily basis, no matter which person within the company is currently handling resolution issues.
- ○ *Implement a handling procedure.* A deduction-handling procedure reduces the risk that open issues will be lost in the system. This follows a tiered approach, where very small deductions are not worth the effort of even a single customer contact and are immediately written off. For larger deductions, a company may require immediate follow-up or follow-up only after the second deduction, or an immediate rebilling — the choice is up to the individual company. The procedure should include such basic steps as:

  1. Ensuring that the customer has provided adequate documentation of the problem.
  2. Collection of data needed to substantiate or refute the claim.
  3. Contacting the customer to obtain missing information.

4. Once collected, reviewing all information to determine a recommended course of action.
5. Depending on the size of the deduction, obtaining necessary approvals.
6. Contacting the customer with resolution information.
7. If approved, entering credit information into the accounting system to clear debit balances representing valid deductions.

   The collections staff must be drilled in the use of this procedure, so there is absolutely no question about how to handle a deduction. This will favorably increase departmental efficiency and require less management time to pass judgment on individual deduction problems.

○ *Stratify deductions.* If there are a multitude of open deductions, resolve deductions for the largest-dollar items first and work down through the deductions list in declining dollar order. This approach is initially designed to take out of the accounts receivable list the largest deductions; but more important, it allows the collections staff to research the reasons why the largest deductions are occurring and to put a stop to them. As the staff gradually fixes these issues and moves down to small deductions, it can address relatively smaller underlying deduction issues.

○ *Report on deduction problems.* Have the collections staff summarize all deductions on a regular basis and forward this information to management. The management team can review the data to see what problems are causing the deductions. It may be best to issue the report sorted in several formats, since problems hidden within one reporting format are more visible in others. This approach calls for the use of a central deductions database.

 ## How Do I Collect Overdue Payments?

There are a multitude of methods for collecting payments from customers. The next list progresses from several milder contact methods into significantly more aggressive collection techniques.

1. *Call sooner.* Begin calling immediately after the invoice due date has passed. By taking this approach, the company instills in its customers the idea that

payment terms are to be taken seriously, and the company absolutely expects payment on the stated date.

2. *Issue dunning letters for small balances.* This is the least expensive way to contact customers and is to be preferred over more labor-intensive activities such as direct personal contacts. Consider mixing up the method and timing of delivery in order to gain the customer's attention. For example, send the letter by fax or e-mail, and distribute it to different people within the customer's organization in hopes of jarring loose a response.

3. *Issue an attorney letter.* This is a letter issued on an attorney's letterhead, threatening legal action if payment is not made. The implication is that the customer is now much closer to a lawsuit, which sometimes brings about a rapid settlement of the outstanding balance. Attorney letters are expensive if custom-written by the attorney. To reduce the cost, write the letter for the attorney and just ask him or her to print it on letterhead.

4. *Insist on payment of undisputed balances.* This keeps customers from using a dispute on a single line item to not pay a larger invoice.

5. *Send a summary of the last discussion.* Document a customer's latest promised payment information in a letter or e-mail and send it to the customer. This confirmation approach tells the customer that the company is monitoring the situation closely. If a customer has agreed to a repetitive series of payments, use this approach to both thank the company for the most recent payment and remind it of the amount and due date of the next payment.

6. *Take product back.* In few cases where a shipped product is still on hand and untouched by the customer, it is possible to accept a merchandise return.

7. *Use cash on delivery terms.* For extremely late-paying customers, consider shifting them to cash-on-delivery (COD) payment terms. If the customer has no other source for goods and so must buy from the company, add the entire open balance or a portion of it to the COD amount, thereby enforcing payment if the customer ever wants to see any additional goods delivered.

8. *Send to a collection agency.* When no other in-house approach works, send the invoice to a collection agency for more aggressive follow-up. Their services are expensive but are usually success-based, so there is no downside in doing so.

When Should I Take Legal Action to Collect from a Customer?

Initiating legal action against a customer is an enormously expensive and prolonged undertaking that is almost never worth the effort. Even if the court awards a substantial settlement, the customer may go to great lengths to hide its assets, so the company never collects a dime. Here are three ways to obtain cash in these situations:

1. *Prescreen customer debts.* Always prescreen a customer's debts prior to initiating a legal action. This should at least involve purchasing a credit report on the customer to determine the number of judgments and tax liens already filed against it as well as other types of outstanding debt. This type of investigation may very well reveal that the customer has so many calls on its assets already that an investment in legal action is completely uneconomical.

2. *Threaten a small claims court filing.* This is a low-cost legal technique that may rattle an intransigent customer into paying. Simply obtain the complaint documentation from the appropriate court, fill it out, and send a copy to the customer, with a note attached stating when the cash has to be in the company's hands or else the paperwork will be filed with the court.

3. *File with a small claims court.* This is usually in the county where the customer resides but can also be where the action over which a complaint is filed took place. In either case, check with the court to verify the maximum amount of money it will address. If the amount being claimed is higher, waive the difference in order to fit under the court's maximum cap. Also, pull a credit report on the customer to verify its official legal name and corporate status, so this information can be correctly listed on the complaint form. Finally, locate a collection attorney located near the small claims court and request representation at the court for a modest fee and percentage of any proceeds. These steps are not difficult, and the cost is minimal.

CHAPTER 12

INVENTORY MANAGEMENT

How Do I Increase the Accuracy of Inventory Records?

*I*ncreasing the accuracy of inventory records involves implementing *all* of the next 17 steps, and in the order presented. This is a difficult implementation to shortcut, for missing any of the steps will have a negative impact on record accuracy. The steps are:

1. *Select and install inventory tracking software.* The primary requirements for this software are:

   - *Track transactions.* The software should list the frequency of product usage, which shows inventory quantities that should be changed and which items may be obsolete.
   - *Update records immediately.* The inventory data must always be up-to-date, because production planners must know what is in stock, while cycle counters require access to accurate data. Batch updating of the system is not acceptable.
   - *Report inventory records by location.* Cycle counters need inventory records that are sorted by location in order to more efficiently locate and count the inventory.

2. *Test inventory tracking software.* Create a set of typical records in the new software, and perform a series of transactions to ensure that the software functions properly. In addition, create a large number of records and perform the transactions again, to see if the response time of the system drops significantly.

3. *Revise the rack layout.* Create aisles that are wide enough for forklift operation if this is needed for larger storage items, and cluster small parts racks together for easier parts picking.

4. *Create rack locations.* A typical rack location is, for example, A-01-B-01. This means that this location code is located in Aisle A, Rack 1. Within Rack 1, it is located on Level B (numbered from the bottom to the top). Within Level B, it is located in Partition 1. As one moves down an aisle, the rack numbers should progress in ascending sequence, with the odd rack numbers on the left and the even numbers on the right. Thus, the first rack on the left side of aisle D is D-01, the first rack on the right is D-02, the second rack on the left is D-03, and so on. This layout allows a stock picker to move down the center of the aisle, efficiently pulling items from stock based on sequential location codes.

5. *Lock the warehouse.* One of the main causes of record inaccuracy is removal of items from the warehouse by outside staff. To stop this removal, all entrances to the warehouse must be locked. Only warehouse personnel should be allowed access to it. All other personnel entering the warehouse should be accompanied by a member of the warehouse staff to prevent the removal of inventory.

6. *Consolidate parts.* To reduce the work of counting the same item in multiple locations, group common parts into one place. This step requires multiple iterations, for it is difficult to combine parts when thousands of them are scattered throughout the warehouse.

7. *Assign part numbers.* Have several experienced personnel verify all part numbers. A mislabeled part is as useless as a missing part, since the computer database will not show that it exists.

8. *Verify units of measure.* Have several experienced people verify all units of measure. Unless the software allows multiple units of measure to be used, the entire organization must adhere to one unit of measure for each item.

9. *Pack the parts.* Pack parts into containers, seal the containers, and label them with the part number, unit of measure, and total quantity stored inside. Leave a few parts free for ready use. Open containers only when additional stock is needed. This method allows cycle counters to verify inventory balances rapidly.

10. *Count items.* Count items when there is no significant activity in the warehouse, such as during a weekend. Elaborate cross-checking of the counts, as would be done during a year-end physical inventory count, is not necessary. It is more important to have the perpetual inventory system operational before the warehouse activity increases again; any errors in the data

will be detected quickly during cycle counts and flushed out of the database. The initial counts must include a review of the part number, location, and quantity.

11. *Train the warehouse staff.* Warehouse staff members should receive software training immediately before using the system, so that they do not forget how to operate the software. Enter a set of test records into the software, and have the staff simulate all common inventory transactions, such as receipts, picks, and cycle count adjustments.

12. *Enter data into the computer.* Have an experienced data entry person input the location, part number, and quantity into the computer. Once the data has been input, another person should cross-check the entered data against the original data for errors.

13. *Quick-check the data.* Scan the data for errors. If all part numbers have the same number of digits, look for items that are too long or short. Review location codes to see if inventory is stored in nonexistent racks. Look for units of measure that do not match the part being described. For example, is it logical to have a pint of steel in stock? Also, if item costs are available, print a list of extended costs. Excessive costs typically point to incorrect units of measure. All of these steps help to spot the most obvious inventory errors.

14. *Initiate cycle counts.* Print out a portion of the inventory list, sorted by location. Using this report, have the warehouse staff count blocks of the inventory on a continuous basis. They should look for accurate part numbers, units of measure, locations, and quantities. The counts should concentrate on high-value or high-use items, though the entire stock should be reviewed regularly. The most important part of this step is to examine *why* mistakes occur. If a cycle counter finds an error, its cause must be investigated and then corrected, so that the mistake will not occur again. It is also useful to assign specific aisles to cycle counters, which tends to make them more familiar with their assigned inventory and the problems causing specific transactional errors.

15. *Initiate inventory audits.* The inventory should be audited frequently, perhaps once a week. This allows the company to monitor changes in the inventory accuracy level and initiate changes if the accuracy drops below acceptable levels. The minimum acceptable accuracy level is 95%, with an error being a mistaken part number, unit of measure, quantity, or location.

This accuracy level is needed to ensure accurate inventory costing as well as to assist the materials department in planning future inventory purchases. In addition, establish a tolerance level when calculating the inventory accuracy. For example, if the computer record of a box of screws yields a quantity of 100 and the actual count results in 105 screws, then the record is accurate if the tolerance is at least 5% but inaccurate if the tolerance is reduced to 1%. The maximum allowable tolerance should be no higher than 5%, with tighter tolerances being used for high-value or high-use items.

16. *Post results.* Inventory accuracy is a team project, and the warehouse staff feels more involved if the audit results are posted against the results of previous audits. Accuracy percentages should be broken out for the counting area assigned to each cycle counter, so that everyone can see who is doing the best job of reviewing and correcting inventory counts.

17. *Reward the staff.* Accurate inventories save a company thousands of dollars in many ways. This makes it cost-effective to encourage the staff to maintain and improve the accuracy level with periodic bonuses that are based on the attainment of higher levels of accuracy with tighter tolerances.

How Do I Reduce the Number of Stock-Keeping Units in Inventory?

Most companies store an inordinate number of inventory stock-keeping units (SKUs), most of which do not sell frequently. Here are some possibilities for proactively shrinking the investment in SKUs.

○ *Include materials staff in the design stage.* A materials manager on a product design team can push for the reuse of existing parts in new products, so that the total number of SKUs is reduced.

○ *Reduce the number of product options.* A product with a broad array of options requires additional SKUs for each of the options, so narrowing the number of options offered reduces the SKU investment.

○ *Reduce the number of products.* Each product requires its own set of SKUs, not only for the product options just noted but also for any special parts that are only used for that product. If a product is not generating much profit and has a large number of unique SKUs, this is a good target for elimination.

○ *Review engineering change orders.* The engineering department may issue change orders to modify existing products. If so, the materials management staff should time the introduction of all change orders to coincide with an appropriate drawdown of all raw materials that will be eliminated as part of the change order.

How Do I Reduce Inventory Purchases?

The bulk of a company's inventory problems arise at the point of purchase. The next points are useful ways to keep from making the wrong purchasing decisions.

○ *Access customer buying information.* Gain direct access to the inventory planning systems of key customers. This gives the purchasing staff perfect information about what it, in turn, needs to order from its suppliers.
○ *Reduce supplier distance.* Distant sourcing lengthens lead times and therefore the amount of safety stock. By sourcing inventory requirements from suppliers located very close, there is a much lower need for safety stock.
○ *Adjust open purchase orders.* Compare the amount of outstanding balances on open purchase orders to current needs, and modify open purchase order amounts to more closely match current requirements.
○ *Use risk pooling.* Safety stock levels can be reduced for parts that are used in a large number of products, because fluctuations in the demand levels of parent products will offset each other, resulting in a lower overall safety stock level.
○ *Use layered replenishment.* In a distributor environment, maintain significant inventory levels for any items that are constantly sold, and do not stock any items at all for low-order items; customers must wait for the company to procure these later items from suppliers.
○ *Shift inventory ownership.* Shift raw material ownership to suppliers, so that they own the inventory located on the company's premises. The company then pays suppliers when it removes inventory from its warehouse. This arrangement usually requires sole sourcing.
○ *Use phased deliveries.* If a supplier imposes a minimum *order* quantity, it may be possible to negotiate for a smaller *delivery* quantity, so that smaller quantities are delivered more frequently.

How Do I Compress Inventory Storage Space?

The next methods can be used to compress inventory into the smallest possible warehouse space, which reduces a company's facility costs.

- ○ *Drop shipping.* A company receives an order from a customer and contacts its supplier with the shipping information, which in turn ships the product directly to the customer.
- ○ *Cross docking.* When an item arrives at the receiving dock, it is immediately moved to a shipping dock for delivery to the customer in a different truck.
- ○ *Use temporary storage for peak storage requirements.* Offload some storage into less-expensive overflow locations, such as rented trailers. By doing so, a company can shift inventory back into its primary warehouse facilities as soon as the peak period is over, thereby paying much less for storage space over the course of the year.
- ○ *Match storage to cubic space.* A great deal of space in a warehouse is unused, because the cubic volumes in storage racks greatly exceed the volume of the items stored in them. These points can be followed to fill this excess space:

  - *Case height adjustment.* Alter the height of storage cases so the optimal pallet height can be achieved to fill all available rack space. Conversely, it may be less expensive to adjust the height of the existing storage racks rather than to modify the cases to match the racks.
  - *Modular storage cabinets.* For items with small storage volumes, use modular storage cabinets. These cabinets have multiple drawers with varying drawer heights, the contents of which can be reconfigured with dividers to achieve the optimal amount of storage space.
  - *Movable racking systems.* These racks are mounted on wheels and pushed together, thereby eliminating all but one aisle. They are expensive.
  - *Double-deep racking.* Set up two rows of racks adjacent to each other, with only one rack exposed to an aisle. This configuration allows for the storage of two pallets of the same item in a single storage location, one behind the other, thereby eliminating one aisle.

- *Stacking lanes.* For many pallets containing the same item, use stacking lanes in an open warehouse area where multiple pallets are stacked on top of each other without any bracing system, many pallets deep.
- *Narrow aisles.* Use narrow aisles where manual putaways and picking are the norm rather than using forklifts.
- *Extended racks.* Extend racks heights up to the ceiling.

How Do I Avoid Inventory Losses on Short Shelf Life Items?

Install gravity-flow racking. This system requires putaway from the rear, where items slide down a slight angle in the rack, assisted by rollers, pushing any items in front to the front of the rack. As soon as a picker removes items from the front of the rack, the weight of items in the rear push the next-oldest item to the front.

For larger case sizes, pallet-flow racking can be used. A pallet-flow rack uses standard racks that are set at an even height, on which are built dynamic flow rails at a slight downward angle from the loading end to the unloading end. The flow rails incorporate rollers and a series of automatic brakes to slow the movement of pallets. A forklift operator places a pallet at the receiving end of the pallet-flow rack, and it slides along the rails, being slowed by the brakes, until it comes to a halt behind the next pallet in line. When someone removes a pallet from the other end of the rack, the whole line of pallets automatically slides forward to fill the void.

How Do I Improve Picking Efficiency?

The next techniques can be used to reduce the labor needed to pick inventory in the warehouse or to increase the efficiency of this operation.

- ○ *Pick in order by location.* Sort all single-line orders in bin location sequence, so a small number of pickers can quickly move through the warehouse and pick all the orders at once. This reduces picker time but requires extra back-end labor to break the picked items into individual orders.
- ○ *Forward picking.* Summarize pick lists over a short time period, so that only a small number of passes through the warehouse will remove all required

items from stock. Picked items are then shifted to a centralized forward picking location, where they can be broken down into individual orders. This works best when there are many orders, each for a small number of items.

○ *Pick-to-light.* Light sensors are mounted on the front of each storage bin. Each sensor unit is linked to the computer system's picking module and contains a light that illuminates to indicate that picking is required for an order, an LCD (liquid crystal diode) readout listing the number of required units, and a button to press to indicate completion of a pick. When a stock picker enters or scans a bar-coded order number into the system, the bin sensors for those bins containing required picks will light up, and their LCD displays will show the number of units to pick. When a stock picker has completed picking from a bin, he or she presses the button, and the indicator lights shut off. This works well for high-volume picking situations.

○ *Voice picking.* Employees wear a portable computer, which accepts picking information from the main corporate computer and translates this information into English, which it communicates to the worker for hands-free picking with no written pick sheet. The worker also talks to the computer via a headset, telling it when items have been picked. The computer converts these spoken words into electronic messages for immediate transfer back to the main computer. This works well for high-volume picking situations.

○ *Wave picking.* Pick groups of orders at the same time, based on common delivery requirements. Since picking is based on common delivery dates, it is easier to ship in full truckload quantities, thereby saving freight costs.

○ *Zone picking.* Consolidate an entire day's picks into a single master pick list, which is then sorted by warehouse location. Different pickers are then sent to specific sections of the warehouse with their portions of the master pick list, where they use less travel time to pick their portions of all picks required for the day. All picked items are then consolidated in a central picking area, where they are broken down to fulfill individual orders. This works best in large warehouse environments where there are many orders to be filled.

○ *Zone picking with order forwarding.* Start an order in one zone picking area and forward the partially

completed order to the next warehouse zone; this
gains some benefit from zone picking while keeping
orders segregated. It avoids the need for any downstream order breakdown area.

How Do I Store Inventory to Reduce Picking Travel?

If the warehouse staff stores inventory in any open space
anywhere in the warehouse, stock pickers will find themselves traveling to distant areas for frequently used items.
This greatly increases travel time by stock pickers, possibly requiring more staff. To eliminate excess travel time,
cluster inventory into ABC classifications. Definitions of
each category are:

- *A classification.* The top 20% of items by transaction
  volume, usually comprising about 60% of all transactions. These items are stored closest to the stock
  pickers.
- *B classification.* The next 20% of items, usually comprising about 20% of all transactions.
- *C classification.* The remaining 60% of items, usually
  comprising about 20% of all transactions. These
  items are stored farthest from the stock pickers.

By organizing warehouse storage around these classifications, a company can save not only warehouse labor
costs but also fuel for forklifts and related machine
maintenance.

How Do I Reduce Inventory Scrap?

Scrap is caused by a number of problems. The next points
present possible ways to reduce the volume of scrap that a
company will experience.

- *Design products with lower tolerances.* All products
  should be designed to operate with components that
  have a broad tolerance range. By doing so, fewer
  parts will be rejected, since it is easier to manufacture such parts.
- *Produce the same parts on the same machine.* No two
  machines are exactly alike, either due to minor tolerance differences or variations in wear and tear.
  When production is assigned to a machine, these differences cause extra scrap during test runs, while the
  machine is "dialed in" to the proper output. The
  solution is to schedule the same part to be run on

the same machine as much as possible. Setups can then be fully documented and used repeatedly with minimal test runs.

○ *Inspect at the next workstation.* Shift the inspection burden to the next downstream workstation. By doing so, inspection is completed as soon after a work step as possible, so that very few additional products will have been made before the error is noticed, resulting in less scrap. Also, having someone besides the producing employee conduct the review will ensure a more objective examination.

○ *Schedule preventive maintenance.* If properly maintained, machines are more likely to produce within expected tolerances, which yield less scrap. This calls for a heightening of scheduled preventive maintenance.

○ *Produce to order.* If items are produced in accordance with a schedule, a large part of a facility's output will go straight to storage, where it will be at risk of becoming obsolete. Instead, produce to order, so that finished goods are shipped straight to customers.

How Do I Identify Obsolete Inventory?

The materials review board (MRB) is responsible for evaluating all obsolete inventory and determining the most appropriate disposition for each item. The MRB is composed of representatives from every department having any interaction with inventory issues: accounting, engineering, logistics, and production. The MRB should use the next methods for identifying obsolete inventory.

○ *Previous obsolete inventory report.* The preceding period's list of obsolete inventory is a good starting point, since not all items on the list may have been dispositioned yet. The MRB should maintain this list in order to track its success in eliminating obsolete items from stock.

○ *Leave count tags in place.* Leave the physical inventory count tags on all inventory items following completion of the annual physical count. The tags taped to any items used during the subsequent year will be thrown away at the time of use, leaving only the oldest unused items still tagged by the end of the year.

○ *Last date of use.* Create a report listing all inventory, starting with those products with the oldest "last used" date, and investigate those items that have not been used in a long time. However, this approach does not yield sufficient proof that an item will never be used again, since it may be an essential component of an item that has not been scheduled for production in some time or a service part for which demand is low.

A more advanced version of the "last used" report is shown in Exhibit 12.1. It compares total inventory withdrawals to the amount on hand, which by itself may be sufficient information to conduct an obsolescence review. It also lists planned usage, which calls for information from a material requirements planning system and which itemizes any upcoming requirements that might keep the MRB from otherwise disposing of an inventory item. An extended cost for each item is also listed, in order to give report users some idea of the write-off that might occur if an item is declared obsolete. In the exhibit, the subwoofer, speaker bracket, and wall bracket appear to be obsolete based on prior usage, but the planned use of more wall brackets would keep that item from being disposed of.

○ *"Where used" report.* If a computer system includes a bill of materials, there is a strong likelihood that it also generates a "where used" report, listing all the bills of material for which an inventory item is used. If there is no "where used" listed on the report for an item, it is likely that a part is no longer needed. This report is most effective if bills of material are removed from the computer system or deactivated as soon as products are withdrawn from the market;

Description	Item No.	Location	Quantity on Hand	Last Year Usage	Planned Usage	Extended Cost
Subwoofer case	0421	A-04-C	872	520	180	$9,053
Speaker case	1098	A-06-D	148	240	120	1,020
Subwoofer	3421	D-12-A	293	14	0	24,724
Circuit board	3600	B-01-A	500	5,090	1,580	2,500
Speaker, bass	4280	C-10-C	621	2,480	578	49,200
Speaker bracket	5391	C-10-C	14	0	0	92
Wall bracket	5080	B-03-B	7400	0	120	2,800
Gold connection	6233	C-04-A	3,025	8,042	5,900	9,725
Tweeter	7552	C-05-B	725	6,740	2,040	5,630

Exhibit 12.1 INVENTORY OBSOLESCENCE REVIEW REPORT

this more clearly reveals those inventory items that are no longer needed.

How Do I Sell Obsolete Inventory?

Here are some methods for realizing some cash flow from the disposition of obsolete inventory that a company cannot use internally.

- *Return to the supplier.* Many suppliers will accept product returns, though it may be in exchange for a substantial restocking fee. Also, they may issue only a credit for the return rather than a cash payment.
- *Sell as service parts.* Some parts may be needed for warranty replacements or can be sold at a premium as service parts for a number of years to come. However, this method usually disposes of only a small proportion of all obsolete parts.
- *Sell to salvage contractors.* Third parties will buy inventory at steep discounts. If this approach is to be used, force the contractors to bid on batches of obsolete inventory, so they cannot pick through the inventory for the choicest items.
- *Donate for a tax deduction.* Some nonprofit organizations will accept inventory, which they typically redistribute to other nonprofit organizations. A company can then recognize a tax credit for the value of the donated inventory.

CHAPTER 13

DEBT MANAGEMENT

What Is Commercial Paper?

Commercial paper is unsecured debt that is issued by a company and that has a fixed maturity ranging from 1 to 270 days. A company uses commercial paper to meet its short-term working capital obligations. It is commonly sold at a discount from face value with the discount (and therefore the interest rate) being higher if the term is longer. A company can sell its commercial paper directly to investors, such as money market funds, or through a dealer in exchange for a small commission.

Because there is no collateral on the debt, commercial paper is an option only for large companies having high-level credit ratings from a recognized credit rating agency. For those companies capable of issuing it, the interest rate on commercial paper is extremely low.

What Is Factoring?

Under a *factoring* arrangement, a finance company agrees to take over a company's accounts receivable collections and keep the money from those collections in exchange for an immediate cash payment to the company. This process typically involves having customers mail their payments to a lockbox that appears to be operated by the company, but which is actually controlled by the finance company. Under a true factoring arrangement, the finance company takes over the risk of loss on any bad debts, though it will have the right to pick which types of receivables it will accept in order to reduce its risk of loss. A finance company is more interested in this type of deal when the size of each receivable is fairly large, since this reduces its per-transaction cost of collection. If each receivable is quite small, the finance company may still be interested in a factoring arrangement, but it will charge the company extra for its increased processing work. The lender will charge an interest rate (at least 2% higher than the prime rate) as well as a transaction fee for processing each invoice as it is received. There may also be a minimum total fee charged, in order to cover the origination fee for the factoring arrangement in the event that few receivables are actually handed to the lender. A company working under this arrangement can be paid by the factor at once or can wait until the invoice due date before payment is sent. The latter arrangement reduces the interest expense that a company would have to pay the factor but tends to go against the reason why the factoring arrangement was established, which is to get money back to the company as rapidly as possible. An added advantage is that no collections staff is required, since the lender handles this chore.

What Is Accounts Receivable Financing?

Under an *accounts receivable financing* arrangement, a lender uses the accounts receivable as collateral for a loan and takes direct receipt of payments from customers rather than waiting for periodic loan payments from the company. A lender typically will loan only a maximum of 80% of the accounts receivable balance to a company and only against those accounts that are less than 90 days old. Also, if an invoice against which a loan has been made is not paid within the required 90-day time period, the lender will require the company to pay back the loan associated with that invoice.

What Is Field Warehouse Financing?

Under a *field warehousing* arrangement, a finance company segregates a portion of a company's warehouse area with a fence. All inventory within it is collateral for a loan from the finance company to the company. The finance company will pay for more raw materials as they are needed, and receives payment on its loan directly from accounts receivable as soon as customer payments are received. If a strict inventory control system is in place, the finance company will also employ someone who will record all additions to and withdrawals from the secured warehouse. If not, the company will be required to count all items within the secure area frequently and report this information back to the finance company. If the level of inventory drops below the amount of the loan, the company must pay back the finance company the difference between the outstanding loan amount and the total inventory valuation. The company is also required under state lien laws to post signs around the secured area, stating that a lien is in place on its contents.

Field warehousing is highly transaction intensive, especially when the finance company employs an onsite warehouse clerk, and so is a very expensive way to obtain funds. This approach is recommended only for those companies that have exhausted all other less expensive forms of financing. However, lenders typically do not require any covenants in association with these loans, giving corporate management more control over company operations.

 ## What Is Floor Planning?

Some lenders will directly pay for large assets that are being procured by a distributor or retailer (such as kitchen appliances or automobiles) and be paid back when the assets are sold to a consumer. In order to protect itself, the lender may require that the price of all assets sold be no lower than the price the lender originally paid for it on behalf of the distributor or retailer. Since the lender's basis for lending is strictly on the underlying collateral (as opposed to its faith in a business plan or general corporate cash flows), it will undertake frequent recounts of the assets and compare them to its list of assets originally purchased for the distributor or retailer. If there is a shortfall in the expected number of assets, the lender will require payment for the missing items. The lender may also require liquidation of the loan after a specific time period, especially if the underlying assets run the risk of becoming outdated in the near term.

This financing option is a good one for smaller or underfunded distributors or retailers, since the interest rate is not excessive (due to the presence of collateral).

What Is an Operating Lease?

Under the terms of an *operating lease*, the lessor carries the asset on its books and records a depreciation expense, while the lessee records the lease payments as an expense on its books. This type of lease typically does not cover the full life of the asset, nor does the buyer have a small-dollar buyout option at the end of the lease.

What Is a Capital Lease?

Under the terms of a *capital lease*, the lessee records it as an asset and is entitled to record all related depreciation as an expense. In this latter case, the lease payments are split into their interest and principal portions and are recorded on the lessee's books as such.

What Is a Line of Credit?

A *line of credit* is a commitment from a lender to pay a company whenever it needs cash, up to a preset maximum level. It is generally secured by company assets and for that reason bears an interest rate not far above the prime rate. The bank typically will charge an annual maintenance fee, irrespective of the amount of funds drawn down on the loan, on the grounds that it has invested in the completion of paperwork for the loan. The bank will also likely require an annual audit of key accounts and asset balances to verify that the company's financial situation is in line with the bank's assumptions. One problem with a line of credit is that the bank can cancel the line or refuse to allow extra funds to be drawn down from it if the bank feels that the company is no longer a good credit risk. Another issue is that the bank may require a company to maintain a compensating balance in an account at the bank; this increases the effective interest rate on the line of credit, since the company earns little or no interest on the funds stored at the bank.

A line of credit is most useful for situations where there may be only short-term cash shortfalls or seasonal needs that result in the line being drawn down to zero at some point during the year.

What Is a Bond?

A *bond* is a fixed obligation to pay, usually at a stated rate of $1,000 per bond, which is issued by a corporation to investors. It may be a *registered bond*, under which a company maintains a list of owners of each bond. The company then periodically sends interest payments, as well as the final principal payment, to the investor of record. It may also be a *coupon bond*, for which the company does not maintain a standard list of bond holders. Instead, each bond contains interest coupons that the bond holders send to the company on the dates when interest payments are due. The coupon bond is more easily transferable between investors, but this ease of transferability makes it more susceptible to loss.

A bond is generally issued with a fixed interest rate. However, if the rate is excessively low in the current market, investors will pay less for the face value of the bond, thereby driving up the net interest rate paid by the company. Similarly, if the rate is too high, investors will pay extra for the bond, thereby driving down the net interest rate paid.

There may be a bond indenture document that itemizes all features of the bond issue. It contains restrictions that the company is imposing on itself, such as limitations on capital expenditures or dividends, in order to make the bond issuance as palatable as possible to investors. If the company does not follow these restrictions, the bonds will be in default.

What Types of Bonds Can Be Issued?

The next list describes the more common types of bonds that a company can issue.

- ○ *Collateral trust bond.* A bond that uses as collateral a company's security investments.
- ○ *Convertible bond.* A bond that can be converted to stock using a predetermined conversion ratio. The presence of conversion rights typically reduces the interest cost of these bonds, since investors assign some value to the conversion privilege.
- ○ *Debenture.* A bond issued with no collateral. A subordinated debenture is one that specifies debt that is senior to it.
- ○ *Deferred interest bond.* A bond that provides for either reduced or no interest in the beginning years of the bond term and compensates for it with increased interest later in the bond term.
- ○ *Floorless bond.* A bond whose terms allow purchasers to convert them as well as any accrued interest to common stock. The reason for the name is that bond holders can convert some shares and sell them on the open market, thereby supposedly driving down the price and allowing them to buy more shares, and so on.
- ○ *Guaranteed bond.* A bond whose payments are guaranteed by another party. Corporate parents will sometimes issue this guarantee for bonds issued by subsidiaries in order to obtain a lower effective interest rate.

○ *Income bond.* A bond that pays interest only if income has been earned. The income can be tied to total corporate earnings or to specific projects. If the bond terms indicate that interest is cumulative, interest will accumulate during nonpayment periods and be paid at a later date when income is available for doing so.

○ *Mortgage bond.* A bond offering can be backed by any real estate owned by the company (called a *real property mortgage bond*), or by company-owned equipment (called an *equipment bond*), or by all assets (called a *general mortgage bond*).

○ *Serial bond.* A bond issuance where a portion of the total number of bonds are paid off each year, resulting in a gradual decline in the total amount of debt outstanding.

○ *Variable rate bond.* A bond whose stated interest rate varies as a percentage of a baseline indicator, such as the prime rate.

○ *Zero-coupon bond.* A bond with no stated interest rate. Investors purchase these bonds at a considerable discount to their face value in order to earn an effective interest rate.

○ *Zero-coupon convertible bond.* A bond that offers no interest rate on its face but that allows investors to convert to stock if the stock price reaches a level higher than its current price on the open market. The attraction to investors is that, even if the conversion price to stock is marked up to a substantial premium over the current market price of the stock, a high level of volatility in the stock price gives investors some hope of a profitable conversion to equity.

What Is a Bridge Loan?

A *bridge loan* is a form of short-term loan that is granted by a lending institution on the understanding that the company will obtain longer-term financing shortly that will pay off the bridge loan. This option is commonly used when a company is seeking to replace a construction loan with a long-term note that it expects to pay down gradually over many years. This type of loan is usually secured by facilities or fixtures in order to obtain a lower interest rate.

What Is Receivables Securitization?

A large company can securitize its accounts receivable, thereby achieving one of the lowest interest rates available for debt. To do so, it creates a special purpose entity (SPE) and transfers a selection of its receivables into the SPE. The SPE then sells the receivables to a bank conduit, which in turn pools the receivables that it has bought from multiple companies and uses the cash flows from the receivables to back the issuance of commercial paper to investors, who in turn are repaid with the cash flows from the receivables.

Receivables securitization is initially a complex process to create; the primary benefit of doing so is that a company's receivables are isolated from the company's other risks, so that the SPE has a higher credit rating than the company, with an attendant decline in borrowing costs. To achieve the AAA credit rating typically needed for receivables securitization, a credit rating agency will review the performance record of receivables previously included in the pool, debtor concentrations in the pool, and the company's credit and collection policies.

A key factor in preserving the stellar credit rating of the SPE is to maintain an adequate degree of separation between the company and the SPE. To do so, the transfer of receivables is supposed to be a nonrecourse sale, so that the company's creditors cannot claim the assets of the SPE if the company goes bankrupt. This means that there should be no mechanism by which the company can regain control of any receivables shifted to the SPE.

What Is a Sale and Leaseback Arrangement?

Under a *sale and leaseback arrangement*, a company sells one of its assets to a lender and then immediately leases it back for a guaranteed minimum time period. By doing so, the company obtains cash from the sale of the asset that it may be able to more profitably use elsewhere, while the leasing company handling the deal obtains a guaranteed lessee for a time period that will allow it to turn a profit on the financing arrangement. A sale and leaseback is most commonly used for the sale of a corporate building but can also be arranged for other large assets, such as production machinery.

A sale and leaseback is useful for companies in any type of financial condition. A financially healthy organization can use the resulting cash to buy back shares and prop up its stock price while a faltering organization can use the cash to fund operations. It has the added advantage of not burdening a company's balance sheet with debt; furthermore, it puts cash back *into* the balance sheet, allowing a company to obtain additional debt.

How Does One Interact with Credit Rating Agencies?

If a publicly held company issues debt, it can elect to have that debt rated by either Moody's, Standard & Poor's, or Fitch. These are the three top-tier credit rating agencies that the Securities and Exchange Commission allows to issue debt ratings. A debt rating results in a credit score that indicates the perceived risk of default on the underlying debt, which in turn impacts the price of the debt on the open market. Having a credit score is essentially mandatory, since most funds are prohibited by their internal investment rules from buying debt that does not have a specific level of credit rating assigned to it.

In order to develop a credit rating, a credit rating agency reviews the company's financial statements as well as its budgets, forecasts, performance against peer companies, internal operating reports, risk management strategies, and financial and operating policies. The focus of this analysis is forward-looking, since the

Definition	Fitch Rating	Moody's Rating	S&P Rating
Prime	AAA	Aaa	AAA
High grade	AA+	Aa1	AA+
	AA	Aa2	AA
	AA−	Aa3	AA−
Upper medium grade	A+	A1	A+
	A	A2	A
	A−	A3	A−
Lower medium grade	BBB+	Baa1	BBB+
	BBB	Baa2	BBB
	BBB−	Baa3	BBB−
Non–investment grade	BB+	Ba1	BB+
Speculative	BB	Ba2	BB
	BB−	Ba3	BB−
Highly speculative	B+	B1	B+
		B2	B
		B3	B−
Substantial risk	CCC	Caa1	CCC+

Exhibit 13.1   Credit Rating Agency Score Comparison

credit score reflects the company's future ability to meet its obligations.

If a company wants to improve its credit rating, then it must take specific steps to make its financial structure more conservative, such as by issuing more stock and using the proceeds to pay down debt. This requires the development of a plan to achieve the higher credit rating and communication of this information to the credit rating agency.

How Do the Credit Rating Agency Scores Compare to Each Other?

The table in Exhibit 13.1 shows how the scores of each agency compare at various levels of credit quality.

CHAPTER 14

EQUITY REGISTRATION

What Methods Are Used to Register Stock for Sale?

A key goal of both a company and its investors is to have its securities registered, so that it can more easily sell the securities and so that investors can freely trade them. The registration process is very time-consuming and expensive, so companies attempt to circumvent it through a variety of exemptions. As noted later in this chapter, the Securities and Exchange Commission's Regulation A provides a reduced filing requirement for small-dollar issuances, while Regulation D allows for the complete absence of registration for security sales to accredited investors, though those investors cannot resell their securities without taking additional steps. If none of these simpler methods is available, a company must use the Form S-1, S-3, or S-8. Form S-3 is an abbreviated registration that is available only to seasoned public companies, while Form S-1 is the "full" version that the remaining public companies must use. The Form S-8 is a highly abbreviated registration that is applicable only to stock issued to employees.

What Are the Contents of a Form S-1?

The Form S-1 is the default registration form to be used if no other registration forms or exemptions from registration (such as would be applicable under Regulations A or D) are available. A key factor in the preparation of a Form S-1 is whether the company can incorporate a number of required items by referencing them in the form, which can save a great deal of work. Incorporation by reference is available *only* if the company has not been for the past three years a blank check company, a shell company, or a registrant for an offering of penny stock. The company must also be current with its various filings of financial information.

The 17 main informational contents of the Form S-1 are:

1. *Forepart of the registration statement.* Include the company name, the title and amount of securities to be registered, and their offering price. Also describe the market for the securities.

2. *Summary information.* Provide a summary of the prospectus contents that contains a brief overview of the key aspects of the offering as well as contact information for the company's principal executive offices.

3. *Risk factors.* Discuss the most significant factors that make the offering speculative or risky, and explain how the risk affects the company or the securities being offered.

4. *Ratio of earnings to fixed charges.* If the registration is for debt securities, show a ratio of earnings to fixed charges. If the registration is for preferred equity securities, show the ratio of combined fixed charges and preference dividends to earnings.

5. *Use of proceeds.* State the principal purpose for which proceeds from the offering are intended.

6. *Determination of offering price.* Describe the factors considered in determining the offering price, both for common equity and for warrants, rights, and convertible securities.

7. *Dilution.* Disclose the net tangible book value per share before and after the distribution, and the amount of shareholder dilution.

8. *Selling security holders.* For those securities being sold for the account of another security holder, name each security holder as well as each person's relationship with the company within the past three years.

9. *Plan of distribution.* Describe the involvement of underwriters and stock exchanges in the distribution, any other form of distribution, and the compensation paid to all parties as part of the distribution.

10. *Description of securities to be registered.* State the title and rights associated with each type of security being offered for sale.

11. *Interests of named experts and counsel.* Identify any experts and counsel who are certifying or preparing the registration document or providing a supporting valuation, and the nature of their compensation relating to the registration.

12. *Information with respect to the registrant.* This section comprises the bulk of the document and includes a description of the business and its property, any legal proceedings, the market price of the company's stock, financial statements, selected financial data, and management's discussion and analysis of the company's financial condition and its results of operations. It also requires disclosure of any disagreements with the company's auditors.

13. *Material changes.* Describe material changes that have occurred since the company's last-filed annual or quarterly report.

14. *Other expenses of issuance and distribution.* Itemize the expenses incurred in connection with the issuance and distribution of the securities to be registered, other than underwriting discounts and commissions.

15. *Indemnification of directors and officers.* Note the effect of any arrangements under which the company's directors and officers are insured or indemnified against liability.

16. *Recent sales of unregistered securities.* Identify all unregistered securities sold by the company within the past three years, including the names of the principal underwriters, consideration received, and the type of exemption from registration claimed.

17. *Exhibits and financial statement schedules.* Provide exhibits, with a related index, for such items as the underwriting agreement, consents, and powers of attorney.

The complete details of these reporting requirements are located in Regulation S-K.

 ## When Is a Form S-3 Used?

The Form S-3 allows a company to incorporate a large amount of information into the form by reference, which is generally not allowed in a Form S-1. Specifically, the company can incorporate the information already filed in its latest Form 10-K, subsequent quarterly 10-Q reports, and 8-K reports, thereby essentially eliminating the ''information with respect to the registration'' that is required for the Form S-1. This represents a considerable time savings, so companies file a Form S-3 whenever possible. However, the Form S-3 is restricted to those companies that meet these four eligibility requirements:

1. It is organized within and has principal business operations within the United States; and
2. It already has a class of registered securities, or has been meeting its periodic reporting requirements to the Securities and Exchange Commission (SEC) for at least the past 12 months; and
3. It cannot have failed to pay dividends, sinking fund installments, or defaulted on scheduled debt or lease payments since the end of the last fiscal year; and
4. The aggregate market value of the common equity held by nonaffiliates of the company is at least $75 million.

If a company has an aggregate market value of common equity held by nonaffiliates of less than $75 million, it can still use the Form S-3, provided that:

1. The aggregate market value of securities sold by the company during the 12 months prior to the Form S-3 filing is no more than one-third of the aggregate market value of the voting and nonvoting common equity held by its nonaffiliated investors; and
2. It is not a shell company, and has not been one for the past 12 months; and
3. It has at least one class of common equity securities listed on a national securities exchange.

The eligibility requirements of the Form S-3 restrict its use to larger public companies. Smaller "nano-cap" firms must search for a registration exemption, such as is provided by Regulation A and Regulation D.

When Is a Form S-8 Used?

The Form S-8 allows a company to register securities that it offers to its employees and consultants under an employee benefit plan. Such a plan can involve a broad array of securities-related issuances, such as common stock, stock options, restricted stock units, and purchases under an employee stock purchase plan. People covered by this type of registration include employees, officers, directors, general partners, and consultants. Securities issued to consultants can be registered only through a Form S-8 if they provide bona fide services to the company, and those services are not related to the sale of its securities or making a market in them. Family members are also covered, if they received company securities through an employee gift.

There are two significant advantages to using a Form S-8.

1. The form is effective immediately upon filing.
2. It is extremely simple to complete. The company must merely state that its regular periodic filings are incorporated by reference and note the manner in which the company indemnifies its officers and directors. The principal accompanying document is the employee benefit plan.

This form of registration is available only if a public company has been current with its filing requirements for at least the past 12 months and has not been a shell company for at least the preceding 60 days.

In short, the Form S-8 presents significant advantages over the normal securities registration process. However, since it is applicable only to employee benefit plans, it usually applies to only a small proportion of a company's outstanding securities.

What Is a Shelf Registration?

Shelf registration is the registration of a new issue of securities that can be filed with the SEC up to three years in advance of the actual distribution of such securities. This allows a company to obtain funds quickly when needed rather than compiling a registration document and waiting for the SEC to declare the registration effective.

A shelf registration can be accomplished through a Form S-3 filing, which in turn is restricted to certain companies that meet the SEC's eligibility rules. It is also possible to use a Form S-1 to initiate a shelf registration, but only if the intent is to sell the securities "on an immediate, continuous, or delayed basis," with all sales being completed within the next two years.

A shelf registration must be declared effective by the SEC before any securities sales related to it can be initiated. However, the SEC allows for some registration statements to be declared effective immediately upon their dates of filing. This automatic shelf registration is available only to *well-known seasoned issuers* (WKSI). A WKSI is a company whose common stock belonging to nonaffiliates has a market value of at least $700 million or which has issued at least $1 billion of nonconvertible securities within the past three years and will register only nonconvertible securities other than common equity. In addition, such filings have reduced information filing requirements.

Why Must a Registration Statement Be Declared Effective?

A registration statement is reviewed by SEC staff members. If they find that it conforms to SEC regulations and clearly states key information about the company, they declare it *effective*. Once the registration statement is declared effective, either the company or those investors on whose behalf it is registering the securities can initiate selling activities.

The SEC normally spends 30 days reviewing the registration document and issues a comment letter, detailing its suggestions for improving the document. The company then responds with its defense of the existing presentation or issues a revised registration document, for which the SEC again has 30 days to conduct a review. Several iterations of this process may occur before the SEC is satisfied with the registration document and declares the document to be effective.

When Can the Regulation A Exemption Be Used?

Regulation A provides an exemption from the securities registration requirements of the Securities Act of 1933, on the grounds that a smaller securities issuance does not warrant registration. Regulation A allows exemption from registration if the offering is no larger than $5 million in aggregate per year. Of this amount, no more than $1.5 million can be attributed to the secondary offering of securities currently held by existing shareholders; the secondary offering cannot include resales by company affiliates if the company has not generated net income from continuing operations in at least one of the past two fiscal years. The exemption is restricted to American and Canadian companies, and it is not available to investment and development-stage companies. Anyone using this exemption must also create an offering circular, similar to the one that would be required for a registered offering.

The regulation has provisions that can disqualify a company from using it. It is not available if a company has had a variety of disclosure problems with the SEC in the past five years, or if the company currently has a registration statement being reviewed by the SEC, or if any affiliates or the company's underwriter have been convicted within the past 10 years of a crime related to a security transaction.

What Are the Advantages of Using a Regulation A Exemption?

There are three advantages to the exemption provided under Regulation A.

1. There is no limit on the number of investors, nor must they pass any kind of qualification test.
2. There are no restrictions on the resale of any securities sold under the regulation.
3. The key difference between a Regulation A offering and a registered offering is the absence of any periodic reporting requirements. This is a major reduction in costs to the company and is the most attractive aspect of the exemption.

In addition, and unlike a registered offering, the regulation allows a company to test the waters with investors in advance of the offering, in order to determine the level of investor interest. To take advantage of this feature, the company must submit the materials used for this initial testing of the waters to the SEC on or before their first date of use. The materials must state that no money is being solicited or will be accepted, that no sales will be made until the company issues an offering circular, that any indication of interest by an investor does not constitute a purchase commitment, and also identify the company's chief executive officer as well as briefly describe the business. The company can test the waters only until it has filed an offering circular with the SEC and can commence securities sales only once at least 20 days have passed since the last document delivery or broadcast.

What Is the Process for Using the Regulation A Exemption?

When a company is ready to notify the SEC of securities sales under this exemption, it does so using Form 1-A. Once the form is filed, the company can conduct a general solicitation, which can include advertising the offering, as long as the solicitation states that sales cannot be completed until the SEC qualifies the company's preliminary offering circular. This preliminary document does not have to include the final security price, though it should contain an estimate of the range of the maximum offering price and the maximum number of shares or debt securities to be offered. Advertising can state only where the offering circular can be obtained, the name of the company, the price and type of security being offered, and the company's general type of business.

While a company is permitted to advertise its offering as soon as the Form 1-A is filed, it must follow a specific procedure to conduct actual security sales. Once the Form 1-A has been qualified by the SEC, the company must furnish an offering circular to each prospective purchaser at least 48 hours prior to mailing a confirmation of sale. If a broker/dealer is involved with the sale, this entity must provide a copy of the offering circular either with or prior to the confirmation of sale.

If the information in an offering circular becomes false or misleading due to changed circumstances or there have been material developments during the course of an offering, the company must revise the offering circular.

Once securities sales are under way, the company must file Form 2-A with the SEC every six months following the qualification of the offering statement, describing ongoing sales from the offering and use of proceeds. In addition, it must file a final Form 2-A within 30 calendar days following the later of the termination of the offering or the application of proceeds from the offering.

What Are the Restrictions on Using the Regulation D Exemption?

Under Regulation D, securities can be sold only to an *accredited investor*. An *accredited investor* is one whom the issuing company reasonably believes falls within any of these five categories at the time of the securities sale:

1. A bank, broker-dealer, insurance company, investment company, or employee benefit plan
2. A director, executive officer, or general partner of the issuing company
3. A person whose individual net worth (or joint net worth with a spouse) exceeds $1 million
4. A person having individual income exceeding $200,000 or joint income with a spouse exceeding $300,000 in each of the last two years, with a reasonable expectation for reaching the same income level in the current year
5. Any trust with total assets exceeding $5 million

The issuing company is not allowed any form of general solicitation for the sale of securities under the regulation. This prohibits the use of advertisements and articles via any medium of publication. It also prohibits the sale of securities through seminars to which attendees were invited through any form of general solicitation. In order to avoid having a general solicitation, a company must pre-screen any investor to whom an inquiry is sent, usually by using an underwriter or promoter who already has a list of qualified potential investors.

Securities sold under a Regulation D offering cannot be resold without registration. For this reason, the issuing company is required under Rule 502 of the regulation to "exercise reasonable care to assure that the purchasers of the securities are not underwriters." To do so, the company must take these three steps:

1. Inquire of purchasers if they are acquiring the securities for themselves or for other parties.
2. Disclose to each purchaser that the securities have not been registered and therefore cannot be resold until they are registered.
3. Add a legend to each securities certificate, stating that the securities have not been registered and stating the restrictions on their sale or transfer.

When Can Rule 144 Be Used to Register Stock?

When an investor acquires restricted securities, the securities bear a restrictive legend, stating that the securities may not be resold unless they are registered with the SEC or exempt from its registration requirements. Rule 144 allows for the resale of restricted securities if five conditions are met, which primarily involve the passage of time. They are:

1. *Holding period.* If the securities issuer is subject to the periodic reporting requirements of the Securities Exchange Act of 1934 (e.g., issues 10-Q, 10-K, and other periodic reports), the securities holder must hold the securities for at least six months. If the securities issuer is not reporting under the Exchange Act, the holding period is one year.
2. *Adequate current information.* The securities issuer must be current in its reporting under the Exchange Act.
3. *Trading volume formula.* If the securities holder is an affiliate of the company (i.e., one who is in a control position), the number of securities available for sale during any three-month period cannot exceed the greater of 1% of the outstanding shares of the same

class being sold, or if the class is listed on a stock exchange, the greater of 1% of the average reported weekly trading volume during the four weeks preceding the investor's filing of a notice of sale using a Form 144. If the securities issuer's stock is traded over the counter only, just the 1% rule applies.

4. *Ordinary brokerage transactions.* If the securities holder is an affiliate, the securities sale must be handled as a routine trading transaction, where the broker cannot receive more than a normal commission. The seller and broker cannot solicit orders to buy the securities, other than to respond to various types of unsolicited inquiries.

5. *File a notice of proposed sale.* If the securities holder is an affiliate, the proposed sale must be filed with the SEC on a Form 144 if the sale involves more than 5,000 shares or if the aggregate dollar amount is greater than $50,000 in any three-month period. The completed form shall be filed concurrently with either the placing with a broker of a sale order or the execution with a market maker of such a sale. The sale must take place within three months of filing the form, or else an amended notice must be filed.

If a securities holder has held the restricted securities for at least one year, and has not been a company affiliate for at least the past three months, the securities can be resold without regard to the preceding conditions. If the company is fulfilling its reporting requirements under the Exchange Act, the holding period is reduced to six months.

Once these conditions are met, the securities holder must have the restrictive legend removed before the securities can be sold. Legend removal must be done by the company's stock transfer agent, which will do so only with the written approval of the issuing company's counsel. This written approval is in the form of an opinion letter.

PART III

FINANCIAL ANALYSIS

CHAPTER 15

FINANCIAL ANALYSIS

How Do I Calculate the Breakeven Point?

*B*reakeven analysis is the revenue level at which a company earns exactly no profit. It is also known as the cost-volume-profit relationship. To determine a breakeven point, add up all the fixed costs for the company or product being analyzed, and divide it by the associated gross margin percentage. This results in the sales level at which a company will neither lose nor make money—its breakeven point. The formula is shown in Exhibit 15.1.

The breakeven chart can also be shown graphically. Exhibit 15.2 shows a horizontal line across the chart that represents the fixed costs that must be covered by gross margins, irrespective of the sales level. There is an upward-sloping line that begins at the left end of the fixed cost line and extends to the right across the chart. This is the percentage of variable costs, such as direct labor and materials, that is needed to create the product. The last major component of the breakeven chart is the sales line, which is based in the lower left corner of the chart and extends to the upper right corner. The amount of the sales volume in dollars is noted on the vertical axis, while the amount of production capacity used to create the sales volume is noted across the horizontal axis. Finally, there is a line that extends from the marked breakeven point to the right, and which is always between the sales line and the variable cost line. This represents income tax costs. These are the main components of the breakeven chart in Exhibit 15.2.

Total Fixed Costs/Gross Margin Percentage = Breakeven Sales Level

Exhibit 15.1 Breakeven Formula

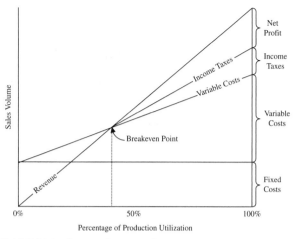

Exhibit 15.2   SIMPLIFIED BREAKEVEN CHART

On the chart, the area beneath the fixed costs line is the total fixed cost to be covered by product margins. The area between the fixed cost line and the variable cost line is the total variable cost at different volume levels. The area beneath the income line and above the variable cost line is the income tax expense at various sales levels. Finally, the area beneath the revenue line and above the income tax line is the amount of net profit to be expected at various sales levels.

What Is the Impact of Fixed Costs on the Breakeven Point?

A common alteration in fixed costs is when additional personnel or equipment are needed in order to support an increased level of sales activity. As noted in the breakeven chart in Exhibit 15.3, the fixed cost will step up to a higher level when a certain capacity level is reached. An example of this situation is when a company has maximized the use of a single shift and must add supervision and other overhead costs, such as electricity and natural gas expenses, in order to run an additional shift. Another example is when a new facility must be brought on line or an additional machine acquired. Whenever this happens, management must take a close look at the amount of fixed costs that will be incurred, because the net profit level may be less after the fixed costs are added, despite the extra sales volume. In Exhibit 15.3, the maximum amount of profit that a company can attain is at the sales level just

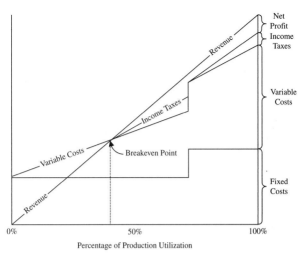

Exhibit 15.3   BREAKEVEN CHART INCLUDING IMPACT OF STEP COSTING

prior to incurring extra fixed costs, because the increase in fixed costs is so high. Though step costing does not always involve such a large increase in costs, this is a point to be aware of when increasing capacity to take on additional sales volume. In short, more sales do not necessarily lead to more profits.

What Is the Impact of Variable Cost Changes on the Breakeven Point?

The variable cost percentage can drop as the sales volume increases, because the purchasing department can cut better deals with suppliers when it orders in larger volumes. In addition, full truckload or railcar deliveries result in lower freight expenses than would be the case if only small quantities were purchased. The result is shown in Exhibit 15.4, where the variable cost percentage is at its highest when sales volume is at its lowest and gradually decreases in concert with an increase in volume.

Another point is that the percentage of variable costs will not decline at a steady rate. Instead, there will be specific volume levels at which costs will drop. This is because the purchasing staff can negotiate price reductions only at specific volume points. Once such a price reduction has been achieved, there will not be another opportunity to reduce prices further until a separate and distinct volume level is reached once again.

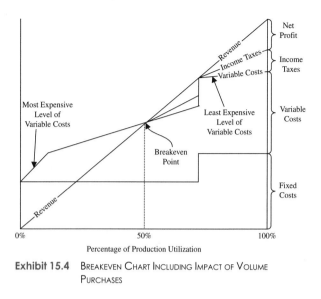

Exhibit 15.4 BREAKEVEN CHART INCLUDING IMPACT OF VOLUME PURCHASES

How Do Pricing Changes Alter the Breakeven Point?

A common problem impacting the volume line in the breakeven calculation is that unit prices do not remain the same when volume increases. Instead, a company finds that it can charge a high price early on, when the product is new and competes with few other products in a small niche market. Later, when management decides to go after larger unit volume, unit prices drop in order to secure sales to a larger array of customers or to resellers that have a choice of competing products to resell. Thus, higher volume translates into lower unit prices. The result appears in Exhibit 15.5, where the revenue per unit gradually declines despite a continuing rise in unit volume, which causes a much slower increase in profits than would be the case if revenues rose in a straight, unaltered line.

This breakeven chart is a good example of what the breakeven analysis really looks like in the marketplace. Fixed costs jump at different capacity levels, variable costs decline at various volume levels, and unit prices drop with increases in volume. Given the fluidity of the model, it is reasonable to revisit it periodically in light of continuing changes in the marketplace in order to update assumptions and make better calculations of breakeven points and projected profit levels.

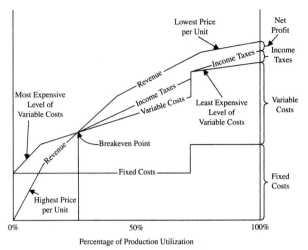

Exhibit 15.5 BREAKEVEN CHART INCLUDING IMPACT OF VARIABLE PRICING LEVELS

How Can the Product Mix Alter Profitability?

Product mix has an enormous impact on corporate profits, except for those very rare cases where all products happen to have the same profit margins. To determine how the change in mix will impact profits, construct a chart, such as the one shown in Exhibit 15.6, that contains the number of units sold and the standard margin for each product or product line, and the resulting gross margin dollars. The resulting average margin will impact the denominator in the standard breakeven formula. For example, if the average mix for a month's sales results in a gross margin of 40%, and fixed costs for the period were $50,000, the breakeven point would be $50,000/40%, or $125,000. If

Product	Unit Sales	Margin %	Margin $
Flow meter	50,000	25%	$12,500
Water collector	12,000	32%	3,840
Ditch digger	51,000	45%	22,950
Evapo-preventor	30,000	50%	15,000
Piping connector	17,000	15%	2,550
Totals	160,000	36%	$56,840

Exhibit 15.6 CALCULATION TABLE FOR MARGIN CHANGES DUE TO PRODUCT MIX

the product mix for the following month were to result in a gross margin of 42%, the breakeven point would shift downward to $50,000/42%, or $119,048. Thus, changes in product mix will alter the breakeven point by changing the gross margin number that is part of the breakeven formula.

 How Do I Calculate Price Variances?

The *price variance* is the difference between the standard and actual price paid for anything, multiplied by the number of units of each item purchased. The derivation of price variances for materials, wages, variable overhead, and fixed overhead are presented next.

- ○ *Material price variance.* This is based on the actual price paid for materials used in the production process, minus their standard cost, multiplied by the number of units used. It is typically reported to the purchasing manager. This calculation is a bit more complicated than it at first seems, since the "actual" cost is probably either the last in, first out; first in, first out; or average cost of an item. Here are four additional areas to investigate if there is a material price variance:

  1. The standard price is based on a different purchase volume.
  2. The standard price is incorrectly derived from a different component.
  3. The material was purchased on a rush basis.
  4. The material was purchased at a premium, due to a supply shortage.

- ○ *Labor price variance.* This is based on the actual price paid for the direct labor used in the production process, minus its standard cost, multiplied by the number of units used. It is typically reported to the managers of both production and human resources; the production manager, because this person is responsible for manning jobs with personnel of the correct wage rates; and the human resources manager, because this person is responsible for setting the allowable wage rates that employees are paid. This tends to be a relatively small variance, as long as the standard labor rate is regularly revised to match actual labor rates in the production facility. Since most job categories tend to be clustered into relatively small pay ranges, there is not much chance that a labor price variance will become excessive. Here are three areas to investigate if there is a labor price variance:

1. The standard labor rate has not been adjusted recently to reflect actual pay changes.
2. The actual labor rate includes overtime or shift differentials that were not included in the standard.
3. The manning of jobs is with employees whose pay levels are different from those used to develop standards for those jobs.

○ *Variable overhead spending variance.* To calculate this variance, subtract the standard variable overhead cost per unit from the actual cost incurred, and multiply the remainder by the total unit quantity of output. This is very similar to the material and labor price variances, since there are some overhead costs that are directly related to the volume of production, as is the case for materials and labor. The detailed report on this variance is usually sent to the production manager, who is responsible for all overhead incurred in the production area. Here are three areas to investigate if there is a variable overhead spending variance:

1. The cost of activities in any of the variable overhead accounts has been altered by the supplier.
2. The company has altered its purchasing methods for the variable overhead costs to or from the use of blanket purchase orders (which tend to result in lower prices due to higher purchase volumes).
3. Costs are being misclassified between the accounts, so that the spending variance appears too low in one account and too high in another.

○ *Fixed overhead spending variance.* This is the total amount by which fixed overhead costs exceed their total standard cost for the reporting period. There is no way to relate this price variance to volume, since it is not directly tied to any sort of activity volume. The detailed variance report on this topic may be distributed to many people, depending on who is responsible for each general ledger account number that it contains. Investigation of variances in this area generally centers on a period-to-period comparison of prices charged to suppliers, with particular attention to those experiencing recent price increases.

How Do I Calculate Efficiency Variances?

The *efficiency variance* is the difference between the actual and standard usage of a resource, multiplied by the standard price of that resource. The efficiency variance applies to materials, labor, and variable overhead. It does not apply to fixed overhead costs, since these costs are incurred independently from any resource usage. Here is a closer examination of the efficiency variance, as applied to each of these areas:

○ *Material yield variance.* This measures the ability of a company to manufacture a product using the exact amount of materials allowed by the standard. A variance will arise if the quantity of materials used differs from the preset standard. It is calculated by subtracting the total standard quantity of materials that are supposed to be used from the actual level of usage, and multiplying the remainder by the standard price per unit. This information is usually issued to the production manager. Here are some of the areas to investigate to correct the material yield variance:

1. Excessive machine-related scrap rates.
2. Poor material quality levels.
3. Excessively tight tolerance for product rejections.
4. Improper machine setup.
5. Substitute materials that cause high reject rates.

○ *Labor efficiency variance.* This measures the ability of a company's direct labor staff to create products with the exact amount of labor set forth in the standard. A variance will arise if the quantity of labor used is different from the standard; note that this variance has nothing to do with the cost per unit of labor (which is the price variance), only the quantity of it that is consumed. It is calculated by subtracting the standard quantity of labor consumed from the actual amount, and multiplying the remainder times the standard labor rate per hour. As was the case for the material yield variance, it is most commonly reported to the production manager. Here are the likely causes of the labor efficiency variance:

1. Employees have poor work instructions.
2. Employees are not adequately trained.
3. Too many employees are manning a work station.

4. The wrong mix of employees is manning a work station.
5. The labor standard used as a comparison is incorrect.

○ *Variable overhead efficiency variance.* This measures the quantity of variable overhead required to produce a unit of production. For example, if the machine used to run a batch of product requires extra time to produce each product, there will be an additional charge to the product's cost that is based on the price of the machine, multiplied by its cost per minute. This variance is not concerned with the machine's cost per minute (which would be examined through a price variance analysis) but with the number of minutes required for the production of each unit. It is calculated by subtracting the budgeted units of activity upon which the variable overhead is charged from the actual units of activity, times the standard variable overhead cost per unit. Depending on the nature of the costs that make up the pool of variable overhead costs, this variance may be reported to several managers, particularly the production manager. The causes of this variance will be tied to the unit of activity on which it is based. For example, if the variable overhead rate varies directly with the quantity of machine time used, the main causes will be any action that changes the rate of machine usage. If the basis is the amount of materials used, the causes will be those just noted for the materials yield variance.

How Do I Conduct a Profitability Analysis for Services?

In the services industry, employee billable hours constitute the prime criterion for overall corporate profitability. Financial analysis should encompass the next three factors, which encompass the primary determinants of profitability in the services sector:

1. Percentage of time billed
2. Full labor cost per hour
3. Billing price per hour

The percentage of time billed can be easily tracked with a spreadsheet, such as the one shown in Exhibit 15.7, where billable employee time is listed by week, with a month-to-date billable percentage listed not only by

			Week Ending			
Name	07 Feb.	14 Feb.	21 Feb.	28 Feb.	Hours	Billable %
Abrams, J.	40	30	0	0	70	46%
Barlow, M.	40	32	27	39	138	91%
Chubby, T.	48	32	42	43	165	109%
Totals	128	94	69	82	373	82%
Billable %	107%	98%	58%	68%	82%	
Workdays	5	4	5	5		

Exhibit 15.7   BILLABLE HOURS REPORT

employee but also for the entire company. This approach easily highlights any staff members who are not meeting minimum billable targets.

In the exhibit, note the "workdays" row at the bottom, which indicates the number of standard working days in each week of the report, as well as the maximum number of hours that employees can bill during the month. The exhibit shows that more than 100% of possible employee hours were billed during the first week of February, due to the billable overtime hours worked by T. Chubby. However, J. Abrams later becomes unbillable, resulting in only a 46% billable percentage for that employee by the end of the month. In total, the group has an 82% billable percentage during the month.

The full labor cost per hour encompasses not only the hourly rate paid per employee but also the hourly cost of payroll taxes, various types of insurance, and other benefits (net of deductions paid by employees). Exhibit 15.8 shows the calculation of the full labor cost per hour for several employees.

A key consideration is that, if the employees providing services are being paid on a salary basis, any overtime hours worked by them that are billable to customers

Name	Labor Rate per Hour	Payroll Taxes	Pension Matching	Medical Insurance	Long-term Disability	Full Labor Cost per Hour
Abrams, J.	$17.50	$1.37	$0.05	$2.93	$0.04	$21.89
Barlow, M.	29.32	2.30	0.05	5.17	0.03	36.87
Chubby, T.	41.07	3.22	0.05	2.93	0.04	47.31

Exhibit 15.8   FULL LABOR COST PER HOUR CALCULATION

Name	Billing Rate per Hour	×	Billable Percentage	=	Net Billing Rate per Hour	−	Full Labor Cost per Hour	=	Gross Margin
Abrams, J.	$45.00		46%		$20.70		$21.89		($1.19)
Barlow, M.	55.00		91%		50.05		36.87		13.18
Chubby, T.	60.00		109%		65.40		47.31		18.09

Exhibit 15.9   EMPLOYEE PROFITABILITY ANALYSIS

represent a pure profit increase, since there is no offsetting labor cost.

The price billed per hour means little unless it is compared to the full labor rate cost per hour, thereby arriving at the margin being earned on each hour worked. Otherwise, a high hourly cost could entirely offset an otherwise impressive billing rate, resulting in no profitability for the company. Exhibit 15.9 shows how the billing rate, full labor cost per hour, and billable percentage can be combined to reveal a complete picture of profitability for billable employees.

In the exhibit, the billable percentage for J. Abrams has dropped so low that the net billing rate per hour is less than that employee's fully burdened labor cost per hour; the solution is to increase the billing rate, increase the billable percentage, reduce the employee's cost, or terminate the employee. The situation for the third employee on the list, T. Chubby, is somewhat different. We assume that Chubby does not receive extra overtime pay; if this were not the case, the labor cost per hour in the exhibit would increase substantially to include the cost of an overtime premium.

The analysis in Exhibit 15.9 could also include a charge for a commission percentage, on the grounds that a salesperson is being paid a commission for having obtained the services contract under which the employee is now billable.

Another use for Exhibit 15.9 is to calculate the breakeven billable percentage for each employee, which management can use as a minimum billable target. This information can be determined by shifting the information in the exhibit slightly and revising the calculation, as shown in Exhibit 15.10.

The analysis in Exhibit 15.10 reveals a different aspect of the situation; although J. Abrams is currently not profitable, a relatively low billing percentage of 49% will result

Name	Full Labor Cost per Hour	÷	Billing Rate per Hour	=	Breakeven Billable %
Abrams, J.	$21.89		$45.00		49%
Barlow, M.	36.87		55.00		67%
Chubby, T.	47.31		60.00		79%

Exhibit 15.10 BREAKEVEN BILLABLE PERCENTAGE CALCULATION

in a profit. Conversely, although T. Chubby is currently profitable on an hourly basis, the breakeven analysis reveals that a much higher billable percentage is required to maintain this situation, because the margin on Chubby's services is lower than for the other two employees.

The analysis of profitability for services is nearly complete and excludes only the consideration of corporate overhead. The gross margins noted for employees in Exhibit 15.9 must be extrapolated by the total number of hours worked in the reporting period to arrive at the grand total gross margin earned during the period. Overhead expenses are then compared to this figure to determine the profit or loss for the period, as shown in Exhibit 15.11. The exhibit reveals that the company must pare overhead expenses drastically, obtain additional billable staff, or greatly increase the gross margin per hour of the existing employees in order to earn a profit.

How Are Profits Affected by the Number of Days in a Month?

In a service-related business, the prime focus of conversation usually includes such factors as billable rates per hour and the percentage of billable time. However, a third

Name	Gross Margin per Hour	×	Hours Worked in Period	=	Total Gross Margin
Abrams, J.	($1.19)		70		($83.30)
Barlow, M.	13.18		138		1,818.84
Chubby, T.	18.09		165		2,984.85
			Total gross margin		$4,720.39
			Overhead expenses		($9,425.00)
			Net loss		($4,704.61)

Exhibit 15.11 CORPORATE PROFITABILITY ANALYSIS

factor is worth a considerable amount of attention as well: the number of business days in the month. Using the standard number of federal holidays in the United States, here are the number of months with different quantities of business days:

Number of Business Days per Month	Number of Months
23	1
22	2
21	1
20	6
19	1
Total Months	**12**

Figure out the number of business days it takes for the consulting or service business to break even. If it takes 21 business days, the company will lose money in 7 months out of 12. If it takes 22 or 23 business days, there is a real problem. If this appears to be an issue, calculate the expense reduction required to reduce the breakeven point by 1 incremental day. This is an excellent approach for monitoring how well the business is structured to make money throughout the year.

Which Research and Development Projects Should Be Funded?

A good way to fund research and development (R&D) projects is to apportion investable funds into multiple categories: a large percentage that is to be used only for highly risky projects with associated high returns and a separate pool of funds specifically designated for lower-risk projects with correspondingly lower levels of return. The exact proportions of funding allocated to each category will depend on management's capacity for risk as well as the size and number of available projects in each category. This approach allows a company the opportunity to achieve a breakthrough product introduction.

If this approach to allocating funds is used, it is likely that a number of new product projects will be abandoned prior to their release into the market, on the grounds that they will not yield a sufficient return on investment or will not be technologically or commercially feasible. This is not a bad situation, since some projects are bound to fail if a sufficiently high level of project risk is acceptable to management. Conversely, if no projects fail, this is a clear sign that management is not investing in sufficiently risky investments. To measure the level of project failure, calculate R&D waste, which is the amount of unrealized product development spending (e.g., the total expenditure on canceled projects during the measurement period). Even better, divide the amount of R&D waste by the total R&D expenditure during the period to determine the proportion of expenses incurred on failed projects.

Though funding may be allocated into broad investment categories, management must still use a reliable method for determining which projects will receive funding and which will not. The standard approach is to apply a discount rate to all possible projects and to select those having the highest net present value (NPV). However, the NPV calculation does not include several key variables found in the expected commercial value (ECV) formula, making the ECV the preferred method. The ECV formula requires one to multiply a prospective project's net present value by the probability of its commercial success, minus the commercialization cost, and then multiply the result by the probability of technical success, minus the development cost. Thus, the intent of using ECV is to include all major success factors into the decision to accept or reject a new product proposal. The formula is:

$$(((\text{Project net present value} \times \text{probability of commercial success}) - \text{commercialization cost}) \times \text{probability of technical success})) - \text{product development cost}$$

EXAMPLE

The Moravia Corporation collects this information about a new project for a battery-powered lawn trimmer, where there is some technical risk that a sufficiently powerful battery cannot be developed for the product:

Project net present value	$4,000,000
Probability of commercial success	90%
Commercialization cost	$750,000
Probability of technical success	65%
Product development cost	$1,750,000

Based on this information, Moravia computes the ECV for the lawn trimmer project:

$$(((\$4,000,000 \text{ project net present value}$$
$$\times \ 90\% \text{ probability of commercial success})$$
$$- \ \$750,000 \text{ commercialization cost})$$
$$\times \ 65\% \text{ probability of technical success}))$$
$$- \ \$1,750,000 \text{ product development cost}$$

$$\text{Expected commercial value} = \$102,500$$

How Do I Create a Throughput Analysis Model?

The primary focus of *throughput analysis* is on how to force as much throughput dollars (sales minus totally variable expenses) as possible through the capacity constraint (i.e., the bottleneck operation). It does this by first determining the throughput dollars per minute of every production job scheduled to run through the capacity constraint and then rearranging the order of production priority so that the products with the highest throughput dollars per minute are completed first. The system is based on the supposition that only a certain amount of production can be squeezed through a bottleneck operation, so the production that yields the highest margin must come first in order of production scheduling priority, to ensure that profits are maximized. The concept is most easily demonstrated in the example shown in Exhibit 15.12.

In the example, we have four types of products that a company can sell. Each requires some machining time on the company's capacity constraint, which is the circuit board manufacturing process (CBMP). The first item is a 19-inch color television, which requires four minutes of the CBMP's time. The television sells for $100.00 and has associated direct materials of $67.56, which gives it a throughput of $32.44. (The price and direct materials cost are not shown in the exhibit; they are inferred from it.) We then divide the throughput of $32.44 by the four minutes of processing time per unit on the capacity constraint to arrive at the throughput dollars per minute of $8.11 that is shown in the second column of the exhibit. We then calculate the throughput per minute for the other three products and sort them in high-low order, based on which

Product Name	Throughput \$\$/minute of Constraint	Required Constraint Usage (minutes)	Units of Scheduled Production	Constraint Utilization (minutes)	Throughput per Product
1. 19" color television	\$8.11	4	500/500	2,000	\$16,220
2. 32" LCD television	7.50	6	350/350	2,100	15,750
3. 50" high-definition TV	6.21	10	150/150	1,500	9,315
4. 42" plasma television	5.00	12	180/400	2,160	10,800
		Total planned constraint time		**7,760**	—
		Maximum constraint time		**8,000**	—
			Throughput total		**\$52,085**
			Operating expense total		47,900
			Profit		\$4,185
			Profit percentage		8.0%
			Investment		\$320,000
			Return on investment*		15.7%

*Annualized

Exhibit 15.12 THROUGHPUT MODEL

ones contribute the most throughput per minute. This leaves the 19-inch color television at the top of the list. Next, we multiply the scheduled production for each item by the time required to move it through the constrained resource. We do this for all four products, and verify that the total planned time required for the constraint operation is equal to or less than the actual time available at the constraint, as shown in the "Total planned constraint time" row. In the exhibit, the maximum available constraint time is listed in bold as 8,000 minutes, which is the approximate usage level for an eight-hour day in a 21-day month of business days, assuming 80% efficiency. This number will vary dramatically, depending on the number of shifts used, scrap levels, and the efficiency of operation of the constrained resource.

A key concept is that the maximum number of units of the highest throughput-per-minute item (in this case, the 19-inch color television) are to be sold as well as the maximum volume for each product listed below it. Only the production volume of the product listed at the bottom of the table (in this case, the 42-inch plasma television) will be reduced in order to meet the limitations of the constrained resource. The amount of planned production as well as the amount of potential sales are shown in the "Units of Scheduled Production" column of the throughput model. For example, "500/500" is shown in this column for the 19-inch color television, which means that there are 500 units of potential sales for this product and the company plans to produce all 500 units. Only for the last product in the table, the 42-inch plasma television, do the units of production not match the potential sales (180 units are being produced instead of the 400 units of potential sales). By matching units of production with potential sales, a company can maximize throughput.

Then, by multiplying the throughput per minute by the number of minutes for each product, and then multiplying the result by the total number of units produced, we arrive at the total throughput for each product, as shown in the final column, as well as for the entire production process for the one-month period, which is $52,085. We must still subtract from the total throughput the sum of all operating expenses for the facility, which is $47,900 in the exhibit. After they are subtracted from the total throughput, we find that we have achieved a profit of 8.0% and a return on investment (annualized, since the results of the model are only for a one-month period) of 15.7%.

When reviewing a proposal with this model, one must review the impact of the decision on the incremental change in net profit caused by a change in throughput minus operating expenses, divided by the change in investment. If there is an incremental improvement in the model, the proposed decision should be accepted. The model makes it easy to determine the exact amount of system improvement (or degradation) occurring by incrementally changing one element of the production system.

How Do I Determine if More Volume at a Lower Price Creates More Profit?

What happens when a customer indicates that a very large order is about to be issued, but only if the company grants a significant price reduction? The typical analysis is for the controller to determine the fully burdened cost of the product in question, compare it to the low requested price, and reject the proposal out of hand because the company cannot cover its overhead costs at such a low price point. Conversely, the sales manager will ram through approval of the proposal, on the grounds that "We will make up the loss with higher volume." Which is right? Based on their logic, neither one, because they are not considering the net impact of this proposal on total system throughput. The next example will clarify the situation.

EXAMPLE

The sales manager of the electronics company in the previous example runs into the corporate headquarters, flush from a meeting with the company's largest account, Electro-Geek Stores (EGS). He has just agreed to a deal that drops the price of the 32-inch LCD television by 20% but that guarantees a doubling in the quantity of EGS orders for this product for the upcoming year. The sales manager points out that the company may have to hold off on a few of the smaller-volume production runs of other products, but no problem — the company is bound to earn more money on the extra volume. To test this assumption, the controller pulls up the throughput model on his computer, shifts the LCD TV to the top of the priority list, adjusts the throughput to reflect the lower price, and obtains the results shown in the next table.

Product Name	Throughput $$/minute of Constraint	Required Constraint Usage (minutes)	Units of Scheduled Production	Constraint Utilization (minutes)	Throughput per Product
1. 32" LCD television	$4.36	6	700/700	4,200	$18,312
2. 19" color television	8.11	4	500/500	2,000	16,220
3. 50" high-definition TV	6.21	10	150/150	1,500	9,315
4. 42" plasma television	5.00	12	25/400	300	1,500
			Total planned constraint time	**8,000**	—
			Maximum constraint time	**8,000**	—
			Throughput total		**$45,347**
			Operating expense total		47,900
			Profit		$(2,553)
			Profit percentage		(5.6%)
			Investment		$320,000
			Return on investment*		(9.6%)

*Annualized

(Continued)

(*Continued*)

In short, the sales manager just skewered the company. By dropping the price of the LCD television by 20%, much of the product's throughput was eliminated while so much of the capacity constraint was used up that there was little room for the production of any other products that might generate enough added throughput to save the company. Specifically, because of its low level of throughput dollars per minute, the planned production of the 42-inch plasma television had to be dropped from 180 units to just 25, nearly eliminating the throughput of this product.

This example clearly shows that one must carefully consider the impact on the capacity constraint when debating whether to accept a high-volume sales deal. This is a particularly dangerous area in which to ignore throughput analysis, for the acceptance of a really large-volume deal can demand all of the time of the capacity constraint, eliminating any chance for the company to manufacture other products and thereby eliminating any chance of offering a wide product mix to the general marketplace.

Should I Outsource Production?

The proper analysis of this question surrounds whether a company can earn more throughput on a combination of the outsourced production and the additional new production that will now be available through the constrained resource.

EXAMPLE

To continue with the information in the original throughput example, one of the company's key suppliers has offered to take over the entire production of the 50-inch high-definition television, package it in the company's boxes, and drop ship the completed goods directly to the company's customers. The catch is that the company's throughput per unit will decrease from its current $62.10 to $30.00. The cost accounting staff would likely reject this deal, on the grounds that profits would be reduced. To see if this is a good deal, we turn once again to the throughput model, which is reproduced in the next table. In this exhibit, we have

Product Name	Throughput $$/minute of Constraint	Required Constraint Usage (minutes)	Units of Scheduled Production	Constraint Utilization (minutes)	Throughput per Product
1. 19" color television	$8.11	4	500/500	2,000	$16,220
2. 32" LCD television	7.50	6	350/350	2,100	15,750
3. 50" high-definition TV	3.00	10	150/150	N/A	4,500
4. 42" plasma television	5.00	12	325/400	3,900	19,500
		Total planned constraint time		**8,000**	—
		Maximum constraint time		**8,000**	—
			Throughput total		**$55,970**
			Operating expense total		47,900
			Profit		$8,070
			Profit percentage		14.4%
			Investment		$320,000
			Return on investment*		30.3%

*Annualized

(*Continued*)

219

(*Continued*)
removed the number from the Units of Scheduled Production column for the high-definition television, since it can now be produced without the use of the capacity constraint. However, we are still able to put a cumulative throughput dollar figure into the final column for this product, since there is some margin to be made by outsourcing it through the supplier. By removing the high-definition television's usage of the capacity constraint, we are now able to produce more of the next product in line, which is the plasma television set. This additional production allows the company to increase the amount of throughput dollars, thereby creating $3,885 more profits than was the case before the outsourcing deal.

The traditional cost accounting approach would have stated that profits would be lowered by accepting an outsourcing deal that clearly cost more than the product's internal cost. However, by using this deal to release some capacity at the bottleneck, the company is able to earn more money on the production of other products.

Should I Add Staff to the Bottleneck Operation?

When a company starts using constraint management as its guiding principle in managing throughput, an early area of decision making will be how to increase the output of the constrained resource. An obvious first step is to add staff to it, with the intent of achieving faster equipment setup time, less equipment downtime, more operational efficiency per machine, and so on. As long as the incremental increase in throughput exceeds the cost of each staff person added to the constraint, this should be a logical step to take. However, traditional accounting analysis will likely find that the additional labor assigned to the constrained resource will not be needed at all times and that it would therefore have a low level of efficiency. Such an analysis would reject the proposal.

EXAMPLE

The same company from the previous examples realizes that it can vastly reduce job setup time by adding an employee to the constrained resource, thereby

Product Name	Throughput $$/minute of Constraint	Required Constraint Usage (minutes)	Units of Scheduled Production	Constraint Utilization (minutes)	Throughput per Product
1. 19" color television	$8.11	4	500/500	2,000	$16,220
2. 32" LCD television	7.50	6	350/350	2,100	15,750
3. 50" high-definition TV	6.21	10	150/150	1,500	9,315
4. 42" plasma television	5.00	12	266/400	3,192	15,960
		Total planned constraint time		8,792	—
		Maximum constraint time		8,800	—
			Throughput total		$57,245
			Operating expense total		52,100
			Profit		$5,145
			Profit percentage		9.0%
			Investment		$320,000
			Return on investment*		19.3%

*Annualized

(*Continued*)

221

(*Continued*)

increasing the maximum constraint time from 8,000 minutes per month to 8,800 minutes. Due to scheduling issues, the employee must be assigned to the constrained resource for an entire eight-hour day, even though she is needed only for a total of one hour per day. Her cost is $25 per hour, or $4,200 per month ($25/hour × 8 hours × 21 business days). The result of this change is shown in the next table.

The exhibit reveals that the company can use the extra capacity to build more units of the 42-inch plasma television, resulting in $5,160 of additional throughput that, even when offset against the $4,200 additional labor cost (which has been added to the operating expense line item), still results in an incremental profit improvement of $960 ($5,160 additional throughput − $4,200 additional labor cost). The main problem is that the employee will be working on the constrained resource for only one hour out of eight, which is a 12.5% utilization percentage that will certainly draw the attention of the cost accounting staff.

Consequently, low incremental labor efficiency on the constrained resource can make sense if the resulting incremental throughput exceeds the cost of the labor.

Should I Produce a New Product?

When adding a new product that requires use of the constrained resource, management may be startled to find that profits actually decline as a result of the introduction, because the new product eliminated an old product that yielded more throughput per minute. The traditional cost accounting system will not spot this problem, because it focuses on the profitability of a product rather than the amount of the constrained resource needed to produce it.

EXAMPLE

The company's engineers have designed a new, lower-cost 32-inch LCD television to replace the existing model. The two products are compared in the next table.

	32″ LCD Television (New)	32″ LCD Television (Old)
Price	$400	$400
Totally variable costs	$340	$355
Throughput	$60	$45
Overhead allocation	$35	$35
Profit	$25	$10
Required constraint usage	10 minutes	6 minutes
Throughput per minute of constraint	$6.00	$7.50

The traditional cost accountant would review this comparative exhibit and conclude that the new model is clearly better, since it costs less to build, resulting in a profit $15 greater than the old model. However, the new model achieves less throughput per minute, because its larger throughput is being spread over a substantial increase in the required amount of time on the constrained resource. By replacing the old model with the new model, we arrive at the results shown in the next table.

The model shows that profits have declined by $570, because the new model has used up so much constraint time that the company is no longer able to produce as many of the 42-inch plasma televisions. Furthermore, the throughput per minute on the new product has declined so much that it is now ranked as the third most profitable product, instead of occupying the new second position, as was the case for its predecessor product.

Let us now modify the analysis so that the company's product engineers have spent their time reducing the required amount of constraint time for the 32-inch LCD television rather than in reducing its cost. In fact, let us assume that they *increase* the product's cost by $5 while *reducing* the amount of required constraint time from six minutes to five minutes, which increases its throughput per minute to $8.00. The result is shown in the next table, where the company's total throughput has increased, because more time is now available at the constrained resource for additional production of the plasma television. However, this new product introduction would almost certainly have been canceled by the cost accountants, because the cost per unit would have increased.

(*Continued*)

(Continued)

NEW PRODUCT ADDITION DECISION (LOWER COST)

Product Name	Throughput $$/minute of Constraint	Required Constraint Usage (minutes)	Units of Scheduled Production	Constraint Utilization (minutes)	Throughput per Product
1. 19" color television	$8.11	4	500/500	2,000	$16,220
2. 50" high-definition TV	6.21	10	150/150	1,500	9,315
3. 32" LCD television (new)	6.00	10	350/350	3,500	21,000
4. 42" plasma television	5.00	12	83/400	996	4,980
		Total planned constraint time		**7,996**	—
		Maximum constraint time		**8,000**	—
		Throughput total			**$51,515**
		Operating expense total			47,900
		Profit			$3,615
		Profit percentage			8.0%
		Investment			$320,000
		Return on investment*			13.6%

*Annualized

224

New Product Addition Decision (Higher Throughput/Minute)

Product Name	Throughput $$/minute of Constraint	Required Constraint Usage (minutes)	Units of Scheduled Production	Constraint Utilization (minutes)	Throughput per Product
1. 19" color television	$8.11	4	500/500	2,000	$16,220
2. 32" LCD television (new)	8.00	5	350/350	1,750	14,000
3. 50" high-definition TV	6.21	10	150/150	1,500	9,315
4. 42" plasma television	5.00	12	229/400	2,748	13,740
		Total planned constraint time		**7,998**	—
		Maximum constraint time		**8,000**	—
			Throughput total		**$53,275**
			Operating expense total		47,900
			Profit		$5,375
			Profit percentage		10.1%
			Investment		$320,000
			Return on investment*		20.2%

* Annualized

225

CHAPTER 16

PRICING ANALYSIS

What Is the Lowest Price that I Should Accept?

A customer offers to buy product at a low price. Should a company accept the deal? The basic rule is that the lowest price is the one that at least covers all variable costs of production, plus a small profit. Anything lower would cost a company money to produce and therefore would make no economic sense. The main issue becomes the determination of what variable costs to include in the variable cost calculation. Variable costs *may* include:

○ Direct labor
○ Direct machine costs
○ Inventory carrying costs
○ Materials
○ Ordering costs
○ Quality costs (testing, inspection, and rework)
○ Receiving costs
○ Scrap costs

The costs in this list are those that may vary directly with production volume. Not every item will be considered a variable cost at some companies; for example, if the purchasing staff is unlikely to be laid off as a result of not taking the customer order, the purchasing cost is probably not a variable one; the same reasoning can be used to assume that the receiving costs and even the direct labor costs are not really variable. Also, the direct machine costs, such as for utilities and any volume-related maintenance or machine labor, still may be be incurred even if the order is not accepted, and so will not be called variable. Given all these exceptions, it is apparent that the product's list of variable costs may be quite small (possibly only the cost of materials), resulting in an equally small cost that must be covered by the customer's price.

There are two objections to the exclusion of overhead costs from the pricing formula.

1. It may result in extremely low price points that will not allow a company to cover all of its expenses, which results in a loss.

   Over the long term, this is an accurate assessment. However, in the short term, if a company has excess production capacity available and can use it to sell additional product that generates throughput (sale minus totally variable costs), it should do so in order to increase profits. If its production capacity is already maximized, proposed sales having lower throughput levels than items already being manufactured should be rejected.

2. Traditional accounting holds that a small proposed order that requires a lengthy machine setup should have the cost of that setup assigned to the product; if the additional cost results in a loss on the proposed transaction, the sale should be rejected.

   However, it is quite likely that a company's existing production capacity can absorb the cost of the incremental setup without incurring any additional cost. Under this logic, if there is excess production capacity, setups are free. This approach tends to result in a company offering a much richer mix of order sizes and products to its customers, which can yield a greater market share. However, this concept must be used with caution, for at some point the ability of the company to continually set up small production jobs will maximize its capacity, at which point there will be an incremental cost to adding more production jobs.

EXAMPLE

A customer of the Low-Ride Bicycle Company wants to buy 1,000 bicycles from it, which it will sell in another country where it has recently opened a sales branch. The customer wants Low-Ride to offer its best possible price for this deal. The manager of Low-Ride knows that the same offer is being made to the company's chief competitor, Easy-Glide Bicycles. The company's cost to create a bicycle in a lot size of 1,000 units is shown next.

	Cost per Unit
Direct labor	$13.50
Direct machine cost	20.17
Inventory carrying cost	None
Materials	72.15
Ordering costs	Fixed
Quality costs	3.02
Receiving costs	Fixed
Scrap costs	7.22
Total Cost	$116.06

The owner of Low-Ride has received the request for pricing at the slowest time of the production year, when he normally lays off several staff members. He sees this as a golden opportunity to retain employees, which is more important to him than earning a profit on this order. Consequently, he can charge a price of as little as $116.06 per bike, as derived in the preceding table, though this will leave him with no profit. He has recently hired the production manager away from Easy-Glide Bicycles and knows that Easy-Glide has a similar cost structure, except for 20% higher scrap costs. Accordingly, he knows that Easy-Glide's minimum variable cost will be higher by $1.44. This means that he can add $1.43 to his price and still be lower than the competing price. Therefore, he quotes $117.49 per unit to the customer.

How Do I Set Long-Range Prices?

The pricing decisions just outlined for short-range situations are ones that will bring a company to the brink of bankruptcy if it uses them at all times, for they do not allow for a sufficient profit margin to pay for a company's overhead, not to mention the profit it needs in order to provide some return to investors on their capital. Proper long-range pricing requires the consideration of several additional costs, which are listed next.

○ *Product-specific overhead costs.* This is the overhead associated with the production of a single unit of production. This tends to be a very small cost category, for if a cost can be accurately identified down to this level, it is considered to be a variable cost instead of a fixed one.

○ *Batch-specific overhead costs.* A number of overhead costs are accumulated at this level, such as the cost of labor required to set up or break down a machine for a batch of production, the utility cost required to run machines for the duration of the batch, the cost of materials handlers needed to move components to the production area as well as remove finished products from it, and an allocation of the depreciation on all machinery used in the process.

○ *Product line – specific overhead costs.* A product line may have associated with it the salary of a product manager, a design team, a production supervisor, quality control personnel, customer service, distribution, advertising costs, and an ongoing investment in inventory. All of these overhead costs can be allocated to the products that are the end result of the overhead costs incurred.

○ *Facility-specific overhead costs.* Production must take place somewhere, and the cost of that "somewhere" should be allocated to the production lines housed within it, usually based on the square footage taken up by the machines used in each production process. The costs of overhead in this category can include building depreciation, taxes, insurance, maintenance, and the cost of any maintenance staff.

The size of the markup added to the variable and fixed costs of a product should at least equal the target rate of return. This rate is founded on a firm's cost of capital, which is the blended cost of all debt and equity currently held. If the markup margin used is lower than this amount, a company will not be able to pay off debt or equity holders over the long term, thereby reducing the value of the company and driving it toward bankruptcy.

EXAMPLE

To continue with the preceding example, if the Low-Ride Bicycle Company wants to determine its long-range bicycle price, it should include the additional factors noted in the next table, which covers all possible fixed costs, plus a markup to cover its cost of capital.

	Cost per Unit
Total variable cost	$116.06
Product-specific overhead costs	0.00
Batch-specific overhead costs	41.32
Product-line specific overhead costs	5.32
Facility-specific overhead costs	1.48
Markup of 12%	19.70
Total long-range price	$183.88

How Should I Set Prices over the Life of a Product?

It may not be sufficient to think of long-range pricing as just the addition of all fixed costs to a product's variable costs. Such thinking does not factor in all changes in a product's costs and expected margins that can reasonably be expected over the course of its market life. For example, if one were to compile the full cost of a product at the point when it has just been developed, the cost per unit will be very high, for sales levels will be quite small; this means that production runs will also be short, so that overhead costs per unit will be very high. Also, it is common for a company with the first new product in a market to add a high margin onto this already high unit cost, resulting in a very high initial price. Later in the product's life, it will gain greater market share, so that more products are manufactured, resulting in lower overhead costs per unit. However, competing products will also appear on the market, which will force the company to reduce its margins in order to offer competitive pricing. Thus, the full cost of a product will vary, depending on the point at which it is currently residing in its life cycle.

The best way to deal with long-range pricing over the course of a product's entire life cycle is to use a company's previous history with variations in cost, margin, and sales volume for similar products to estimate likely cost changes in a new product during its life cycle. An example of this is shown in Exhibit 16.1.

The exhibit shows that a company will have a considerable amount of overhead costs to recoup during the start-up phase of a new product life cycle, which will require a high price per unit, given the low expected sales volume at this point. However, setting a very high initial price for a product leaves a great deal of pricing room for

	Start-up Phase	Growth Phase	Maturity Phase	Totals for All Phases
Unit volume	10,000	200,000	170,000	380,000
Variable cost/ea	$ 4.50	$ 4.25	$ 4.15	$ 4.21
Fixed cost pool	$300,000	$650,000	$575,000	$1,525,000
Fixed cost/ea	$ 30.00	$ 3.25	$ 3.38	$ 4.01
Total cost/ea	$ 34.50	$ 7.50	$ 7.53	$ 8.22
Expected margin	30%	20%	15%	19%
	$ 44.85	$ 9.00	$ 8.66	$ 9.79
Total revenue	$448,500	$1,800,000	$1,472,200	$3,720,700
Total variable cost	$ 45,000	$ 850,000	$ 705,500	$1,600,500
Total fixed cost	$300,000	$ 650,000	$ 575,000	$1,525,000
Total margin	$103,500	$ 300,000	$ 191,700	$ 595,200

Exhibit 16.1 LIFE CYCLE PRICING

competitors to enter the market; accordingly, many companies choose to initially lose money on new product introductions by setting their prices at the long-range price rather than the short-range price that is needed to recoup start-up costs. By doing so, they send a signal to potential market entrants that they are willing to compete at low initial price points that will leave little room for outsize profits by new market entrants.

 ## How Should I Set Prices against a Price Leader?

There may be a price leader in the marketplace that sets product prices. This tends to be a company with a dominant share of the market, and usually the lowest cost structure, and which therefore can control the price of a large share of all products sold in a particular market niche. If another company tries to sell its products at a higher price, it will find customers will not accept the increase, for they can still buy products from the price leader at a lower rate. If a company wants to sell its products for less than the prices set by the price leader, it can do so, but the leader's dominance will probably prevent the company from gaining much market share through this strategy. Consequently, companies in such industries tend to adopt whatever price points are set by the price leader.

How Do I Handle a Price War?

When there is too much production capacity in an industry and not enough available customer sales to use up that capacity, a common outcome is a price war, where one company lowers its prices in order to steal customers away from a competitor, which in turn matches or reduces these prices in order to retain its customers. During a price war, the only winner is the customer, who experiences greatly reduced prices; however, it is ruinous for companies that are slashing prices.

One way to avoid a price war is to analyze the perceived value of each feature of a company's products in relation to similar products produced by competitors. If a company can clearly identify selected product features that a competitor's offerings do not contain, these features can be heavily promoted in order to raise the perceived overall value of the products in the eyes of customers, which allows a company to avoid a price war. A discerning competitor will be able to see this differentiation and may realize that a price war will not work.

Another option is to conduct a competitive analysis of the company that is initiating a price war, to see if its cost structure will not allow it to cut prices to sustainable levels that are lower than what the company can support. If not, a rational pricing move is to briefly cut prices to levels below the variable cost of the competitor, thereby sending it a clear message that further price competition will put it out of business. This is a particularly effective approach if the competitor is outsourcing its production. If so, the *entire* cost of the outsourced product is variable, as opposed to a mix of fixed and variable costs when production is kept in house. This gives an in-house manufacturer an advantage over an outsourced manufacturer, because the in-house manufacturer has the option of not including fixed costs in its pricing calculations in the short run, whereas the outsourced manufacturer has no fixed costs to exclude.

EXAMPLE

Companies A and B produce exactly the same product. Company A manufactures it in house and incurs a $10 cost that is half fixed and half variable cost. Company B, however, outsources its production and must pay $10 to its supplier for each unit it buys. This manufacturing scenario gives Company A a clear advantage over

(Continued)

> (*Continued*)
> Company B in the event of a price war, for Company
> A can slash its price down to its variable cost of $5,
> whereas B can only drop prices to its variable cost of
> $10. Thus, the type of manufacturing system used has
> a direct bearing on the competitive positioning of
> companies that are locked in a price war.

Another strategy is to contact key customers and offer
them special long-term deals, which locks them into set
pricing levels for what will presumably be the duration of
the price war.

Another option is to create a new product or product
line, with new features and market positioning, while let-
ting the old product gradually be eliminated by a price
war. By doing so, a company allows competitors to reduce their margins to dangerous levels while it neatly
sidesteps the entire problem by concentrating on a slightly
different market. The approach can also be reversed by
leaving the price point of the old product alone and instead designing a new and much lower-cost product that
can compete more effectively in a price war. Yet another
variation is to design a new product that is sufficiently different that customers are faced with an apples-to-oranges
comparison of competing products; they cannot judge
which competing product is the better value, and so the
price war never gets started.

If all of these options fail, the only alternative left is to
participate in a price war. If this becomes necessary, the
best way to do so is to cut prices at the first hint of a price
war, to set deeply discounted prices, and to do so with
great fanfare. By taking this aggressive approach, competitors will know that a company is serious about its partici-
pation in a price war and that it intends to pursue the war
until all other competitors back off.

How Do I Handle Dumping by a Foreign Competitor?

A U.S. industry can experience a severe drop in sales if
a competitor located in a foreign country imports competing goods into the United States at extremely low
prices. This is known as *dumping*. When this occurs, an
injured U.S. company can sue the competitor directly or
can bring the issue to the attention of the Federal Trade
Commission, which is empowered under the Federal

Trade Commission Act to investigate and increase import duties to a sufficient level to erase the pricing advantage. A company can recover three times its proven damages if it wins such a lawsuit.

To prove a dumping allegation, the litigant must prove that the foreign competitor is selling at a lower price in the United States than it is selling in its other markets, after factoring in the cost of transporting the goods to the United States. The litigant must also prove that the pricing activity is intended to destroy or injure competition.

When Is Transfer Pricing Important?

Many organizations sell their own products internally — from one division to another. Each division sells its products to a downstream division that includes those products in its own production processes. When this happens, management must determine the prices at which components will be sold between divisions. This is known as *transfer pricing*. It is most common in vertically integrated companies, where each division in succession produces a component that is a necessary part of the product being created by the next division in line. Any incorrect transfer pricing can cause considerable dysfunctional purchasing behavior.

How Do Transfer Prices Alter Corporate Decision Making?

A company must set its transfer prices at levels that will result in the highest possible levels of profits, not for individual divisions but rather for the entire organization. For example, if a transfer price is set at a product's cost, the selling division would rather not sell the product at all, even though the buying division can sell it externally for a profit that more than makes up for the lack of profit experienced by the division that originally sold it the product. The typical division manager will select the product sales that result in the highest level of profit only for his or her division, since the manager has no insight (or interest) in the financial results of the rest of the organization. Only by finding some way for the selling division to also realize a profit will a company have an incentive to sell its products internally, thereby resulting in greater overall profits.

An example of such a solution is when a selling division creates a by-product that it cannot sell but that another division can use as an input for the products it manufactures.

The selling division scraps the by-product, because it has no incentive to do anything else with it. However, by assigning the selling division a small profit on sale of the by-product, it now has an incentive to ship it to the buying division. Such a pricing strategy assists a company in deriving the greatest possible profit from all of its activities.

Another factor is that the amount of profit allocated to a division through the transfer pricing method used will impact its reported level of profitability and therefore the performance review for that division and its management team. If the management team is compensated in large part through performance-based bonuses, its actions will be heavily influenced by the profit it can earn on intercompany transfers. For example, an excessively low transfer price will result in low production priority for that item, as long as the selling division has some other product available that it can sell for a greater profit.

Finally, altering the transfer price used can have a dramatic impact on the amount of income taxes a company pays, if it has divisions located in different countries that use different tax rates.

Companies that are frequent users of transfer pricing must create prices that are based on a proper balance of the goals of overall company profitability, divisional performance evaluation, and (in some cases) the reduction of income taxes. The attainment of all these goals by using a single transfer pricing method should not be expected. Instead, focus on the attainment of the most critical goals, while keeping the adverse affects of not meeting other goals at a minimum. This process may result in the use of several transfer pricing methods, depending on the circumstances surrounding each interdivisional transfer.

How Does the External Market Price Work as a Transfer Pricing Method?

The most commonly used transfer pricing technique is based on the existing *external market price*. Under this approach, the selling division matches its transfer price to the current market rate. By doing so, a company can achieve four goals:

1. *Maximize profits.* A company can achieve the highest possible corporate-wide profit. This happens because the selling division can earn just as much profit by selling all of its production outside of the company as

it can by doing so internally — there is no reason for using a transfer price that results in incorrect behavior of either selling externally at an excessively low price or selling internally when a better deal could have been obtained by selling externally.

2. *Profit center structure.* Using the market price allows a division to earn a profit on its sales, no matter whether it sells internally or externally. By avoiding all transfers at cost, the senior management group can structure its divisions as profit centers, thereby allowing it to determine the performance of each division manager.

3. *Simplified information sources.* The market price is simple to obtain — it can be taken from regulated price sheets, posted prices, or quoted prices, and applied directly to all sales. No complicated calculations are required, and arguments over the correct price to charge between divisions are kept to a minimum.

4. *Outside shopping.* A market-based transfer price allows both buying and selling divisions to shop anywhere they want to buy or sell their products. For example, a buying division will be indifferent as to where it obtains its supplies, for it can buy them at the same price, whether that source is a fellow company division or not. This leads to a minimum of incorrect buying and selling behavior that would otherwise be driven by transfer prices that do not reflect market conditions.

However, market prices are not always available. This happens when the products being transferred do not exactly match those sold on the market, or if they are intermediate-level products that have not yet been converted into final products, so there is no market price available for them. Another problem with market-based pricing is that there must truly be an alternative for a selling division to sell its entire production externally. This is a common problem for specialty products, where the number of potential buyers is small, and their annual buying needs are limited in size. A final issue is that market-based pricing can drive divisions to sell their production outside of the company.

How Does Adjusted Market Pricing Work as a Transfer Pricing Method?

Adjusted market pricing involves price setting in order to simplify transfer prices and adjust for the absence of sales-related costs. For example, if market prices vary considerably by the unit volume ordered, there may be a broad range of transfer prices in use, which can be very complicated to track. A single adjusted market price can be used instead, which is based on the average shipment or order size. If a buying division turns out to have purchased in significantly different quantities from the ones that were assumed at the time prices were set, a company can retroactively adjust transfer prices at the end of the year; or it can leave the pricing alone and let the divisions do a better job of planning their interdivisional transfer volumes in the next year. As another example, there should be no bad debts when selling between divisions, as opposed to the occasional losses incurred when dealing with outside firms; accordingly, this cost can be deducted from the transfer price. The same argument can be made for the sales staff, whose services are presumably not required for interdepartmental sales. However, these price adjustments are subject to negotiation, so more aggressive division managers are more likely to resist reductions from their market-based prices while those managing the buying divisions will push hard for excessively large price deductions. The result may be pricing anomalies that do not yield the optimum profit for the company as a whole.

How Do Negotiated Transfer Prices Work as a Transfer Pricing Method?

The managers of buying and selling divisions can negotiate a transfer price between themselves, using a product's variable cost as the lower boundary of an acceptable negotiated price and the market price (if one is available) as the upper boundary. The price that is agreed on, as long as it falls between these two boundaries, should give some profit to each division, with more profit going to the division with better negotiating skills. The method has the advantage of allowing division managers to operate their businesses in a more independent manner, not relying on preset pricing. It also results in better performance evaluations for those managers with greater negotiation skills. However, it also suffers from these flaws:

○ *Suboptimal behavior.* If the negotiated price excessively favors one division over another, the losing division will search outside the company for a better deal on the open market and will direct its sales and purchases in that direction; this may result in suboptimal company-wide profitability levels.

○ *Negotiation time.* The negotiation process can take up a substantial proportion of a manager's time, not leaving enough for other management activities. This is a particular problem if prices require constant renegotiation.

○ *Brokered deals.* Interdivisional conflicts over negotiated prices can become so severe that the problem is kicked up corporate headquarters, which must step in and set prices that the divisions are incapable of determining by themselves.

For all these reasons, the negotiated transfer price is a method that is generally relegated to special or low-volume pricing situations.

How Does the Contribution Margin Work as a Transfer Pricing Method?

What if there is no market price at all for a product? A company then has no basis for creating a transfer price from any external source of information, so it must use internal information instead. One approach is to create transfer prices based on a product's *contribution margin*. Under this pricing system, a company determines the total contribution margin earned after a product is sold externally and allocates this margin back to each division, based on their respective proportions of the total product cost. There are several good reasons for using this approach, which:

○ *Converts a cost center into a profit center.* By using this method to assign profits to internal product sales, divisional managers are forced to pay stricter attention to their profitability, which helps the overall profitability of the organization.

○ *Encourages divisions to work together.* When every supplying division shares in the margin when a product is sold, it stands to reason that it will be much more eager to work together to achieve profitable sales rather than bickering over the transfer prices to be charged internally. Also, any profit improvements that can be brought about only by changes that span several divisions are much more likely to receive general approval and cooperation under this pricing method, since the changes will increase profits for all divisions.

These arguments make the contribution margin approach popular as a secondary transfer pricing method, after the market price approach. Despite its useful attributes, there are a number of issues with it that a company must guard against in order to avoid behavior by divisions that will lead to less-than-optimal overall levels of profitability. The contribution margin approach:

○ *Can increase assigned profits by increasing costs.* When the contribution margin is assigned based on a division's relative proportion of total product costs, the divisions will realize that they will receive a greater share of the profits if they can increase their overall proportion of costs.

○ *Must share cost reductions.* If a division finds a way to reduce its costs, it will receive an increased share of the resulting profits that is in proportion to its share of the total contribution margin distributed. For example, if Division A's costs are 20% of a product's total costs and Division B's share is 80%, then 80% of a $1 cost reduction achieved by Division A will be allocated to Division B, even though it has done nothing to deserve the increase in margin.

○ *Requires the involvement of the corporate headquarters staff.* The contribution margin allocation must be calculated by somebody, and since the divisions all have a profit motive to skew the allocation in their favor, the only party left that can make the allocation is the headquarters staff. This may increase the cost of corporate overhead.

○ *Results in arguments.* When costs and profits can be skewed by the system, there will inevitably be arguments between the buying and selling divisions, which the corporate headquarters team may have to mediate. These issues detract from an organization's focus on profitability.

The contribution margin approach is not a perfect one, but it does give companies a reasonably understandable and workable method for determining transfer prices. It has more problems than market-based pricing but can be used as an alternative or as the primary approach if there is no way to obtain market pricing for transferred products.

How Does the Cost-Plus Method Work as a Transfer Pricing Method?

The *cost-plus* approach is an alternative when there is no market from which to determine a transfer price. This method is based on its name—just accumulate a product's

Type of Transfer Pricing Method	Profitability Enhancement	Performance Review	Ease of Use	Problems
Market Pricing	Creates highest level of profits for entire company.	Creates profits centers for all divisions.	Simple applicability.	Market prices not always available; may not be large enough external market; does not reflect slight reduced internal selling costs; selling divisions may deny sales to other divisions in favor of outside sales.
Adjusted Market Pricing	Creates highest level of profits for entire company.	Creates profits centers for all divisions.	Requires negotiation to determine reductions from, market price.	Possible arguments over size of reductions; may need headquarters' intervention.
Negotiated Prices	Less optimal than market-based pricing, especially if negotiated prices vary substantially from the market.	May reflect manager negotiating skills more than division performance.	Easy to understand but requires substantial preparation for negotiations.	May result in better deals for divisions if they buy or sell outside the company; negotiations are time consuming; may require headquarters' intervention.
Contribution Margins	Allocates final profits among cost centers; divisions tend to work together to achieve large profit.	Allows for some basis of measurement based on profits, where cost center performance is only other alternative.	Can be difficult to calculate if many divisions involved.	A division can increase its share of the profit margin by increasing its costs; a cost reduction by one division must be shared among all divisions; requires headquarters' involvement.
Cost Plus	May result in profit buildup problem, so that division selling externally has no incentive to do so.	Poor for performance evaluation, since will earn a profit no matter what cost is incurred.	Easy to calculate profit add-on.	Margins assigned do not equate to market-driven profit margins; no incentive to reduce costs.

Exhibit 16.2 COMPARISON OF TRANSFER PRICING METHODS

full cost and add a standard margin percentage to the cost; this is the transfer price. This approach has the singular advantage of being very easy to understand and calculate, and can convert a cost center into a profit center, which may be useful for evaluating the performance of a division manager.

This method's flaw is that the margin percentage added to a product's full cost may have no relationship to the margin that would actually be used if the product were to be sold externally. If a number of successive divisions were to add a standard margin to their products, the price paid by the final division in line—the one that must sell the completed product externally—may be so high that there is no room for its own margin, which gives it no incentive to sell the product. Because of this issue, the cost-plus method is not recommended in most situations.

 ## How Do the Transfer Pricing Methods Compare to Each Other?

A comparison of all the transfer pricing methods just discussed is noted in Exhibit 16.2, which notes each approach's problems, ease of use, and applicability to profitability enhancement and divisional performance reviews.

CHAPTER 17

COST REDUCTION ANALYSIS

What Reports Are Used for Cost Reduction Projects?

A cost reduction analysis project should start with a general overview of the target area that results in a graphical presentation of potential cost reductions. The format in Exhibit 17.1 shows the potential cost reduction impact of numerous projects across the bottom axis and implementation difficulty on the vertical axis. Cost reductions in the lower right corner are low-hanging fruit that generate significant returns in exchange for a modest effort. Conversely, items in the upper left corner require a great deal of effort and produce minimal returns. This format is a good guideline for deciding which projects to address first and which can safely be delayed.

In the exhibit, the commission restructuring in the upper left corner is projected to have such a low payback and high difficulty of implementation that it is not worth doing, whereas the procurement card program is highly worthwhile, since it has the reverse characteristics.

A variation on the cost reduction payoff matrix is one that itemizes a number of additional factors, such as the risk of project failure, implementation duration, and level of support. If any prospective project has a high risk score in any category, the project manager should either consider alternative projects or work on risk mitigation strategies. A sample risk matrix is shown in Exhibit 17.2. In the exhibit, the riskiest project appears to be the office merger, which contains three high-risk scores, while the single MRO (maintenance, repair, and operations) distributor option is the safest, with four low-risk scores.

Exhibits 17.1 and 17.2 provide only an overview of potential cost reduction projects. The next step in an organized cost reduction system is to generate greater detail regarding potential reductions. The format is shown in

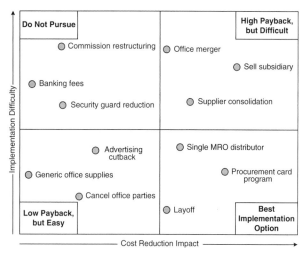

Exhibit 17.1   Cost Reduction Payoff Matrix

Exhibit 17.3, which begins with the general topics already shown in the cost reduction payoff matrix and then notes and quantifies specific opportunities. The matrix is split into two parts, with those projects estimated to have low levels of implementation difficulty listed at the top and those with more difficult implementation difficulty listed at the bottom.

What Is Spend Analysis?

Spend analysis is the process of organizing procurement information by suppliers and commodities and then using this information to achieve volume discounts and rebates with a reduced number of suppliers. A spend analysis system requires the creation and enhancement of a spend

	Cost Overrun	Customer Turnover	Extended Implementation	Management Support	Project Failure
Advertising cutback	1	4	3	2	1
Layoffs	2	1	2	4	1
Office merger	3	1	4	5	4
Single MRO distributor	1	1	4	1	2
Supplier consolidation	2	1	5	1	3
Scoring	1 = low risk	1 < 1 month	1 < 1 month	1 = high	1 = low risk
	5 = high risk	5 > 1 year	5 > 1 year	5 = low	5 = high risk

Exhibit 17.2   Cost Reduction Risk Matrix

Topic Area	Opportunity	Action	Implementation Difficulty	Cost Reduction (000s)
Advertising cutback	All of advertising is spent on NASCAR sponsorship	Drop sponsorship and switch to mix of Internet and magazine advertising	Low	$ 380
Cancel office parties	Currently have Christmas and summer parties for 14 offices	Eliminate all summer office parties	Low	170
Generic office supplies	Using brand names for 140+ types of office supplies	Standardize on generic office supplies	Low	30
Layoff	10% of production staff is currently idle	Conduct a layoff of 5% of the production staff, leaving the remainder on staff to maintain capacity	Low	490
Procurement card program	Purchase orders used for virtually all purchases	Implement a procurement card program, and mandate its usage for purchases under $500	Low	640
Single MRO distributor	Currently use 15 MRO distributors	Centralize orders and shift to standard generic supplies	Low	520
		Total Cost Reduction		**$2,230**

Exhibit 17.3 COST REDUCTION ITEMIZATION MATRIX

(Continued)

Topic Area	Opportunity	Action	Implementation Dificulty	Cost Reduction (000s)
Banking fees	Currently paying account fees for a separate bank account for each office and not aggregating cash for investing purposes	Switch all accounts to a single bank, and roll all cash, into an investment account, using zero-balance accounts	High	40
Commission restructuring	Junior-level base pay is 25% higher than comparable rates in the market	Drop base pay to market rate for all new hires	High	75
Office merger	The Denver and Boulder offices service approximately the same group of customers	Eliminate the Boulder office, sublease the space, and shift staff to the Denver office	High	390
Security guard reduction	Currently have evening on-site security guards for all 14 offices	Switch to a private contractor that patrols the area periodically	High	85
Sell subsidiary	The Wynona Brewery is the only brewery still owned by the company	Sell the subsidiary	High	790
Supplier consolidation	Have over 1,000 suppliers for 5,400 stock-keeping units	Consolidate the supply base to 300 suppliers and realize a 3% overall cost reduction	High	500
		Total Cost Reduction		**$1,880**

Exhibit 17.3 Cost Reduction Itemization Matrix (Continued)

database as the source of a spend analysis, followed by the gradual concentration of ordering volume with a select group of suppliers; this is followed by continual efforts to monitor the company's compliance with the new system. This lengthy process can result in major cost reductions.

How Is the Spend Database Constructed?

The *spend database* is a highly organized cluster of files containing key information about *what* a company buys, *how much* it spends, and *who* it buys from. The database needs input feeds from the procurement systems of every company subsidiary, which should be updated on at least a quarterly basis. By aggregating all of this purchasing information, a company can see cost-saving opportunities at the corporate level that would not have been present at the subsidiary level.

Next, the information must be cleansed and enriched. *Cleansing* is improving on and correcting the information already contained within a database, while *enrichment* is adding new information to the database. As an example of cleansing, the same supplier may be recorded under a slightly different name in the feeds coming from different subsidiaries, such as International Business Machines, IBM, and I.B.M. When this happens, it is difficult to determine the amount of a company's total spend with a specific supplier. To fix the problem, the spend database should link all of the name variations for a single supplier to a single parent-level supplier name. For example, IBM could be used as the parent supplier name, and I.B.M. and International Business Machines are linked to it.

A considerable amount of cleansing may be required for item descriptions. An identical item listed in the item master records of five subsidiaries can easily have five wildly different descriptions, and it can be very difficult to match them. One way to correct the situation is to load supplier part numbers and part descriptions into the spend database, so that a part number arriving through a feed from a subsidiary will automatically pull in the correct part description.

Part of the database enrichment process includes adding commodity codes to each purchase. A commodity code assigns a general spend category to a supplier. The company can then aggregate purchase dollars for each commodity code to see where it is spending the bulk of its money and use this information to negotiate volume purchase discounts with suppliers.

It may also be useful to enrich the spend database with a supplier credit rating. This information is periodically updated through an input feed from a third-party credit rating agency. The spend analysis system then issues reports containing just those suppliers whose credit ratings indicate that they are in financial difficulty, which the company uses to resource with different suppliers.

Another possible enrichment is to periodically update the spend database with the company's in-house supplier ratings. These ratings are useful for steering more work toward those suppliers that consistently have high ratings on such issues as quality and on-time performance.

A fully loaded spend database is not usable unless it has an excellent report writing package, since the ability to drill down through the data is of paramount importance to spend management. Consequently, the database should be equipped with a report writer that can report on information at multiple levels, including by subsidiary, commodity code, and geographic region.

How Does Supplier Consolidation Work?

The primary spend analysis strategy is to consolidate purchases in order to increase buying volume with a smaller number of preferred suppliers. These consolidation activities should be based on the number of available suppliers and the dollar volume of goods purchased. If there are few suppliers available, single sourcing in exchange for a cooperative approach to cost reduction may be the only cost reduction strategy. However, if there are many suppliers available and the dollar volume of purchased quantities is high, a company can engage in a global search for the lowest-cost provider or reverse auctions to bid down prices. If there are many suppliers but dollar volumes are low, global sourcing is probably not cost-effective, but sourcing through a single distributor may yield the lowest overall cost. These options are shown in Exhibit 17.4.

If a company elects to follow a global sourcing strategy, this will yield the greatest cost reductions if products have a very high labor content; international suppliers typically have access to labor rates far below those in the domestic market. Global sourcing does not work as well for raw materials, since international suppliers probably have no better access to low-cost raw materials than do

○ *Maverick spenders.* Some employees do not rout[ine]
purchase requests through the purchasing depar[t]
ment, and they do not purchase through the ap[-]
proved corporate online purchasing catalog. The[ir]
mind-set is either to buy their favorite brand or [to]
use their favorite supplier. By doing so, they redu[ce]
a company's purchase volumes with preferred su[p-]
pliers, which results in fewer rebates and discoun[ts.]
Some ways to deal with maverick spenders inclu[de]
bringing their activities to the attention of seni[or]
management, including maverick spending in th[eir]
annual performance reviews, and charging their [de-]
partments for lost savings.

Which Reports Should Be Used for Spend Analysis?

[T]here is no better spend analysis report than one t[hat]
[cl]early states exactly how much money a company [will]
[sa]ve if it complies with directing orders to the lowest-[cost]
[su]pplier. The table shown in Exhibit 17.5 for a single [part]
[nu]mber illustrates the concept. The exhibit shows the l[owest]
[cost] (and approved) price in the top row and then the v[ariou]
[s] prices being paid to other suppliers (and even [the]
[sa]me supplier by a different subsidiary—see the fo[llow]
[ro]w), along with the additional costs being incurre[d by]
[co]ntinuing to use the other suppliers. This is a pow[erful]
[ar]gument for showing exactly how to reduce expense[s by]
[ea]ch subsidiary, supplier, and component.

Commodity codes are multilevel, and reporting on[ly at]
[th]e topmost level may not provide a sufficient lev[el]

[Bud]get, Part #123

[Subs]idiary	Supplier	Approved?	Unit Price	12-Month Purchase Volume (Units)	Va[...] Ap[...] Ur[...]
[...]hridge	J.C. Hammonds	X	$1.00	25,000	
[...]oma	Dithers & Sons		1.05	15,000	
[...]ver	Arbuthnot Corp.		1.08	18,000	
[...]ta	J.C. Hammonds		1.10	42,000	
[...]ngham	Checkers Ltd.		1.15	15,000	
				Total profit impact	

[Exhi]bit 17.5 COMPLIANCE PROFIT IMPACT

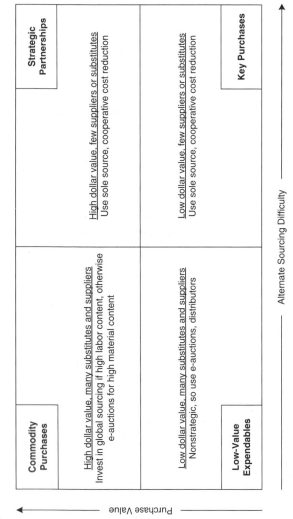

Exhibit 17.4 COST REDUCTION STRATEGY MATRIX

domestic suppliers (and must incur higher freight costs to deliver to the company).

As a company gradually shifts its business toward its preferred suppliers, its spend analysis will focus on the remaining nonpreferred suppliers. This will be a substantial list but one toward which an ever-shrinking proportion of the company's spend is directed. The most cost-effective approach is to continually review the highest-dollar commodities that have not yet been addressed, pick a preferred supplier within each one, and direct the bulk of the business in that commodity to that supplier.

How Does Parts Consolidation Work?

Spend analysis highlights problems with parts duplication. This issue arises when different subsidiaries use slightly different versions of the same parts. If the parts description fields in the spend database have been normalized so that descriptions are comparable, the spend analysis team can spot opportunities for standardizing on a smaller number of parts. If essentially the same part is coming from different suppliers, immediate consolidation of parts with a single supplier is possible. However, this analysis may also call for a longer-term solution, which is designing parts standardization into new versions of the company's products. In the latter case, cost savings may take years to realize.

Parts duplication analysis tends to be a distant second effort behind supplier consolidation, but it can provide significant savings. For example, if a smaller firm can standardize its parts, it can order the remaining parts in greater volumes; its cost per unit may therefore decline to the point where it can effectively compete on price against a much larger competitor that has not taken advantage of parts standardization. This effect comes from buying large quantities of a smaller number of items.

Can Spend Analysis Work for MRO Items?

Maintenance, repair, and operations (MRO) items are typically bought in great variety and very small quantities, which makes them difficult to consolidate for volume purchases. Instead, enroll the services of a distributor in examining the company's MRO purchases. The distributor can recommend replacing stock-keeping units with

less expensive ones, or which can be shipped a freight expense, or have lower support costs. The c tor deals with these MRO items every day in much volumes than the company does and so has knowledge of cost effectiveness. Distributors will this service if the company consolidates its M chases with them.

This is the single most important MRO cost r initiative, because a company can essentially shi part of its investigative labor to a third party.

What Is Spend Compliance?

The end result of spend analysis is a much great tration of a company's spend with a much sm ber of preferred suppliers. However, given the of locations from which a large corporation c purchases, and its ever-changing needs, it can b ficult to keep this small and select supplier bas idly expanding again, thereby diluting the e original spend analysis. There are a number improve compliance with a completed sper project, which are:

○ *Contracts database.* The foundation for sp ance is to construct a database contair tracts that the company has entered i approved suppliers. This database is us subsequent purchasing information a should have been purchased through th pliers and the terms at which items we from them. As an example of how database can be used, Contractor ABC issue Smith Company a 2% rebate onc chases 30,000 widgets from ABC. T matches its purchases against the contr and finds that Contractor ABC did Smith the rebate once the 30,000-unit t surpassed. Smith contacts ABC and ext the rebate but also interest income fc payment.

○ *Incumbent rebates and discounts.* The c base can be loaded immediately wit supplier contracts; by doing so, and l against the spend database, a compar an immediate benefit, which is that not have issued rebates and disco *existing* contracts and purchase volun

Level 1 Commodity	Level 2 Commodity	Level 3 Commodity	Total Suppliers	Total Spend (000s)
Metal manufacturing	Steel product	Iron and steel pipe	8	$13,540
		Rolled steel	4	4,710
		Steel wire	3	3,900
	Steel product total		15	$22,150
	Aluminum product	Aluminum sheets	2	2,370
		Extruded aluminum	9	970
		Other aluminum	11	320
	Aluminum product total		22	$3,660
	Nonferrous metal	Extruded copper	14	1,900
		Copper wire	2	1,110
		Other nonferrous	5	880
	Nonferrous metal total		21	$3,890
Supplies total			50	$29,700

Exhibit 17.6 MULTILEVEL COMMODITY SPEND REPORT

detail regarding the volume of spend or the number of suppliers. The report shown in Exhibit 17.6 drills down through multiple levels of commodity codes to provide this additional detail.

Another useful report is to show a quarterly trend of spend with the company's suppliers. Not only does it show the ongoing concentration of spend with top suppliers, but (of more importance) it can be used in ongoing negotiations to obtain further price reductions, discounts, and rebates as the company directs more business toward its top suppliers. The report also shows the remaining spend *not* with the top suppliers, which shows the company the extent of additional spend concentration that it can achieve. An example is shown in Exhibit 17.7.

It is also possible to aggregate information at a considerably higher level to see what proportion of total spend has been shifted to approved suppliers by commodity type. The purpose of this report is to measure progress toward gradually shifting spend into a small cluster of preferred suppliers. It does not measure cost savings, focusing instead on general levels of concentration. An example is shown in Exhibit 17.8.

An overall result of spend analysis is to reduce the number of suppliers. At a general level, it is useful to aggregate this information to see how much concentration is occurring. The intent is not to shift *all* spend into a small number of suppliers, since it is not cost effective to spend time eliminating the smallest tier of suppliers. Instead, the focus of the report is to highlight the *proportion* of spend

		Spend (000s)			
Ranking	Supplier Name	Quarter 1	Quarter 2	Quarter 3	Quarter 4
1	Columbus Framing	$17,980	$18,020	$18,400	$18,940
2	Masonic Metalcastings	9,730	10,030	10,170	10,500
3	Jacobean Fittings	7,090	7,260	7,605	7,865
4	Bricklin Supply	5,995	6,190	6,430	6,990
5	J.C. Hammonds Corp.	5,450	5,780	6,000	6,150
	Subtotals	$46,245	$47,280	$48,605	$50,445
Remaining suppliers		90,410	89,045	86,830	84,060
	Grand totals	$136,655	$136,325	$135,435	$134,505
Remaining suppliers percent of total		**66%**	**65%**	**64%**	**62%**

Exhibit 17.7   SUPPLIER SPEND TREND REPORT

	20 × 1		20 × 2		20 × 3	
Commodity	Preferred Supplier Spend (000s)	Percent of Total Spend	Preferred Supplier Spend (000s)	Percent of Total Spend	Preferred Supplier Spend (000s)	Percent of Total Spend
Facilities	$1,400	14%	$1,623	18%	$2,044	29%
Fittings	170	3%	350	8%	482	11%
Fixed assets	13,079	32%	16,080	39%	15,750	37%
Materials	2,450	10%	5,030	20%	5,850	24%
Supplies	—	0%	80	4%	130	10%

Exhibit 17.8   PREFERRED SUPPLIER CONCENTRATION BY COMMODITY

concentrated in the top tier of suppliers. An example is shown in Exhibit 17.9.

The example spend concentration report reveals that the company has a considerable amount of supplier consolidation work to do; the suppliers with 80% of total spend in each commodity category comprise roughly 20% of the total number of suppliers, which does not depart

For the Year Ended December 31, 20X3					
	Facilities	Fittings	Fixed Assets	Materials	Supplies
Total spend (000s)	$7,048	$4,382	$42,568	$24,375	$1,300
Total suppliers	108	240	42	289	98
Suppliers with 80% of spend	22	50	10	63	25
Suppliers with 90% of spend	51	82	18	90	31
Suppliers with 95% of spend	73	129	25	135	43

Exhibit 17.9   SPEND CONCENTRATION REPORT

appreciably from what a Pareto analysis would reveal. In other words, the supplier distribution does not depart significantly from what would be expected if the company had taken no action at all to concentrate its spend with preferred suppliers.

What Is the Analysis for a Workforce Reduction?

The first step in workforce cost reduction is to determine the cost directly attributable to each employee. Exhibit 17.10 shows a good format for this calculation. From left to right, it shows base-level annual compensation, followed by all related payroll taxes and net benefit costs. It continues with several additional expenses that can be traced directly to each employee. The social security tax is applicable only below a certain maximum wage level, which is noted in the lower left corner of the exhibit. The 401(k) pension withholding for each employee is not an expense but is included in order to show the company 401(k) match, which *is* an expense. The exhibit is sorted in alphabetical order by employee last name.

Overhead costs should be considered if a sufficient number of positions are eliminated to also trigger an immediate overhead reduction. Exhibit 17.11 uses the same format as Exhibit 17.10, but now the assumption is that by laying off entire *groups* of employees, a block of clearly identifiable overhead expenses can be eliminated. In the exhibit, employees are now sorted by store location, so that the elimination of an entire group of employees and their associated overhead costs can be clumped together. The cost reduction decision point is no longer the individual employee but rather an entire company location.

Thus far, the analysis has only addressed the cost of each employee or group of employees but does not incorporate any revenue that employees may directly generate, such as in a service environment. Without this information, a company may lay off its most expensive employee, without considering that the same person also generates a great deal of revenue for the company.

Exhibit 17.12 shows a breakdown of both revenue and cost for employees, so that profitability can now be ascertained on an individual level. The exhibit compresses the level of expense detail, thereby making room for revenue and profit information. The exhibit includes a column for a commission expense, which is subtracted from the revenues to arrive at a net revenue amount for each employee.

Employee Name	Annual Pay	Social Security	Medicare	401K Withhold	50% 401K Match	Medical	Medical Deducts	Annual Phone	Annual T&E	Total Cost
Andrews, Bill	$ 42,750	$ 2,651	$ 620	$ 4,000	$ 2,000	$ 14,185	$ (5,242)	$ 1,200	$ 5,000	$ 63,163
Brennan, Charles	$ 125,000	$ 6,622	$ 1,813	$ 16,500	$ 8,250	$ 17,265	$ (6,780)	$ —	$ —	$ 152,169
Cantor, David	$ 80,000	$ 4,960	$ 1,160	$ 7,250	$ 3,625	$ 6,175	$ (1,225)	$ 1,200	$ 8,500	$ 104,395
DiMaggio, Earnest	$ 77,500	$ 4,805	$ 1,124	$ 2,500	$ 1,250	$ 17,265	$ (6,780)	$ 1,450	$ 500	$ 97,114
Entenmann, Franklin	$ 142,500	$ 6,622	$ 2,066	$ 16,500	$ 8,250	$ 17,265	$ (6,780)	$ 1,200	$ 18,500	$ 189,623
Fairview, George	$ 37,500	$ 2,325	$ 544	$ 500	$ 250	$ —	$ —	$ 1,200	$ 1,250	$ 43,069
Gorman, Hercules	$ 225,000	$ 6,622	$ 3,263	$ 16,500	$ 8,250	$ —	$ —	$ 1,200	$ 32,750	$ 277,084
Henderson, Ian	$ 85,000	$ 5,270	$ 1,233	$ 4,000	$ 2,000	$ 17,265	$ (6,780)	$ 1,200	$ 1,750	$ 106,938
Innes, Julie	$ 73,000	$ 4,526	$ 1,059	$ —	$ —	$ —	$ —	$ —	$ —	$ 78,585
Jackson, Kari	$ 119,000	$ 6,622	$ 1,726	$ 14,250	$ 7,125	$ 6,175	$ (1,225)	$ —	$ —	$ 139,422
Klerk, Larry	$ 170,000	$ 6,622	$ 2,465	$ 16,500	$ 8,250	$ 14,185	$ (5,242)	$ 1,450	$ 800	$ 198,530
Lincoln, Mandy	$ 95,000	$ 5,890	$ 1,378	$ 9,000	$ 4,500	$ 6,175	$ (1,225)	$ 1,200	$ 4,250	$ 117,168
Masters, Nancy	$ 62,500	$ 3,875	$ 906	$ 1,000	$ 500	$ 14,185	$ (5,242)	$ 1,200	$ —	$ 77,924
	$ 1,334,750	$ 67,410	$ 19,354		$ 54,250	$ 130,140	$ (46,521)	$ 12,500	$ 73,300	$ 1,645,182
Percent of total	81%	4%	1%		3%	8%	-3%	1%	4%	100%

Tax percentage	6.20%	1.45%
Maximum cap	$ 106,800	None

Exhibit 17.10 Employee Cost Roll-up

Napa Store:	Annual Pay	Social Security	Medicare	401K Withhold	50% 401K Match	Medical	Medical Deducts	Annual Phone	Annual T&E	Total Cost
Andrews, Bill	$ 42,750	$2,651	$ 620	$ 4,000	$2,000	$14,185	$ (5,242)	$ 1,200	$ 5,000	$ 63,163
Entenmann, Franklin	$ 142,500	$6,622	$2,066	$16,500	$8,250	$17,265	$ (6,780)	$ 1,200	$ 18,500	$ 189,623
Jackson, Kari	$ 119,000	$6,622	$1,726	$14,250	$7,125	$ 6,175	$ (1,225)	$ —	$ —	$ 139,422
Klerk, Larry	$ 170,000	$6,622	$2,465	$16,500	$8,250	$14,185	$ (5,242)	$ 1,450	$ 800	$ 198,530
Lincoln, Mandy	$ 95,000	$5,890	$1,378	$ 9,000	$4,500	$ 6,175	$ (1,225)	$ 1,200	$ 4,250	$ 117,168
Masters, Nancy	$ 62,500	$3,875	$ 906	$ 1,000	$ 500	$14,185	$ (5,242)	$ 1,200	$ —	$ 77,924
										$ 785,830
									Annual Rent:	$ 156,000
									Annual utilities:	$ 28,000
										$ 969,830
Santa Rosa Store:										
Brennart, Charles	$ 125,000	$6,622	$1,813	$16,500	$8,250	$17,265	$ (6,780)	$ —	$ —	$ 152,169
Cantor, David	$ 80,000	$4,960	$1,160	$ 7,250	$3,625	$ 6,175	$ (1,225)	$ 1,200	$ 8,500	$ 104,395
DiMaggio, Earnest	$ 77,500	$4,805	$1,124	$ 2,500	$1,250	$17,265	$ (6,780)	$ 1,450	$ 500	$ 97,114

Exhibit 17.11 EMPLOYEE COST ROLL-UP WITH OVERHEAD

(Continued)

Napa Store:	Annual Pay	Social Security	Medicare	401K Withhold	50% 401K Match	Medical	Medical Deducts	Annual Phone	Annual T&E	Total Cost
Fairview, George	$ 37,500	$ 2,325	$ 544	$ 500	$ 250	$ —	$ —	$ 1,200	$ 1,250	$ 43,069
Gorman, Hercules	$ 225,000	$ 6,622	$ 3,263	$ 16,500	$ 8,250	$ —	$ —	$ 1,200	$ 32,750	$ 277,084
Henderson, Ian	$ 85,000	$ 5,270	$ 1,233	$ 4,000	$ 2,000	$ 17,265	$ (6,780)	$ 1,200	$ 1,750	$ 106,938
Innes, Julie	$ 73,000	$ 4,526	$ 1,059	$ —	$ —	$ —	$ —	$ —	$ —	$ 78,585
										$ 859,353
									Annual Rent:	$ 172,000
									Annual utilities:	$ 32,500
										$ 1,063,853

Exhibit 17.11 EMPLOYEE COST ROLL-UP WITH OVERHEAD (Continued)

Employee Name	Revenues			Expenses				Profit	Profit %
	Annual Revenues	Commission	Net Revenues	Annual Pay	Payroll Taxes	Benefits	Total Cost		
Andrews, Bill	$ 101,890	$ 4,076	$ 97,814	$ 42,750	$ 3,270	$ 17,143	$ 63,163	$ 34,651	35%
Brennan, Charles	$ 234,750	$ 9,390	$ 225,360	$ 125,000	$ 8,434	$ 18,735	$ 152,169	$ 73,191	32%
Cantor, David	$ 119,250	$ 4,770	$ 114,480	$ 80,000	$ 6,120	$ 18,275	$ 104,395	$ 10,085	9%
DiMaggio, Earnest	$ 142,120	$ 5,685	$ 136,435	$ 77,500	$ 5,929	$ 13,685	$ 97,114	$ 39,321	29%
Entenmann, Franklin	$ 267,040	$ 10,682	$ 256,358	$ 142,500	$ 8,688	$ 38,435	$ 189,623	$ 66,736	26%
Fairview, George	$ 71,020	$ 2,841	$ 68,179	$ 37,500	$ 2,869	$ 2,700	$ 43,069	$ 25,110	37%
Gorman, Hercules	$ 203,150	$ 8,126	$ 195,024	$ 225,000	$ 9,884	$ 42,200	$ 277,084	$ (82,060)	-42%
Henderson, Ian	$ 173,350	$ 6,934	$ 166,416	$ 85,000	$ 6,503	$ 15,435	$ 106,938	$ 59,479	36%
Innes, Julie	$ 123,950	$ 4,958	$ 118,992	$ 73,000	$ 5,585	$ —	$ 78,585	$ 40,408	34%
Jackson, Kari	$ 225,290	$ 9,012	$ 216,278	$ 119,000	$ 8,347	$ 12,075	$ 139,422	$ 76,856	36%
Klerk, Larry	$ 274,040	$ 10,962	$ 263,078	$ 170,000	$ 9,087	$ 19,443	$ 198,530	$ 64,549	25%
Lincoln, Mandy	$ 92,650	$ 3,706	$ 88,944	$ 95,000	$ 7,268	$ 14,900	$ 117,168	$ (28,224)	-32%
Masters, Nancy	$ 129,740	$ 5,190	$ 124,550	$ 62,500	$ 4,781	$ 10,643	$ 77,924	$ 46,626	37%
	$ 2,158,240	$ 86,330	$ 2,071,910	$ 1,334,750	$ 86,763	$ 223,669	$ 1,645,182	$ 426,728	21%

Exhibit 17.12 EMPLOYEE PROFITABILITY CALCULATION

What Is the Cost of a Workforce Reduction?

A workforce reduction is designed to save money, but it may do the reverse in the short term, since there are a number of expenses associated with it. Here are several expenses to consider, followed by several ways to mitigate them.

- ○ *Severance package.* The most minimal severance package is simply severance pay, but it can also include a number of other costs, such as benefits continuation, the use of a company phone or computer, and outplacement services. Severance pay is typically linked to the number of years of employee service, so the payout can be severe if the workforce reduction includes personnel with high seniority.
- ○ *Accrued vacation.* If an employee has not used any portion of earned vacation, the company must pay it to the employee at the time of the workforce reduction.
- ○ *Stock grant acceleration.* If an employee is part of a stock grant program, the program will likely have an award acceleration clause, where vesting in the shares is accelerated in the event of a change in control of the company. If the employee is being laid off because of the change in control, it is likely that he or she will receive the stock grant at termination. If so, the company must record a noncash expense at the time of vesting to reflect the recognition of all remaining expense associated with the stock grant.
- ○ *Unemployment insurance.* If a company continually lays off its employees, they in turn will draw down the state's unemployment fund, which the state government must replenish by increasing the company's unemployment contribution rate in the following year.
- ○ *Potential lawsuits.* There is always a risk that some employees will sue the company for wrongful termination. Even if there is no likelihood of a payout, the company must still pay legal fees to defend its position. To avoid this issue, make any severance payment conditional upon employee agreement not file a claim against the company.

The severance and vacation expenses just described can be mitigated to some extent by paying them out based on an average of an employee's pay for the past few years rather than on the final pay level (which is presumably higher). This pay calculation should be fully documented in the employee manual.

What Are the Alternatives to a Workforce Reduction?

Many companies try to avoid a workforce reduction. However, there are still prospects for reducing payroll costs. The next techniques are still available.

○ *Review overtime pay.* There should be a formal supervisory review of all overtime hours claimed, which can be triggered by an automated timekeeping system. Better yet, an analyst should review the reasons why the bulk of the overtime hours were incurred and see if there are any alternatives that can avoid the future incurrence of this cost.

○ *Use vacation time.* By encouraging its staff to take unused vacation time, a company still incurs a cash outflow to pay for the vacations, but this may also soak up a considerable amount of unused vacation time, so that employees will be more available later, when they may be needed for revenue-generating activities.

○ *Delay new hires.* If there is a reasonable expectation that business will improve shortly, hold off on making offers to new hire candidates. If offers have already been extended, consider delaying their start dates while paying them a stipend and moving expenses.

○ *Attrition.* The most noninvasive form of workforce reduction is simply to not replace employees when they retire or leave the company for other reasons. This is a long-term solution, since employee departures may occur over quite a few years before a company has reduced its headcount to its targeted level.

○ *Delay or reduce scheduled pay raises.* If a medium-term business downturn is expected, management can authorize a significant delay in scheduled pay raises or reduce the amount of raises that will be granted. This approach should be shared by all, to gain acceptance.

○ *Require unpaid days off.* There may be cases where occasional unpaid days off for the entire workforce will resolve financial difficulties. If so, reduce the sting for employees by allowing them to pick which days to take off. For example, the days off may coincide with school vacations or be adjacent to federal holidays.

○ *Shorten the workweek.* If there is not enough work for a large part of the company, the company can elect to shorten the workweek for some period of time, with reduced pay to match the shorter work period. This alternative works best for a single-day reduction from a five-day to a four-day work week, since the result is a 20% pay cut for everyone in the company.

○ *Shorten working hours.* In a retail environment, it may make sense to determine when the bulk of customers are shopping and contract store hours to match.

○ *Use unpaid leaves of absence.* An unpaid leave of absence only encourages employees to look for new jobs and so will likely result in a very high turnover level in the near term. However, if the company offers to continue paying benefits to employees during their leaves of absence, they may be more inclined to stay out of work longer and still return to the company at the end of their leaves.

○ *Offer paid sabbaticals.* If the business downturn is expected to be extensive, management can offer a sabbatical with a moderate rate of pay to those employees judged to have sufficient seniority. The amount paid can be viewed as a retainer for consulting services, which the company can exercise by occasionally calling in employees on sabbatical to assist during high-volume periods.

○ *Freeze pay.* The workforce may accept a complete pay freeze for a limited period of time, if employees understand that the situation is caused by economic conditions that put the company at risk. This approach works best if everyone is included in the pay freeze.

○ *Implement a pay cut.* A more drastic alternative is to mandate a pay cut. If implemented, this should be universal, so that no charges of favoritism can be levied. Further, the pay cut should be even greater for the management team, which creates a solid reason for the management group to work the company back into profitability.

If the company enacts either a shorter workweek or fewer working hours during the business day, this will also reduce the amount of vacation and sick hours accrued, so there is a cumulative cost reduction effect.

How Does 5S Analysis Reduce Costs?

The 5S system is about organizing the workplace in order to eliminate waste. From a cost reduction perspective, it promotes workplace efficiency. As the name of this tool implies, there are five steps, and their names all begin with the letter *s*. They are:

1. *Sort.* Review all of the items within a work area; retain those needed for daily operations, and dispose of all other items.
2. *Straighten.* Reposition furniture and equipment to best serve the process flow, and move all other items out of the way.
3. *Scrub.* Clean the area completely.
4. *Systematize.* Establish schedules for repetitively cleaning the area.
5. *Standardize.* Incorporate the 5S system into standard company operations, so that it is performed on an ongoing basis. This should include a formal system for monitoring the results of the program.

A company should not embark on a total 5S clean sweep of an entire company all at the same time, since that would create a great deal of disruption. Instead, this is a methodical process that is used to gradually address all locations, after which it starts over again in a continuous cycle.

How Are Check Sheets Used?

The *check sheet* is a structured form used for the collection and analysis of data. Its most common application is for the collection of data about the frequency or patterns of events. Data entry on the form is designed to be as simple as possible, with check marks or similar symbols. The check sheet is used most frequently in a production setting but can be easily applied anywhere in a company.

For example, what if the controller is trying to increase the efficiency of the cash application process? Her first step is to determine the frequency of various issues impacting the process, so that she can focus her efforts on efficiency improvement. She discusses the project with the cash application staff and uses their input to construct the check sheet shown in Exhibit 17.13. The cash application staff fills it in during a one-week period, resulting in the determination that unauthorized payment deductions are the most frequent problem encountered during cash application, followed by missing remittance detail information. This information can be used to prioritize efficiency improvement (and the resulting cost reduction) activities.

Reason	Day					
	Mon.	Tue.	Wed.	Thu.	Fri.	Total
Customer double pay		II		I		3
No remittance advice enclosed	I	~~IIII~~	II	I	IIII	13
Pays with multiple checks			I		I	2
Unauthorized deductions taken	~~IIII~~	~~IIII~~ II	IIII	~~IIII~~ II	II	25
Total	6	14	7	9	7	43

Exhibit 17.13 CASH APPLICATION CHECK SHEET

How Is Error Quantification Used?

Any error that results in a scrapped or reworked product or document causes costs to pile up. A company can create an information tracking system to aggregate error information, which is then summarized into a report such as the one shown in Exhibit 17.14. The report notes the number of incidences of an error event during the measurement period. It also notes the lost throughput of each item. If an item is scrapped, the associated throughput (revenue minus totally variable costs) is lost forever. If an item is reworked, the cost of the rework labor is offset against the lost throughput to yield a reduced level of throughput. Further, the report indicates the time and labor cost required for rework.

The error quantification report example reveals that the worst scrap issue to investigate is dented electronics, since the company loses the most throughput dollars from this problem. Among the rework issues, the cost of additional labor must be offset against the potential lost throughput to see if rework is worthwhile. The redrilling work is costing more than the throughput that would otherwise be lost, so these items can be scrapped instead. The other rework efforts all yield a higher throughput than would be the case if no rework were done.

How Is Fixed Cost Analysis Used?

A common decision point is whether to incur a large fixed cost (such as a high-capacity machine) in order to achieve higher margins through greater production efficiency. The answer, in many cases, is no. The reason is

Error Type	Number of Incidents	Lost Throughput per Incident	Total Lost Throughput	Total Rework Time	Total Rework Cost
Rework—Adjust paint gaps	14	$11.14	$155.96	3:30	$70.00
Rework—Cut off excess trim	29	8.23	238.67	5:00	100.00
Rework—Redrill unaligned hole	8	4.88	39.04	2:00	40.00
Rework—Smooth rough edges	11	7.35	80.85	1:00	20.00
Scrap—Broken base unit	10	19.20	192.00	—	—
Scrap—Crushed packaging	4	6.10	24.40	—	—
Scrap—Dented electronics	17	12.05	204.85	—	—

Exhibit 17.14 ERROR QUANTIFICATION REPORT

that a large fixed cost increases a company's breakeven point, so that it must make more sales before it can begin to earn a profit. This can be a risky scenario in a volatile market. The issue can even be reversed: Should existing fixed costs be eliminated in exchange for variable costs that result in somewhat lower margins? In many cases, yes. It is worthwhile to be somewhat less profitable in exchange for having a more flexible company that can earn a profit over a broader range of revenues and margins. This issue can extend to a variety of nonproduction issues, such as leasing office space rather than buying a building.

How Are Ishikawa Diagrams Used?

The *Ishikawa diagram* reveals the causes of a specified event. The diagram, as shown in Exhibit 17.15, has the general appearance of the bones of a fish. The problem to be solved lies at the head. Major bones represent groups of major causes, while minor bones represent subcauses. An Ishikawa diagram is an excellent starting point for a cost reduction analysis, since solving the issues listed along the various branches of the diagram will likely solve the initial problem, which may have been a source of considerable expense.

The exhibit shows the categories of issues causing late product deliveries to customers. The issues are clustered under general categories, such as Policy, Product, and Machine. For example, under the Machine category, incorrect machine setups are delaying the production of goods and inadequate preventive maintenance is increasing machine downtime. Each of the items on the diagram can be addressed in order to ultimately reduce the incidence of late product deliveries to customers.

There are a large number of major causes under which subcauses can be clustered. Possible headings include environment, equipment, inspection, manpower, materials, maintenance, management, policies, prices, procedures, processing, products, promotions, and suppliers.

How Is Value Stream Mapping Used?

Value stream mapping (VSM) focuses on the identification of waste across an entire process. A VSM chart identifies all of the actions required to complete a process while also identifying key information about each action item. Key information will vary by the process under review but can

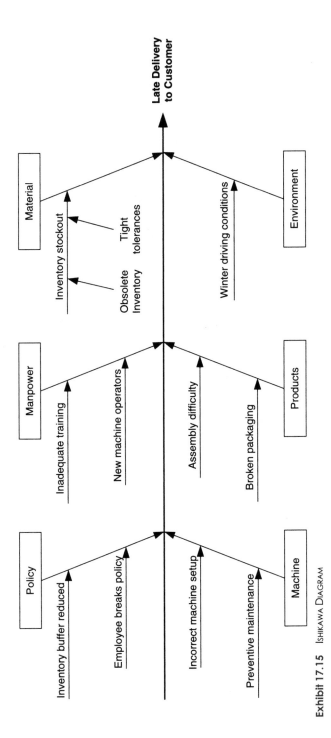

Exhibit 17.15 ISHIKAWA DIAGRAM

include total hours worked, overtime hours, cycle time to complete a transaction, error rates, and absenteeism.

The VSM chart shown in Exhibit 17.16 addresses the entire procurement cycle, from the initial placement of a requisition through processing of the resulting supplier invoice. Under each processing step, the VSM chart itemizes the amount of overtime, staffing, work shifts, process uptime, and transaction error rate. The chart then shows the total time required for each processing step as well as the time required between steps, and also identifies the types of time spent *between* steps (e.g., outbound batching, transit time, and inbound queue time).

The chart reveals that most of the procurement cycle time is used between processing steps, especially in the transit time of orders from suppliers to the company. If total cycle time is an issue, a reasonable conclusion would be either to source locally or to spend more for faster delivery services. However, if the emphasis is on speedier in-house processing, the chart shows that the purchase order processing stage is the most time consuming; it is also probably a bottleneck operation, given the amount of overtime incurred. Likely conclusions would be to reduce the error rate in the purchasing area by working on a reduction of errors in the upstream requisitioning area, offloading purchasing work with procurement cards, or bolstering capacity by adding purchasing staff.

Another option for shrinking the long cycle time is to have the receiving staff send receiving documents to the payables department more frequently than once every four hours; cutting the outbound batch time in half would eliminate two hours from the total cycle time.

VSM works best in highly focused, high-volume processes where it makes sense to spend time wringing a few seconds out of repetitive processes.

What Is Waste Analysis?

Cost reduction can be performed simply by identifying the various types of waste and working to reduce them. Here are seven types of waste to be aware of:

1. *Additional processing.* This is any production process that does not directly add value to a product, such as a quality control review.
2. *Defects.* Any processing that destroys or harms production that has already passed through the bottleneck operation is a form of waste, because it

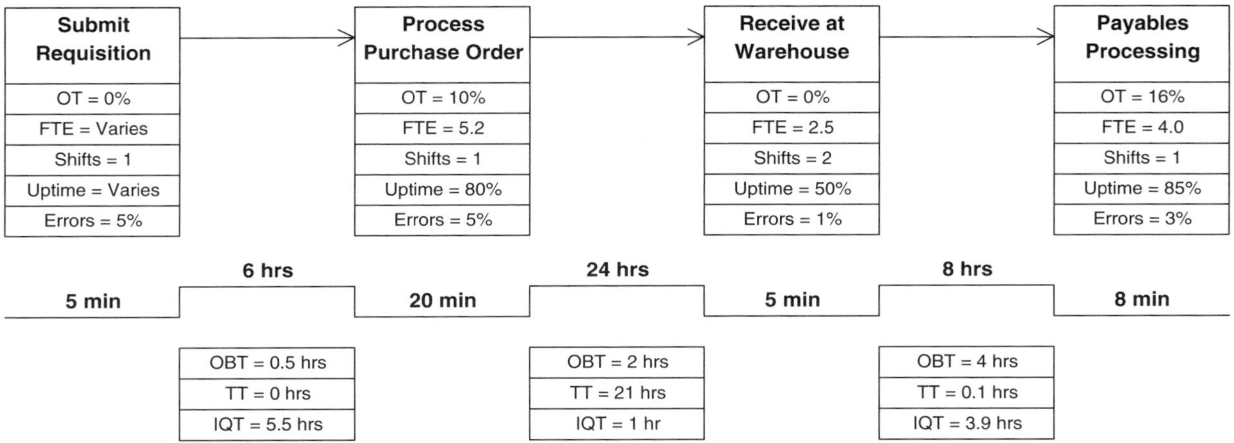

Submit Requisition		Process Purchase Order		Receive at Warehouse		Payables Processing
OT = 0%		OT = 10%		OT = 0%		OT = 16%
FTE = Varies		FTE = 5.2		FTE = 2.5		FTE = 4.0
Shifts = 1		Shifts = 1		Shifts = 2		Shifts = 1
Uptime = Varies		Uptime = 80%		Uptime = 50%		Uptime = 85%
Errors = 5%		Errors = 5%		Errors = 1%		Errors = 3%

5 min   6 hrs   20 min   24 hrs   5 min   8 hrs   8 min

OBT = 0.5 hrs	OBT = 2 hrs	OBT = 4 hrs
TT = 0 hrs	TT = 21 hrs	TT = 0.1 hrs
IQT = 5.5 hrs	IQT = 1 hr	IQT = 3.9 hrs

Key:

FTE = Full-Time Equivalent   **OT** = Overtime

IQT = Inbound Queue Time   **TT** = Transit Time

OBT = Outbound Batch Time

Exhibit 17.16   VALUE STREAM MAP

269

eliminates valuable throughput and may require additional expenditures for rework.

3. *Inventory.* Inventory of all types requires a working capital investment, incurs storage costs, and is at risk of obsolescence. It also hides other cost issues, such as production imbalances and poor work practices.

4. *Motion.* Any motion by employees that does not add value is a waste. This includes any equipment setup time.

5. *Overproduction.* Any production exceeding specific customer orders is a waste, because it uses materials and other resources, which then incur storage costs and are subject to obsolescence.

6. *Transportation.* This is the movement of materials between any operations that transform them, such as between workstations in a production process. The more materials move, the more opportunity there is to damage them. Spending on materials handling equipment or conveyor belts is also a form of waste.

7. *Waiting.* Any time when a machine or its operator is waiting is considered a waste of that resource. Waiting can be caused by unbalanced workloads, overstaffing, materials shortages, and so forth.

CHAPTER 18

METRICS

How Do I Calculate Accounts Payable Turnover?

A*ccounts payable turnover* yields the number of times per year that purchases are being paid off. For example, turnover of 12 times per year is the equivalent of 30 accounts payable days while turnover of 24 times per year is the equivalent of 15 accounts payable days. Accounts payable turnover is most understandable when tracked on a trend line; an increasing turnover trend indicates more rapid payment of accounts payable while a declining trend indicates the reverse.

To calculate accounts payable turnover, divide total annual purchases by the ending accounts payable balance. An alternative approach is to use the average accounts payable for the reporting period, since the ending figure may be disproportionately high or low. The amount of purchases should be derived from all nonpayroll expenses incurred during the year; payroll is not included, because it is not a part of the accounts payable listed in the numerator. Also, depreciation and amortization should be excluded from the purchases figure, since they do not involve cash payments. The formula is:

$$\frac{\text{Total purchases}}{\text{Ending accounts payable balance}}$$

EXAMPLE
The Drain-Away Toilet Company has ending accounts payable of \$157,000 and annualized purchases of \$1,750,000. To determine its accounts payable turnover, we plug this information into the formula: $$\frac{\text{Total purchases}}{\text{Ending accounts payable balance}} = \frac{\$1,750,000}{\$157,000}$$ $$= \underline{11.1} \text{ Accounts payable turnover}$$

The most difficult part of this formulation is determining the amount of annualized purchases. If a company has an irregular flow of business over the course of a year, estimating the amount of purchases can be quite difficult. In such cases, annualizing the amount of purchases for just the past month or two will yield the most accurate comparison to the current level of accounts payable, since these purchases are directly reflected within the accounts payable in the numerator.

How Do I Calculate Accounts Receivable Turnover?

The speed with which a company can obtain payment from customers for outstanding receivable balances is crucial for the reduction of cash requirements. A very high level of accounts receivable turnover indicates that a company's credit and collections function is very good at avoiding potentially delinquent customers as well as collecting overdue funds.

To calculate accounts receivable turnover, divide annualized credit sales by the combination of average accounts receivable and notes due from customers. The key issue in this calculation is the concept of annualized credit sales. If a company is estimating very high sales levels later in the year, this can result in an inordinately large figure in the numerator, against which current receivables are compared, which results in an inaccurately high level of turnover. A better approach is to multiply the current month's sales by 12 to derive the annualized credit sales figure. Another alternative is to annualize the last two months of sales, on the grounds that the receivables balance relates primarily to sales in those two months. The exact measurement method used can result in some variation in the reported level of turnover, so one should model the results using several different approaches in order to arrive at the one that most closely approximates reality. The basic formula is:

$$\frac{\text{Annualized credit sales}}{\text{Average accounts receivable} + \text{Notes payable by customers}}$$

EXAMPLE

The Samson Baggage Company, maker of indestructible luggage for adventure travelers, is growing at a very fast clip—so fast that it is running out of money.

The management team needs to conserve cash and decides to review accounts receivable to see if this might be a likely source. The controller accumulates the data in the next table.

	One Year Ago	Today
Annualized credit sales	$ 13,100,000	$28,500,000
Average accounts receivable	$ 1,637,500	$ 4,750,000
Accounts receivable turnover	8	6

The table indicates that accounts receivable turnover has worsened from 8 to 6 within the past year. If the turnover rate had remained the same as one year ago, the amount of accounts receivable outstanding would have been $3,562,500, which is derived by dividing annualized sales of $28,500,000 by turnover of 8. The difference between the $3,562,500 in receivables at 8 turns and the current $4,750,000 at 6 turns is $1,187,500 that could be converted into cash. Based on this information, the management team decides to tighten credit policies, purchase collection software, and add more collections staff.

Many accounting software packages derive the accounts receivable turnover figure for the user. However, these packages use a different calculation, which is to calculate the average number of days outstanding for each open invoice. This method works fine, but only if the calculation is a weighted average that is based on the amount of each receivable. Otherwise, a very small invoice that is many days overdue can skew the turnover figure considerably.

 ## How Do I Calculate the Average Receivable Collection Period?

The accounts receivable turnover figure may be easier to understand if it is expressed in terms of the average number of days that accounts receivable are outstanding. This format is particularly useful when it is compared to the standard number of days of credit granted to customers. For example, if the average collection period is 60 days and the standard days of credit is 30, customers are taking

much too long to pay their invoices. A sign of good performance is when the average receivable collection
period is only a few days longer than the standard days
of credit.

To calculate the average receivable collection period,
divide annual credit sales by 365 days, and divide the
result into average accounts receivable. The formula is:

$$\frac{\text{Average accounts receivable}}{\text{Annual sales}/365}$$

EXAMPLE

The new controller of the Flexo Paneling Company,
makers of modularized office equipment, wants to
determine the company's accounts receivable collection period. In the June accounting period, the beginning accounts receivable balance was $318,000 and
the ending balance was $383,000. Sales for May and
June totaled $625,000. Based on this information, the
controller calculates the average receivable collection
period as:

$$\frac{\text{Average accounts receivable}}{\text{Annual sales}/365}$$

$$= \frac{(\$318,000 \text{ Beginning receivables} + \$383,000 \text{ Ending receivables})/2}{(\$625,000 \times 6)/365}$$

$$= \frac{\$350,500 \text{ Average accounts receivable}}{\$10,273 \text{ Sales per day}}$$

$$= \underline{34.1} \text{ Days}$$

Note that the controller derived the annual sales
figure used in the denominator by multiplying the
two-month sales period in May and June by six.
Since the company has a stated due date of 30 days
after the billing date, the 34.1-day collection period
appears reasonable.

The main issue is what figure to use for annual sales.
If the total sales for the year are used, this may result in
a skewed measurement, since the sales associated with
the current outstanding accounts receivable may be significantly higher or lower than the average level of sales
represented by the annual sales figure. This problem is
especially common when sales are highly seasonal. A
better approach is to annualize the sales figure for the
period covered by the bulk of the existing accounts
receivable.

How Do I Calculate the Cash–to–Working-Capital Ratio?

The cash–to–working-capital ratio is useful for determining the proportion of working capital that is made up of either cash or investments that can be readily converted into cash. A low ratio can be an indication that a company may have trouble meeting its short-term commitments, due to a potential lack of cash. If this is the case, the next formula to calculate would be the number of expense coverage days in order to determine exactly how many days of operations can be covered by existing cash levels.

To calculate the cash–to–working-capital ratio, add together the current cash balance as well as any marketable securities that can be liquidated in the short term, and divide it by current assets less current liabilities. The key issue is which investments to include in the measurement; since this is intended to be a measure of short-term cash availability, any investments that cannot be liquidated in one month or less should be excluded from the calculation. The formula is:

$$\frac{\text{Cash} + \text{Short-term marketable securities}}{\text{Current assets} - \text{Current liabilities}}$$

EXAMPLE

The Arbor Valley Tree Company has a large inventory of potted plants and trees on hand, which comprises a large proportion of its inventory and is recorded as part of current assets. However, inventory turns over only three times per year, which does not make it very liquid for the purposes of generating short-term cash. The company's financial analyst wants to know what proportion of the current ratio is really comprised of cash or cash equivalents, since it appears that a large part of working capital is skewed in the direction of this slow-moving inventory. She has this information:

Fund Type	Amount	Liquidity
Cash	$55,000	Immediately available
Money market funds	180,000	Available in 1 day
Officer loan	200,000	Due in 90 days
Accounts receivable	450,000	Due in 45 days
Inventory	850,000	Turnover every 4 months
Current liabilities	450,000	Due in 30 days

(*Continued*)

(*Continued*)

Based on this information, she calculates the cash–to–working capital ratio as:

$$\frac{\text{Cash} + \text{Short-term marketable securities}}{\text{Current assets} - \text{Current liabilities}}$$

$$= \frac{\$55,000 + \$180,000}{(\$55,000 + \$180,000 + \$200,000 + \$450,000 + \$850,000) - (\$450,000)}$$

$$= \frac{\$235,000}{\$1,285,000}$$

$$= \underline{\underline{18\%}}$$

She did not include the note receivable from the company officer, since it would be available for 90 days. This nearly halved the amount of the ratio to 18%, which reveals that the company should be extremely careful in its use of cash until more of the accounts receivable or inventory balances can be liquidated.

This measurement can be considerably skewed by the timing of the measurement within the reporting period. For example, if a company has one large accounts payable check run scheduled each month, its cash reserves will look quite large just prior to the check run and much lower afterward; the same situation will apply to the expenditure for a payroll. In these situations, the measurement will drop precipitously right after the payment event, making the company cash situation look much worse that it really is.

How Do I Calculate the Core Growth Rate?

Companies regularly trumpet their ability to increase revenues year after year. But how much of that growth is due to acquisitions, accounting changes, or product price increases? By stripping out these forms of manufactured revenue, it is much easier to see if a company's core operations are actually growing, and by how much.

To calculate the core growth rate, subtract from the current annual revenue the annual revenue from five years ago as well as revenue from acquisitions at the point of acquisition and any revenue changes arising from altered revenue recognition policies. Divide the result by the annual revenue from five years ago, then divide this result by 5 to annualize it, and subtract the company's average annual price increase over the five-year measurement period. The formula is presented next.

$$\frac{((\text{Current annual revenue} - \text{Annual revenue 5 years ago} - \\ \text{Acquired revenue} - \text{Revenue recognition changes}))/ \\ (\text{Annual revenue 5 years ago})}{5 - \text{Average annual price increase}}$$

If information about the company's average annual price increase is not available, consider using the change in price of the underlying commodity or industry segment, as measured by either the Consumer Price Index or the Product Price Index.

EXAMPLE

The president of the Premier Concrete Group (PCG) has recently claimed that the company has experienced average annual compounded growth of 12%. An outside analyst wants to verify this claim by calculating PCG's core growth rate. PCG's current revenue is $88 million, and its revenue five years ago was $50 million. During that period, PCG acquired companies having a total of $27 million in revenues when they were acquired. Also, PCG benefited from altered revenue recognition policies that increased its revenue by $5 million. The analyst also learns that the concrete industry's average annual price increase during the measurement period was 2%. The analyst determines PCG's core growth rate with the next calculation:

$$\frac{(($88 \text{ million current revenue}) - \\ ($50 \text{ million revenue 5 years ago}) - $27 \text{ million} \\ \text{acquired revenue}) - ($5 \text{ million from revenue} \\ \text{recognition changes}))/($50 \text{ million revenue 5 years ago})}{5 \text{ Years} - 2\% \text{ average annual price increase}} = 0.4\%$$

The information used in this formula can be difficult to obtain and may involve the use of approximations, especially for the determination of changes caused by revenue recognition policies and the determination of an average annual price increase. Consequently, the results should be considered *approximations* of the actual core growth rate.

 ## How Do I Calculate the Cost of Capital?

The *cost of capital* is the blended cost of debt and equity that a company has acquired in order to fund its operations. It is important, because a company's investment decisions related to new operations should always result in a return that exceeds its cost of capital; if not, the company is not generating a return for its investors.

The cost of capital is comprised of the costs of debt, preferred stock, and common stock. The formula for the cost of capital is comprised of separate calculations for all three of these items, which must be combined to derive the total cost of capital on a weighted average basis. To derive the cost of debt, multiply the interest expense associated with the debt by the inverse of the tax rate percentage, and divide the result by the amount of debt outstanding. The amount of debt outstanding that is used in the denominator should include any transactional fees associated with the acquisition of the debt as well as any premiums or discounts on sale of the debt. These fees, premiums, or discounts should be gradually amortized over the life of the debt, so that the amount included in the denominator will decrease over time. The formula for the cost of debt is:

$$\frac{(\text{Interest expense} \times (1 - \text{Tax rate})}{\text{Amount of debt} - \text{Debt acquisition fees} + \text{Premium on debt} - \text{Discount on debt}}$$

The cost of preferred stock is a simpler calculation, since interest payments made on this form of funding are not tax deductible. The formula is:

$$\frac{\text{Interest expense}}{\text{Amount of preferred stock}}$$

The calculation of the cost of common stock requires a different type of calculation. It is composed of three types of return: a risk-free return, an average rate of return to be expected from a typical broad-based group of stocks, and a differential return that is based on the risk of the specific stock in comparison to the larger group of stocks. The risk-free rate of return is derived from the return on a U.S. government security. The average rate of return can be derived from any large cluster of stocks, such as the Standard & Poor's 500 or the Dow Jones Industrials. The return related to risk is called a stock's *beta*; it is regularly calculated and published by several investment services for publicly held companies. A beta value of less than 1 indicates a level of rate-of-return risk that is lower than average, while a beta greater than 1 would indicate an increasing degree of risk in the rate of return. Given these components, the formula for the cost of common stock is:

$$\text{Risk-free return} + (\text{Beta} \times (\text{Average stock return} - \text{Risk-free return}))$$

Once all of these calculations have been made, they must be combined on a weighted-average basis to derive the blended cost of capital for a company. We do this by multiplying the cost of each item by the amount of outstanding funding associated with it, as noted in the next table.

Total debt funding	× Percentage cost	= Dollar cost of debt
Total preferred stock funding	× Percentage cost	= Dollar cost of preferred stock
Total common funding	× Percentage cost	= Dollar cost of common stock
		= Total cost of capital

EXAMPLE

An investment analyst wants to determine the cost of capital of the Jolt Electric Company, to see if it is generating returns that exceed its cost of capital. The return it reported for its last fiscal year was 11.8%. The company's bonds are currently priced on the open market at a total price of $50,800,000, its preferred stock at $12,875,000, and its common stock at $72,375,000. Its incremental tax rate is 34%. It pays $4,625,000 in interest on its bonds, and there is an unamortized debt premium of $1,750,000 currently on the company's books. The preferred stock pays interest of $1,030,000. The risk-free rate of return is 5%, the return on the Dow Jones Industrials is 12%, and Jolt's beta is 1.5. To calculate Jolt's cost of capital, we first determine its cost of debt, which is:

$$\frac{(\$4,625,000\ \text{Interest expense}) \times (1 - .34\ \text{Tax rate})}{\$50,800,000\ \text{Debt} + \$1,750,000\ \text{Unamortized premium}}$$
$$= \underline{\underline{5.8\%}}$$

The investment analyst proceeds to the cost of preferred stock, which is calculated as:

$$\frac{\$1,030,000\ \text{Interest expense}}{\$12,875,000\ \text{Preferred stock}} = \underline{\underline{8.0\%}}$$

Finally, the analyst calculates the cost of common stock, which is:

(*Continued*)

(*Continued*)

5% Risk-free return + (1.5 Beta × (12% Average return − 5% Risk-free return) = 15.5%

The analyst then creates the next weighted-average table to determine the combined cost of capital for Jolt:

Type of Funding	Amount of Funding	Percentage Cost	Dollar Cost
Debt	$ 50,800,000	5.8%	$ 2,946,400
Preferred stock	$ 12,875,000	8.0%	$ 1,030,000
Common stock	$ 72,375,000	15.5%	$11,218,125
Totals	$136,050,000	11.2%	$15,194,525

Based on these calculations, Jolt's return of 11.8% is a marginal improvement over its cost of capital of 11.2%.

How Do I Calculate the Current Ratio?

The *current ratio* is heavily used by lenders to see if a company has a sufficient level of liquidity to pay its liabilities. A current ratio of 1:1 is considered to be the absolute minimum level of acceptable liquidity; a ratio closer to 2:1 is preferred.

To calculate the current ratio, divide all current assets by all current liabilities. The formula is:

$$\frac{\text{Current assets}}{\text{Current liabilities}}$$

EXAMPLE

A prospective purchaser is interested in the current financial health of the Ginseng Plus retail chain, which sells herbal remedies for common maladies. She obtains this information about the company for the past three years:

	2010	2011	2012
Current assets	$4,000,000	$8,200,000	$11,700,000
Current liabilities	$2,000,000	$4,825,000	$ 9,000,000
Current ratio	2:1	1.7:1	1.3:1

The rapid increase in current assets indicates that the retail chain probably has gone through a rapid expansion over the past few years. The sudden jump in current liabilities in the last year is particularly disturbing and indicates that the company suddenly is unable to pay its accounts payable, which have correspondingly ballooned. The investor elects to greatly reduce her offer for the company, in light of the likely prospect of an additional cash infusion in order to bring its operations onto an even keel.

This measurement can be misleading if a company's current assets are heavily weighted in favor of inventories, since this current asset can be difficult to liquidate in the short term. The presence of this problem can be revealed by using the inventory turnover ratio.

Another problem is that the current ratio will look abnormally low for those companies that are drawing down cash from a line of credit, since they will tend to keep cash balances at a minimum and replenish their cash only when it is absolutely required to pay for liabilities. In these cases, a current ratio of 1:1 or less is common, even though the presence of the line of credit makes it very unlikely that there will be a problem with the payment of liabilities.

How Do I Calculate Customer Turnover?

The *customer turnover measure* is extremely useful for determining the impact of customer service on a company's customers. A very low turnover rate is important in situations where the cost of acquiring new customers is quite high.

The calculation of customer turnover is subject to some interpretation; the key issue is how long to wait before a customer is assumed to have stopped buying from the company. In some cases, this may be anyone who has not placed an order within the past month and in other cases within the past year. The correct formulation will depend on the nature of the business. With this in mind, the formula is to subtract from the total customer list those that have been invoiced (or sold to on a cash basis) within the appropriate time period and divide the remainder by the total number of customers on the customer list.

$$\frac{\text{Total number of customers} - \text{Invoiced customers}}{\text{Total number of customers}}$$

EXAMPLE

The customer service department of the Indonesian Linens Company is being inundated with requests from the president to reduce the company's high rate of customer turnover, which is currently 30% per year. The department manager does not have enough staff available to contact all customers regularly. She asks the controller for assistance in finding out which customers are most important, so that she can focus her department's attention on them. Mr. Noteworthy, the controller, conducts an activity-based costing analysis of all customers and determines which 50 customers produce the largest amount of gross margin dollars for the company. The customer service manager gratefully shifts her department's focus to these key customers. A few months later, Mr. Noteworthy calculates customer turnover both in total and for this smaller group of key customers, using the next information.

	Total Customer Base	Key Customer Base
Total number of customers	450	50
Customers not placing order in the last three months	135	5
Customer turnover	30%	10%

The table shows that, although overall customer turnover has not changed, the increased focus on high-profit customers has resulted in greatly reduced turnover in this key area.

There may be a number of customers who purchase only small amounts each year; one may not want to include these customers in the turnover calculation, focusing instead on those that provide a significant level of sales volume. Another variation on the ratio is to determine the top customers who provide the company with the bulk of its profits, and measure the turnover rate only among that group. By subdividing customers in this manner, a company can focus its customer retention strategy on those who have the largest financial impact on the company.

How Do I Calculate the Debt Coverage Ratio?

A key solvency issue is the ability of a company to pay its debts. This can be measured with the *debt coverage ratio*, which compares reported earnings to the amount of scheduled after-tax interest and principal payments to see if there is enough income available to cover the payments. If the ratio is less than 1, this indicates that a company will probably be unable to make its debt payments. The measure is of particular interest to lenders, who are concerned about a company's ability to repay them for issued loans.

To calculate the debt coverage ratio, divide the scheduled amount of principal payments by the inverse of the corporate tax rate. This yields the amount of after-tax income required by a company to pay back the principal. Then add the interest expense to be paid, and divide the sum into the net amount of earnings before interest and taxes. An alternative treatment of the numerator is to use earnings before interest, taxes, depreciation, and amortization, since this yields a closer approximation of available cash flow. The formula is:

$$\frac{\text{Earnings before interest \& taxes}}{\text{Interest} + \dfrac{\text{Scheduled principal payments}}{(1 - \text{Tax rate})}}$$

EXAMPLE

The Egyptian Antiques Company's controller wants to be sure that earnings will be sufficient to pay upcoming debt requirements prior to implementing the owner's suggested round of Christmas bonuses. The expected operating income for the year, prior to bonuses, is $135,000. The interest expense is expected to be $18,500. The tax rate is 34%. Upcoming principal payments will be $59,000. The controller uses this debt coverage calculation to see if Christmas bonuses can still be paid:

$$\frac{\text{Earnings before interest \& taxes}}{\text{Interest} + \dfrac{\text{Scheduled principal payments}}{(1 - \text{Tax rate})}}$$

$$= \frac{\$135,000 \, \text{Operating income}}{\$18,500 \, \text{Invest} + \dfrac{\$59,000 \, \text{Principal payments}}{(1 - 34\% \, \text{Tax rate})}}$$

$$= \frac{\$135,000 \, \text{Operating income}}{\$107,894 \, \text{Debt payments}} = \underline{125\%} \, \text{Debt coverage ratio}$$

(Continued)

> (*Continued*)
> The ratio indicates that extra funds will be available for Christmas bonuses since operating income exceeds the amount of scheduled debt payments.

The primary difficulty with this measurement is that it is focused strictly in the near term — it is usually derived from information contained within the financial statements, which report earnings on a historical basis; this gives one no view of expected earnings levels, which may be considerably different. Consequently, it is best to accompany this measurement with another one that includes budgeted earnings levels for the next few earnings periods, which gives one better insight into a company's ability to pay its debts.

How Do I Calculate the Debt-to-Equity Ratio?

The *debt-to-equity ratio* is closely watched by lenders, since an excessively high ratio of debt to equity will put their loans at risk of not being repaid. Possible requirements by lenders to counteract this problem are the use of restrictive covenants that force excess cash flow into debt repayment, restrictions on alternative uses of cash, and a requirement for investors to put more equity into the company.

To calculate the debt-to-equity ratio, divide total debt by total equity. For a true picture of the amount of debt that a company has obtained, the debt figure should include all operating and capital lease payments. The formula is:

$$\frac{\text{Debt}}{\text{Equity}}$$

EXAMPLE

The Conemaugh Cell Phone Company has piled up a great deal of debt while purchasing new bandwidth from the federal government in the key St. Louis marketplace. Its existing debt covenants already stipulate that the company cannot exceed a debt-to-equity ratio of 1½ to 1. Its latest prospective purchase of a rival company, Grand Lake Wireless, will cost $55,000,000. Given its existing equity level of $182,000,000 and outstanding debt of $243,000,000, will it exceed the covenanted debt-to-equity ratio? To answer this question, we use this formula:

$$\frac{\text{Debt}}{\text{Equity}} = \frac{\$243,000,000 \text{ Outstanding debt} + \$55,000,000 \text{ Required debt}}{\$182,000,000 \text{ Existing equity}}$$

$$= \frac{\$298,000,000 \text{ Total debt}}{\$182,000,000 \text{ Total equity}}$$

$$= \underline{164\%} \text{ Debt-to-equity ratio}$$

The debt-to-equity ratio resulting from the proposed deal will exceed the covenant, so Conemaugh must either renegotiate the covenant or complete the acquisition with a mix of debt and equity that will not violate it.

One should consider calculating the debt-to-equity ratio for several years into the future, focusing on the relationship between interest and principal payments (rather than total debt) and equity for each year. The reason for doing so is that a large amount of total debt on the balance sheet may not reveal a true picture of a company's ability to pay it off if the debt is not due for payment until a required balloon payment at some point well into the future. A much smaller amount of debt on the balance sheet, however, may be completely unsupportable if the bulk of it is due for payment in the near term.

How Do I Calculate the Dividend Payout Ratio?

The *dividend payout ratio* is used by investors to see if a company is generating a sufficient level of cash flow to ensure a continued stream of dividends to them. A ratio of less than 1 indicates that existing dividends are at a level that cannot be sustained over the long term.

To calculate the dividend payout ratio, divide total annual dividend payments by annual cash flow. If there is a long-standing tradition by the board of directors of continually increasing the amount of the dividend, then annualize just the last (and presumably largest) dividend and use the resulting figure in the numerator of the calculation. The formula is:

$$\frac{\text{Total dividend payments}}{\text{Net income} + \text{Noncash expenses} - \text{Noncash sales}}$$

EXAMPLE

The Williams Funds are a major investor in the Continental Gas and Electric Company. The fund is controlled by the Williams family, whose primary concern is a long-term, predictable flow of cash from its various investments. The family is concerned that the impact of electricity deregulation on Continental Gas may be impacting its ability to pay dividends. It has collected this information about Continental for the past three years:

	2002	2003	2004
Total dividend	$ 43,000,000	$ 45,000,000	$ 48,000,000
Cash flow	$215,000,000	$180,000,000	$144,000,000
Dividend payout ratio	5:1	4:1	3:1

The table reveals that Continental's board of directors is continuing to grant increasing amounts of dividends, despite a steady drop in cash flow. At the current pace of cash flow decline, Continental will be unable to support its current dividend rate in no more than two years.

Cash flows can vary significantly by year, so calculating this ratio for just one year may not yield sufficient information about a company's ability to pay dividends over the long term. A better approach, as was used in the example, is to run a trend line on the ratio for several years to see if a general pattern of decline emerges.

How Do I Calculate Economic Value Added?

Economic value added shows the incremental rate of return in excess of a firm's total cost of capital. Stated differently, it is the surplus value created on an initial investment. It is *not* just the difference between a firm's percentage cost of capital and its actual rate of return percentage, since it is designed to yield a *dollar* surplus value. If the measurement is negative, a company is not generating a return in excess of its capital costs. It is extremely important to break down the drivers of the measurement in order to determine what parts of a company are keeping the measure from reaching its maximum potential.

To calculate economic value added, multiply the net investment by the difference between the actual rate of return on assets and the percentage cost of capital. The three elements of the calculation are:

1. *Net investment.* The net investment figure used in the formula is subject to a great deal of variation. In its most limited form, one can use the net valuation for all fixed assets. However, some assets may be subject to accelerated depreciation calculations, which greatly reduce the amount of investment used in the calculation; a better approach is to use the straight-line depreciation methodology for all assets, with only the depreciation period varying by type of asset. A variation on this approach is to also add research and development as well as training costs back into the net investment, on the grounds that these expenditures are made to enhance the company's value over the long term. Also, if assets are leased rather than owned, they should be itemized as assets at their fair market value and included in the net investment figure.

2. *Actual return on Investment.* When calculating the return on investment, research and development as well as training expenses should be shifted out of operating expenses and into net investment (as noted in point 1). In addition, any unusual adjustments to net income that do not involve ongoing operations should be eliminated. This results in an income figure that is related to just those costs that can be legitimately expensed within the current period.

3. *Cost of capital.* The formulation of the cost of capital was noted earlier in this chapter.

The economic value added formula is:

(Net investment) × (Actual return on investment
   − Percentage cost of capital)

EXAMPLE

The controller of the Miraflores Manufacturing Company wants to see if the company has a positive economic value added. Based on her calculation of

(Continued)

(*Continued*)
outstanding debt, preferred stock, and common stock, as noted in the next table, she estimates that the firm's cost of capital is 13.7%.

Type of Funding	Amount of Funding	Cost of Funding
Debt	$ 2,500,000	8.5%
Preferred stock	$ 4,250,000	12.5%
Common stock	$ 8,000,000	16.0%
Total	$14,750,000	13.7%

She then takes the balance sheet and income statement and redistributes some of the accounts in them, in accordance with the next table, so that some items that are usually expensed under generally accepted accounting principles are shifted into the investment category.

Account Description	Performance	Net Investment
Revenue	$8,250,000	
Cost of goods sold	5,950,000	
General & administrative	825,000	
Sales department	675,000	
Training department		$ 100,000
Research & development		585,000
Marketing department	380,000	
Net income	**$ 420,000**	
Fixed assets		2,080,000
Cost of patent protection		125,000
Cost of trademark protection		225,000
Total net investment		**$3,115,000**

The return on investment, as based on the net income and investment figures in the preceding table, is 13.5% (net income divided by the total net investment). Using this information, she derives the next calculation to determine the amount of economic value added:

(Net investment) × (Actual return on assets
  − Percentage cost of capital)

> $= (\$3,115,000 \text{ Net investment})$
> $\times (13.5\% \text{ Actual return} - 13.7\% \text{ Cost of capital})$
> $= \$3,115,000 \text{ Net investment} \times -.2\%$
> $= \underline{-\$6,230} \text{ Economic value added}$
>
> In short, the company is destroying its capital base by creating actual returns that are slightly less than its cost of capital.

The focus of this measure is to increase the return on capital employed. However, this measure may keep managers from investing in assets that have problematic returns but that may yield excellent returns if the company is willing to wait a few years to see if the market or the product matures.

 How Do I Calculate Expense Coverage Days?

The *expense coverage days calculation* yields the number of days that a company can cover its ongoing expenditures with existing liquid assets. This is a most useful calculation in situations where the further inflow of liquid assets may be cut off, so the management team needs to know how long the company will last without an extra cash infusion. The calculation is also useful for seeing if there is an excessive amount of liquid assets on hand, which could lead to a decision to pay down debt or buy back stock rather than keep the assets on hand.

To calculate expense coverage days, summarize all annual cash expenditures and divide by 360. Then divide the result into the summary of all assets that can be easily converted into cash. The largest problem with the formulation of this ratio is the amount of the annual cash expenditures, for there are always unusual expenses, such as fees associated with lawsuits, warranty claims, and severance payments that may not be likely to occur again. However, if all of these additional expenses were to be stripped out of the calculation, the ratio would always be incorrect, for there will inevitably be some unusual expenditures. To correct for this problem, a company with steady long-term expenditure levels could average its expenditures over multiple years. Companies experiencing rapid changes in expenditure levels will not have this option and so will have to make judgment calls regarding the most appropriate expenditures to include in the calculation. The formula is:

$$\frac{\text{Cash} + \text{Short-term marketable securities} + \text{Accounts receivable}}{\text{Annual cash expenditures}/360}$$

EXAMPLE

The Chemical Detection Consortium (CDC) obtains 100% of its business from the federal government, which pays it to conduct random chemical warfare tests of airports. The CDC president is concerned that the government has not yet approved the budget for the upcoming year and cannot release funds to CDC until the date of approval. Consequently, he asks the controller to calculate expense coverage days, in order to determine how long the company can last without the receipt of more federal funds. The controller finds that total expenditures in the preceding 12-month period were $7,450,000. These funds are currently on hand:

Fund Type	Amount
Cash	$ 48,500
Short-term marketable securities	425,000
Accounts receivable	620,000
Total	$1,093,500

The calculation of expense coverage days is:

$$\frac{\text{Cash} + \text{Short-term marketable securities} + \text{Accounts receivable}}{\text{Annual cash expenditures}/360}$$

$$= \frac{\$48,500 + \$425,000 + \$620,000}{\$7,450,000/360}$$

$$= \frac{\$1,093,500 \text{ Cash available}}{\$20,694 \text{ Expenses per day}}$$

$$= \underline{\underline{52.8}} \text{ Days of expense coverage}$$

How Do I Calculate Fixed Charge Coverage?

A company may have such a high level of fixed costs that it cannot survive a sudden downturn in sales. The *fixed charge coverage ratio* can be used to see if this is the case. It summarizes a company's fixed commitments, such as principal payments, long-term rent payments, and lease payments, and divides them by the total cash flow from operations. A ratio close to 1 reveals that a company must use nearly all of its cash flows to cover fixed costs and is a strong indicator of future problems if sales drop to any extent. A company in this position can also be expected to drop prices in order to retain business, since it cannot afford to lose any sales.

To calculate fixed charge coverage, summarize all fixed expenses, leases, and principal payments for the year and divide them by the cash flow from operations. It is generally not necessary to include dividend payments in this calculation, since this should not be considered fixed over the long term. The types of expenses and other payments that are fixed can be subject to some interpretation; for example, if a lease is close to expiring, there is no need to include it in the formula, since it is a forward-looking measure, and there will be no lease payments in the future. Also, if a company is expecting to reduce its principal payments by extending a loan over a longer time period, this may also be grounds for reducing the amount of fixed payment listed in the ratio. The formula is:

$$\frac{\text{Fixed expenses} + \text{Fixed payments}}{\text{Cash flow from operations}}$$

EXAMPLE

The owner of Dinky Dinosaur Toys is anticipating a slowdown in the sales of his high-end wooden toys in the upcoming year and wants to know what his company's exposure will be. He itemizes the company's annual fixed expenses and cash flow from operations, which are:

Cash flow from operations	$ 850,000
Interest on line of credit	80,000
Interest on long-term debt	150,000
Office equipment leases	45,000
Leases expiring within current year	10,000
Expected lease on company car	20,000
Principal payments on long-term debt	200,000
Balloon payment on long-term debt	150,000

If all of the fixed expenses and payments in this list were to be added together, they would total $655,000, which would represent a potentially dangerous fixed
(*Continued*)

(Continued)
charge coverage ratio of $655,000 to $850,000, or 77%. However, there are some line items on the list that are open to interpretation. First, the upcoming balloon payment is a one-time payment; it is up to the owner's judgment if this is to be included in the ratio, since it is meant to be a long-term ratio that is comprised of ongoing fixed expenses and payments. Second, the expected lease on the company car is not really a fixed cost, since it has not yet been incurred and can be stopped at the owner's option. Also, the leases expiring within the current year can be ignored, unless new leases on replacement equipment must be obtained. Another issue is the interest on the line of credit; most lines of credit require a complete payoff at least once a year, which means that this line can theoretically be zero. For the purposes of this calculation, the owner should estimate the average interest and principal payment on the line of credit and include it in the ratio. Consequently, there is considerable room for the judgmental inclusion or exclusion of items in this ratio that are highly dependent on the purposes to which the ratio is to be put and what constitutes a "fixed" charge.

How Do I Calculate Inventory Accuracy?

A company's inventory records should have a high level of accuracy, in order to complete production and fulfill orders in an organized manner. Record accuracy activities must ensure not only that the quantity and location of a raw material are correct, but also that units of measure and part numbers are accurate. If any of these four items are wrong, there is a strong chance that the production process will be negatively impacted.

To calculate inventory accuracy, divide the number of accurate test items sampled by the total number of items sampled. The definition of an *accurate test item* is one whose actual quantity, unit of measure, description, and location match those indicated in the warehouse records. If any one of these items is incorrect, the test item should be considered inaccurate. The formula is:

$$\frac{\text{Number of accurate test items}}{\text{Total number of items sampled}}$$

EXAMPLE

An internal auditor for the Meridian and Baseline Company, maker of surveying instruments, is conducting an inventory accuracy review in the company's warehouse. She records the next incorrect information for a sample count of eight items:

	Audited Description	Audited Location	Audited Quantity	Audited Unit of Measure
Aneroid barometer	No	No		
Battery pack	No			
Connection jack		No		
GPS casing	No	No		
GPS circuit board		No		
Heavy-duty tripod	No			No
Plumb line				No
Sextant frame				No

The warehouse manager has spent a great deal of time ensuring that the inventory record accuracy in his warehouse is perfect. He is astounded when the auditor's measurement reveals an accuracy level of zero, despite perfect quantity accuracy; he has completely ignored the record accuracy of part descriptions, locations, and units of measure and as a result has had multiple incorrect components of the measurement for some inventory items.

It is extremely important to conduct this measurement using all four of the criteria noted in the formula derivation. The quantity, unit of measure, description, and location must match the inventory record. If this is not the case, the reason for using it—to ensure that the correct amount of inventory is on hand for production needs—will be invalidated. For example, even if the inventory is available in the correct quantity, if its location code is wrong, no one can find it in order to use it in the production process. Similarly, the quantity recorded may exactly match the amount located in the warehouse, but this will still lead to an incorrect quantity if the unit of measure in the inventory record is something different, such as dozens instead of eaches.

How Do I Calculate Inventory Turnover?

Keeping close track of the rate of inventory turnover is a significant function of management. There are several variations on the inventory turnover measurement, which may be combined to yield the most complete turnover reporting for management to peruse. In all cases, these measurements should be tracked on a trend line in order to see if there are gradual reductions in the rate of turnover, which can indicate to management that corrective action is required in order to eliminate excess inventory stocks.

The most simple turnover calculation is to divide the period-end inventory into the annualized cost of sales. One can also use an *average* inventory figure in the denominator, which avoids sudden changes in the inventory level that are likely to occur on any specific period-end date. The formula is:

$$\frac{\text{Cost of goods sold}}{\text{Inventory}}$$

A variation on the preceding formula is to divide it into 365 days, which yields the number of days of inventory on hand. This may be more understandable to the layman; for example, 43 days of inventory is clearer than 8.5 inventory turns, even though they represent the same situation. The formula is:

$$365 / \frac{\text{Cost of goods sold}}{\text{Inventory}}$$

The preceding two formulas use the entire cost of goods sold in the numerator, which includes direct labor, direct materials, and overhead. However, only direct materials costs relate directly to the level of raw materials inventory. Consequently, a cleaner relationship is to compare the value of direct materials expense to raw materials inventory, yielding a raw materials turnover figure. This measurement can also be divided into 365 days in order to yield the number of days of raw materials on hand. The formula is:

$$\frac{\text{Direct materials expense}}{\text{Raw materials inventory}}$$

The preceding formula does not yield as clean a relationship between direct materials expense and work in process or finished goods, since these two categories of inventory also include cost allocations for direct labor and overhead. However, if these added costs can be stripped out of the work in process and finished goods valuations, there are reasonable grounds for comparing them to the direct materials expense as a valid ratio.

EXAMPLE

The Rotary Mower Company, maker of the only lawn mower driven by a Wankel rotary engine, is going through its annual management review of inventory. Its controller has this information:

Balance Sheet Line Item	Amount
Cost of goods sold	$4,075,000
Direct materials expense	$1,550,000
Raw materials inventory	$388,000
Total inventory	$815,000

To calculate total inventory turnover, the controller creates the next calculation:

$$\frac{\text{Cost of goods sold}}{\text{Inventory}} = \frac{\$4,075,000 \text{ Cost of goods sold}}{\$815,000 \text{ Inventory}}$$
$$= \underline{5} \text{ Turns per year}$$

To determine the number of days of inventory on hand, the controller divides the number of turns per year into 365 days:

$$365 \Big/ \frac{\text{Cost of goods sold}}{\text{Inventory}}$$
$$= 365 \Big/ \frac{\$4,075,000 \text{ Cost of goods sold}}{\$815,000 \text{ Inventory}}$$
$$= \underline{73} \text{ Days of inventory}$$

The controller is also interested in the turnover level of raw materials when compared just to direct materials expenses. He determines this amount with this calculation:

$$\frac{\text{Direct materials expense}}{\text{Raw materials inventory}}$$
$$= \frac{\$1,550,000 \text{ Direct materials expense}}{\$388 \text{ Raw materials inventory}}$$
$$= \underline{4} \text{ Turns per year}$$

The next logical step for the controller is to compare these results to those for previous years as well as to the results achieved by other companies in the industry. One result that is probably not good in any industry is the comparison of direct materials to raw materials inventory, which yielded only 4 turns per year. This means that the average component sits in the warehouse for 90 days prior to being used, which is far too long if any reliable materials planning system is used.

The turnover ratio can be skewed by changes in the underlying costing methods used to allocate direct labor and especially overhead cost pools to the inventory. For example, if additional categories of costs are added to the overhead cost pool, the allocation to inventory will increase, which will reduce the reported level of inventory turnover—even though the turnover level under the original calculation method has not changed at all. The problem can also arise if the method of allocating costs is changed; for example, it may be shifted from an allocation based on labor hours worked to one based on machine hours worked, which can alter the total amount of overhead costs assigned to inventory. The problem can also arise if the inventory valuation is based on standard costs and the underlying standards are altered. In all three cases, the amount of inventory on hand has not changed, but the costing systems used have altered the reported level of inventory costs, which impacts the reported level of turnover.

 ## How Do I Calculate the Margin of Safety?

The *margin of safety* is the amount by which sales can drop before a company's breakeven point is reached. It is particularly useful in situations where large portions of a company's sales are at risk, such as when they are tied up in a single customer contract that can be canceled. Knowing the margin of safety gives an analyst a good idea of the probability that a company may find itself in difficult financial circumstances caused by sales fluctuations.

To calculate the margin of safety, subtract the breakeven point from the current sales level and divide the result by the current sales level. To calculate the breakeven point, divide the gross margin percentage into total fixed costs. This formula can be broken down into individual product lines for a better view of risk levels within business units. The formula is:

$$\frac{\text{Current sales level} - \text{Breakeven point}}{\text{Current sales level}}$$

EXAMPLE
The Fat Tire Publishing House, Inc. is contemplating the purchase of several delivery trucks to assist in the delivery of its Fat Tire Weekly mountain biking magazine to a new sales region. The addition of these

trucks will add $200,000 to the operating costs of the company. Key information related to this decision is noted in the next table.

	Before Truck Purchase	After Truck Purchase
Sales	$2,300,000	$2,700,000
Gross margin percentage	55%	55%
Fixed expenses	$1,000,000	$1,200,000
Breakeven point	$1,818,000	$2,182,000
Profits	$ 265,000	$ 285,000
Margin of safety	21%	19%

The table shows that the margin of safety is reduced from 21% to 19% as a result of the truck acquisition. However, profits are expected to increase by $20,000, so the management team must weigh the risk of adding expenses to the benefit of increased profitability.

How Do I Calculate Net Worth?

A company's *net worth* is the amount of money that is left over after all liabilities have been deducted from its assets. This is theoretically the amount of funds that would be left over for distribution to investors if a company were to be liquidated. If the amount of net worth is negative, this is a reasonable indicator of serious fiscal problems. Net worth is sometimes used by lenders, which may require that a minimum net worth be maintained for a loan to be left outstanding.

The net worth calculation is total liabilities subtracted from total assets. The formula is:

$$\text{Total assets} - \text{Total liabilities}$$

A more detailed version of the measurement is to subtract any preferred stock dividends from total assets; dividends may only be listed alongside the balance sheet as a footnote and so would not otherwise be included in the calculation. In essence, every obligation of the company to make a payment, whether it is included on the balance sheet as a liability or not, should be subtracted from total assets in order to arrive at a company's net worth. The revised calculation is:

$$\text{Total assets} - \text{Total liabilities} - \text{Preferred stock dividends}$$

EXAMPLE

The Bottomless Bathtub Company, maker of fine porcelain tubs, has obtained a $2,000,000 loan from the First Federal Bank to cover the cost of a facility expansion. One condition of the loan is that the company's net worth at the end of each quarterly reporting period does not drop below $500,000. The controller is reviewing the balance sheet for February, which is one month prior to its quarterly report to the bank. The balance sheet is:

Cash and receivables	$ 475,000
Inventory	800,000
Fixed assets	4,305,000
Total assets	$5,580,000
Accounts payable	590,000
Loans outstanding	4,500,000
Total liabilities	$5,090,000
Stockholders' equity	490,000
Total liabilities and equity	$5,580,000

The company's net worth is currently $490,000, which is derived as:

$$\text{Total assets} - \text{Total liabilities}$$
$$= \$5,580,000 - \$5,090,000 = \underline{\$490,000}$$

The company needs to increase its net worth by $10,000 by the end of the following month, so that the quarterly report to the bank will meet the minimum net worth requirement. The controller knows that March is expected to be a breakeven month, so that liabilities will not be reduced. Accordingly, he recommends to the chief financial officer either an investment of $10,000 in equity that is used to reduce the loan balance or increase cash or an immediate layoff that will reduce liabilities in the short run.

The primary difficulty with the net worth measurement is that it is based on historical valuations that may have little basis in present market conditions. For example, if a company has a production line that is composed of several custom-built machines, there may be no resale market for the machines, rendering them valueless in the event of a corporate liquidation. Similarly, if a company holds title to a valuable patent, only the capitalized legal costs associated with the patent will appear as an asset, even though the value of the patent itself may be much higher. For these reasons, a detailed knowledge of a company's individual assets and liabilities is a better approach to determining net worth than the simple calculation presented here.

How Do I Calculate the Price/Earnings Ratio?

By comparing earnings to the current market price of the stock, one can obtain a general idea of the perception of investors of the quality of corporate earnings. For example, if this ratio is substantially lower than the average rate for the industry, it can indicate an expectation among investors that a company's future earnings are expected to trend lower. Alternatively, a high ratio could indicate the excitement of investors over a new patent that a company has just been granted or the expected favorable results of a lawsuit — the possible explanations are legion. The key point when using this ratio is that a result that varies from the industry average probably indicates a change in investor perceptions from the rest of the industry in regard to a company's ability to continue to generate income.

To calculate the *price/earnings ratio*, divide the average common stock price by the net income per share. The net income per share figure typically is used on a fully diluted basis, accounting for the impact of options, warrants, and conversions from debt that may increase the number of shares outstanding. The formula is:

$$\frac{\text{Average common stock price}}{\text{Net income per share}}$$

EXAMPLE

An investment analyst wants to determine the price/earnings ratio for the Mile-High Dirigible Company. The industry average price/earnings ratio for lighter-than-air transport manufacturers is 18:1. She accumulates this information:

(Continued)

(Continued)

Most recent stock price	$ 32.87
Number of shares outstanding	3,875,000
Net income	$8,500,000
Extraordinary income	$2,250,000

If she chooses to leave the extraordinary income in the total net income figure, she uses the next calculation to derive the price/earnings ratio:

$$\frac{\$32.87 \text{ Stock price}}{(\$8,500,000 \text{ Net income}/3,875,000 \text{ Shares outstanding})}$$

$$= 15:1 \text{ Price/earnings}$$

So far, the price/earnings ratio appears to compare favorably to the industry average. However, if she excludes the extraordinary gain from net income, the earnings per share figure drops to $1.61 per share. When incorporated into the price/earnings formula, this change increases the ratio to 20:1, which is higher than the industry average. Accordingly, she considers the stock to be overpriced relative to the industry and forbears from recommending it to her clients.

If a stock tends to fluctuate widely over the short term, it is difficult to arrive at an average common stock price that yields a valid price/earnings ratio. In such cases, it is better to calculate the price/earnings ratio with the most current common stock price as the numerator and view it on a trend line to monitor changes.

Another issue is that the stock price is based on a number of factors besides net income, such as an industry-wide drop in revenue prospects, legal action against the company, well-publicized warranty claims, the presence of valuable patents, and so on. These other factors may result in a stock price that is substantially different from what would otherwise be the case if net income were the only driving factor behind the stock price.

How Do I Calculate the Quick Ratio?

Because of the presence of inventory in the current ratio, one may be reluctant to use it as the best measure of a company's liquidity. One alternative is to use the *quick ratio*, which excludes inventory from the current assets portion of the current ratio. By doing so, one can gain a better understanding of a company's very short-term ability to generate cash from more liquid assets, such as accounts receivable and marketable securities.

To calculate the quick ratio, add together cash, marketable securities, and accounts receivable, and divide the result by current liabilities. Be sure to include only those marketable securities that can be liquidated in the short term and those receivables that are not significantly overdue. The formula is:

$$\frac{\text{Cash} + \text{Marketable securities} + \text{Accounts receivable}}{\text{Current liabilities}}$$

EXAMPLE

The Huff-Puff Shed Company, makers of sheds that are guaranteed not to blow down in any wind under 100 miles per hour, appears to have a comfortably high current ratio of 2.5:1. The components of that ratio are broken down as shown next.

Account	Amount
Cash	$ 120,000
Marketable securities	$ 53,000
Accounts receivable	$ 418,000
Inventory	$2,364,000
Current liabilities	$ 985,000
Current ratio	3:1
Quick ratio	0.6:1

This more detailed analysis reveals that the presence of an excessive amount of inventory is making the company's liquidity look too high with the current ratio. Only by switching to the quick ratio is this problem revealed.

How Do I Calculate Times Interest Earned?

An investor or lender should be interested in a company's ability to pay its debts. The *times interest earned ratio* reveals the amount of excess funding that a company still has available after it has paid off its interest expense. If this ratio is close to 1, the company runs a high risk of defaulting on its debt; any higher ratio shows that it is operating with a comfortable amount of extra cash flow that can cushion it if its business falters.

To calculate times interest earned, divide the average interest expense by the average cash flow. Cash flow is a company's net income, to which all noncash expenses (such as depreciation and amortization) have been added back. This ratio should be run on a monthly basis rather than annually, since short-term changes in the amount of debt carried or cash flow realized can have a sudden and dramatic impact on it. The formula is:

$$\frac{\text{Average cash flow}}{\text{Average interest expense}}$$

	January	February	March
Interest expense	$45,000	$43,000	$41,000
Net income	83,500	65,000	47,000
Depreciation	17,000	17,250	17,500
Amortization	2,500	2,500	2,500
Net cash flow	103,000	84,750	67,000
Times interest earned	2.3	2.0	1.6

EXAMPLE

The Cautious Bankers Corporation (CBC) is investigating the possibility of lending money to the Grasp & Sons Door Handle Corporation (GSR). It collects the next information for the last few months of GSR's operations:

The table reveals that, though GSR's interest expense is dropping, its cash flow is dropping so much faster that the company will soon have difficulty meeting its interest payment obligations. The CBC examiner elects to pass on providing the company with any additional debt.

This ratio assumes that there is no ongoing or balloon principal payment on debt; any such principal payments can greatly exceed the amount of cash outflow required by interest payments and so must also be factored into the determination of a company's ability to pay its debt. Though many companies simply roll over expiring debt into new debt instruments, this is not always possible for those in difficult financial situations.

How Do I Calculate Working Capital Productivity?

The *working capital productivity* measure is quite useful for determining the presence of a possible liquidity problem. If a company is forced to use such financing techniques as accounts receivable factoring to pay for its ongoing operations, the amount of its current assets will be very low. Consequently, if the ratio is extremely high, indicating the presence of few assets to support sales, a company is likely not only to have trouble filling orders (since it has an inadequate inventory) but also may go out of business suddenly if it cannot cover its short-term accounts payable. The size of the ratio will vary considerably by industry, so a better sign of problems is a steady increase in the ratio over time, no matter what the exact ratio measurement may be.

To calculate working capital productivity, divide annual sales by total working capital. It may be useful to also calculate average working capital, in case the ending working capital for the reporting period is unusually high or low. The formula is:

$$\frac{\text{Annual sales}}{\text{Working capital}}$$

EXAMPLE

The Twosome Toboggan Company, makers of extra-large toboggans for wide loads, has reported a reasonable sales to current assets ratio of 4:1, which is comparable to the rest of the industry. However, one lender has heard rumors that the company is very slow in paying its bills, which indicates that its liquidity is not as good as indicated by the sales–to–current assets ratio. Accordingly, the lender obtains the company's most recent balance sheet, which contains this information:

Annual sales	$6,500,000
Cash	$ 150,000
Accounts receivable	$ 400,000
Inventory	$1,075,000
Accounts payable	$ 695,000

(Continued)

(*Continued*)

With this information, the lender derives this working capital productivity measurement:

$$\frac{\text{Annual sales}}{\text{Working capital}}$$

$$= \frac{\$6,500,000 \text{ Annual sales}}{\$150,000 \text{ Cash} + \$400,000 \text{ Receivables} + \$1,075,000 \text{ Inventory} - \$695,000 \text{ Payables}}$$

$$= \frac{\$6,500,000 \text{ Annual sales}}{\$930,000 \text{ Working capital}}$$

$$= \underline{7:1} \text{ Working capital productivity}$$

The presence of an inordinate amount of accounts payable greatly reduces the amount of working capital available to support sales, resulting in far fewer net assets than was initially indicated by the sales–to–current assets ratio. The lender should be extremely concerned about the ability of the company to continue as a going concern.

This is generally a reliable measure. Its main failing is in the derivation of the annual sales figure in the numerator. If the sales figure used here departs considerably from the annualized amount of sales within the recent past, it does not result in a good comparison of sales level to working capital requirements. This can also be a problem if the measurement is made at the end of a high seasonal sales peak, since annualized sales will appear to be quite high while the inventory component associated with working capital will have been greatly reduced, resulting in a ratio that appears to be too high.

PART IV

CONTROL SYSTEMS

CHAPTER 19

BUDGETING

Why Is Budgeting Important?

Budgeting provides the basis for the orderly management of activities within a company. A properly created budget will funnel funding into those activities that a company has determined to be most essential, as defined in its strategic plan. Furthermore, it provides a bridge between strategy and tactics by itemizing the precise tactical events that will be funded, such as the hiring of personnel or acquisition of equipment in a key department. Once the budget has been approved, it also acts as the primary control point over expenditures, since it should be compared to purchase requisitions prior to purchases being made, so that the level of allowed funding can be ascertained. In addition, the results of specific departments can be compared to their budgets, providing an excellent tool for determining the performance of department managers.

How Do the Various Budgets Fit Together?

A properly designed budget is a web of subsidiary-level budgets that account for the activities of virtually all areas within a company. As noted in Exhibit 19.1, the budget begins in two places, with both the revenue budget and research and development budget. The revenue budget contains the revenue figures that the company believes it can achieve for each upcoming reporting period.

Another budget that initiates other activities within the system of budgets is the research and development budget. This is not related to the sales level at all but instead is a discretionary budget that is based on the company's strategy to derive new or improved products. The decision to fund a certain amount of project-related activity in

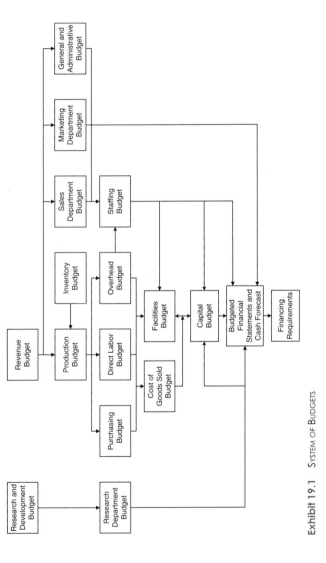

Exhibit 19.1 System of Budgets

this area will drive a departmental staffing and capital budget that is, for the most part, completely unrelated to the activity conducted by the rest of the company.

These additional budgets are positioned beneath the revenue budget and the research and development budget:

- *Production budget.* This budget is largely driven by the sales estimates contained within the revenue budget. However, it is also driven by the inventory-level assumptions in the inventory budget. The production budget is used to derive the unit quantity of required products that must be manufactured in order to meet revenue targets for each budget period.
- *Inventory budget.* This budget contains estimates by the materials management supervisor regarding the inventory levels that will be required for the upcoming budget period.
- *Purchasing budget.* This budget is driven by several factors, such as cost reduction initiatives, planned supplier consolidation, planned scrap levels, and long-term contracts.
- *Direct labor budget.* This budget is based on such factors as crewing rates by machine center, planned efficiency levels, contracted union rates, and labor rates by seniority or experience level.
- *Overhead budget.* This budget includes such items as machine maintenance, utilities, supervisory salaries, wages for the materials management, production scheduling, and quality assurance personnel, facilities maintenance, and depreciation expenses.
- *Cost of goods sold.* The purchasing, direct labor, and overhead budgets are summarized into a cost of goods sold budget. Since it is a summary-level budget for the production side of the budgeting process, this is a good place to itemize any production-related metrics.
- *Sales department budget.* This budget includes the expenses that the sales staff must incur in order to achieve the revenue budget, such as travel and entertainment, as well as sales training.
- *Marketing budget.* This budget is closely tied to the revenue budget, for it contains all of the funding required to roll out new products, merchandise them properly, advertise for them, test new products, and so on.
- *General and administrative budget.* This budget contains the cost of the corporate management staff

plus all accounting, finance, and human resources personnel.

○ *Staffing budget.* This budget involves a feedback loop with the direct labor budget, the general and administrative budget, and the revenue budget.

○ *Facilities budget.* This budget is based on the level of activity that is estimated in many of the budgeted already described. It typically contains expense line items for building insurance, maintenance, repairs, janitorial services, utilities, and the salaries of the maintenance personnel employed in this function.

○ *Capital budget.* This budget comprises either a summary listing of all main fixed asset categories for which purchases are anticipated or a detailed listing of the same information.

○ *Financial statements.* All of the preceding budgets are summarized in a set of financial statements, which should at least include the income statement and cash flow statement.

○ *Financing alternatives.* This category itemizes funding needs during each period itemized in the budget. Problems with required funding as noted in this document will lead to iterations of the rest of the budget, in order to make financing availability match the company's operational considerations.

How Is the Revenue Budget Constructed?

A sample revenue budget is shown in Exhibit 19.2. The exhibit contains revenue estimates for three different product lines that are designated as Alpha, Beta, and Charlie.

The Alpha product line uses a budgeting format that identifies the specific quantities that are expected to be sold in each quarter as well as the average price per unit sold. This format is most useful when there are not so many products that such a detailed delineation would create an excessively lengthy budget. It is a very useful format, for the sales staff can go into the budget model and alter unit volumes and prices quite easily. An alternative format is to reveal this level of detail only for the most important products and to lump the revenue from other products into a single line item, as is the case for the Beta product line.

The most common budgeting format is used for the Beta product line, which avoids the use of detailed unit volumes and prices in favor of a single lump-sum revenue

	Revenue Budget for the Fiscal Year Ended xx/xx/10				
	Quarter 1	Quarter 2	Quarter 3	Quarter 4	Totals
Product Line Alpha:					
Unit price	$ 15.00	$ 14.85	$ 14.80	$ 14.75	—
Unit volume	14,000	21,000	25,000	31,000	91,000
Revenue subtotal	$ 210,000	$ 311,850	$ 370,000	$ 457,250	$1,349,100
Product Line Beta:					
Revenue subtotal	$1,048,000	$1,057,000	$1,061,000	$1,053,000	$4,219,000
Product Line Charlie:					
Region 1	$ 123,000	$ 95,000	$ 82,000	$ 70,000	$ 370,000
Region 2	$ 80,000	$ 89,000	$ 95,000	$ 101,000	$ 365,000
Region 3	$ 95,000	$ 95,000	$ 65,000	$ 16,000	$ 271,000
Region 4	$ 265,000	$ 265,000	$ 320,000	$ 375,000	$1,225,000
Revenue subtotal	$ 563,000	$ 544,000	$ 562,000	$ 562,000	$2,231,000
Revenue grand total	$1,821,000	$1,912,850	$1,993,000	$2,072,250	$7,799,100
Quarterly revenue proportion	23.3%	24.5%	25.6%	26.6%	100.0%
Statistics:					
Product line proportion:					
Alpha	11.5%	16.3%	18.6%	22.1%	17.3%
Beta	57.6%	55.3%	53.2%	50.8%	54.1%
Charlie	30.9%	28.4%	28.2%	27.1%	28.6%
Product line total	100.0%	100.0%	100.0%	100.0%	100.0%

Exhibit 19.2 Revenue Budget

total for each reporting period. This format is used when there are multiple products within each product line, making it cumbersome to create a detailed list of individual products. However, this format is the least informative and gives no easy way to update the supporting information.

Yet another budgeting format is shown for the Charlie product line, where projected sales are grouped by region. This format is most useful when there are many sales personnel, each of whom has been assigned a specific territory in which to operate. This budget can be used to judge the ongoing performance of each salesperson.

There is also a metrics section at the bottom of the revenue budget that itemizes the proportion of total sales that occurs in each quarter, plus the proportion of product line sales within each quarter. Though it is not necessary to use these exact measurements, it is useful to include some type of measure that informs the reader of any variations in sales from period to period.

How Are the Production and Inventory Budgets Constructed?

Both the production and inventory budgets are shown in Exhibit 19.3. The inventory budget is itemized at the top of the exhibit, where we itemize the amount of planned inventory turnover in all three inventory categories. There is a considerable ramp-up in work-in-process (WIP) inventory turnover, indicating the planned installation of a manufacturing planning system that will control the flow of materials through the facility.

The production budget for just the Alpha product line is shown directly below the inventory goals. This budget is not concerned with the cost of production but with the number of units that will be produced. In this instance, we begin with an on-hand inventory of 15,000 units and try to keep enough units on hand through the remainder of the budget year to meet both the finished goods inventory goal at the top of the exhibit and the number of required units to be sold, which is referenced from the revenue budget. The main problem is that the maximum capacity of the bottleneck operation is 20,000 units per quarter. In order to meet the revenue target, we must run that operation at full bore through the first three quarters, irrespective of the inventory turnover target. This is especially important because the budget indicates a jump in bottleneck capacity in the fourth quarter from 20,000 to 40,000

Production and Inventory Budget for the Fiscal Year Ended xx/xx/10

	Quarter 1	Quarter 2	Quarter 3	Quarter 4	Totals
Inventory Turnover Goals:					
Raw Materials Turnover	4.0	4.5	5.0	5.5	4.8
WIP Turnover	12.0	15.0	18.0	21.0	16.5
Finished Goods Turnover	6.0	6.0	9.0	9.0	7.5
Product Line Alpha Production:					
Beginning Inventory Units	15,000	21,000	20,000	15,000	—
Unit Sales Budget	14,000	21,000	25,000	31,000	91,000
Planned Production	20,000	20,000	20,000	27,375	87,375
Ending Inventory Units	21,000	20,000	15,000	11,375	
Bottleneck Unit Capacity	20,000	20,000	20,000	40,000	
Bottleneck Utilization	100%	100%	100%	68%	
Planned Finished Goods Turnover	15,167	15,167	11,375	11,375	

Exhibit 19.3 PRODUCTION AND INVENTORY BUDGETS

units—this will occur when the bottleneck operation is stopped for a short time while additional equipment is added to it. During this stoppage, there must be enough excess inventory on hand to cover any sales that will arise. Consequently, production is planned for 20,000 units per quarter for the first three quarters, followed by a more precisely derived figure in the fourth quarter that will result in inventory turns of 9.0 at the end of the year, exactly as planned.

 How Is the Purchasing Budget Constructed?

The purchasing budget is shown in Exhibit 19.4. This contains several different formats for planning budgeted purchases for the Alpha product line. The first option summarizes the planned production for each quarter; this information is brought forward from the production budget. We then multiply this by the standard unit cost of materials to arrive at the total amount of purchases that must be made in order to adequately support sales. The second option identifies the specific cost of each component of the product, so that management can see where cost increases are expected to occur. Although this version provides more information, it occupies a great deal of space on the budget if there are many components in each product, or many products. A third option is shown at the bottom of the exhibit that summarizes all purchases by commodity type. This format is most useful for the company's buyers, who usually specialize in certain commodity types.

 How Is the Direct Labor Budget Constructed?

The direct labor budget is shown in Exhibit 19.5. This budget assumes that only one labor category will vary directly with revenue volume—that category is the final assembly department, where a percentage in the far right column indicates that the cost in this area will be budgeted at a fixed 3.5% of total revenues. In all other cases, there are assumptions for a fixed number of personnel in each position within each production department. All of the wage figures for each department (except for final assembly) are derived from the planned hourly rates and headcount figures noted at the bottom of the page. This budget can be enhanced with the addition of separate line items for

Purchasing Budget for the Fiscal Year Ended xx/xx/10

	Quarter 1	Quarter 2	Quarter 3	Quarter 4	Totals
Inventory Turnover Goals:					
Raw Materials Turnover	4.0	4.5	5.0	5.5	4.8
Product Line Alpha Purchasing (Option 1):					
Planned Production	20,000	20,000	20,000	27,375	
Standard Material Cost/Unit	$ 5.42	$ 5.42	$ 5.67	$ 5.67	
Total Material Cost	$108,400	$108,400	$113,400	$155,216	$485,416
Product Line Alpha Purchasing (Option 2):					
Planned Production	20,000	20,000	20,000	27,375	
Molded Part	$ 4.62	$ 4.62	$ 4.85	$ 4.85	
Labels	$ 0.42	$ 0.42	$ 0.42	$ 0.42	
Fittings and Fasteners	$ 0.38	$ 0.38	$ 0.40	$ 0.40	
Total Cost of Components	$ 5.42	$ 5.42	$ 5.67	$ 5.67	
Product Line Alpha Purchasing (Option 2):					
Plastic Commodities					
Molded Part Units	20,000	20,000	20,000	27,375	
Molded Part Cost	$ 4.62	$ 4.62	$ 4.85	$ 4.85	
Adhesives Commodity					
Labels Units	20,000	20,000	20,000	27,375	
Labels Cost	$ 0.42	$ 0.42	$ 0.42	$ 0.42	
Fasteners Commodity					
Fasteners Units	20,000	20,000	20,000	27,375	
Fasteners Cost	$ 0.38	$ 0.38	$ 0.40	$ 0.40	
Statistics:					
Materials as Percent of Revenue	36%	36%	38%	38%	

Exhibit 19.4 PURCHASING BUDGET

Direct Labor Budget for the Fiscal Year Ended xx/xx/10						
	Quarter 1	Quarter 2	Quarter 3	Quarter 4	Totals	Notes
Machining Department:						
Sr. Machine Operator	$ 15,120	$15,372	$23,058	$23,058	$ 76,608	
Machining Apprentice	$ 4,914	$ 4,964	$ 9,929	$ 9,929	$ 29,736	
Expense subtotal	$ 20,034	$20,336	$32,987	$32,987	$106,344	
Paint Department:						
Sr. Paint Shop Staff	$ 15,876	$16,128	$16,128	$16,128	$ 64,260	
Painter Apprentice	$ 5,065	$ 5,216	$ 5,216	$ 5,216	$ 20,714	
Expense subtotal	$ 20,941	$21,344	$21,344	$21,344	$ 84,974	
Polishing Department:						
Sr. Polishing Staff	$ 16,632	$11,844	$11,844	$11,844	$ 52,164	
Polishing Apprentice	$ 4,360	$ 4,511	$ 4,511	$ 4,511	$ 17,892	
Expense subtotal	$ 20,992	$16,355	$16,355	$16,355	$ 70,056	
Final Assembly Department:						
General Laborer	$ 63,735	$66,950	$69,755	$72,529	$272,969	3.5
Expense subtotal	$ 63,735	$66,950	$69,755	$72,529	$272,969	
Expense grand total	$125,702	$124,985	$140,441	$143,215	$534,343	

Statistics:

<u>Union Hourly Rates:</u>

Sr. Machine Operator	$15.00	$15.25	$15.25	$15.25
Machining Apprentice	$ 9.75	$ 9.85	$ 9.85	$ 9.85
Sr. Paint Shop Staff	$15.75	$16.00	$16.00	$16.00
Painter Apprentice	$10.05	$10.35	$10.35	$10.35
Sr. Polishing Staff	$11.00	$11.75	$11.75	$11.75
Polishing Apprentice	$ 8.65	$ 8.95	$ 8.95	$ 8.95
Headcount by Position:				
Sr. Machine Operator	2	2	3	3
Machining Apprentice	1	1	2	2
Sr. Paint Shop Staff	2	2	2	2
Painter Apprentice	1	1	1	1
Sr. Polishing Staff	3	2	2	2
Polishing Apprentice	1	1	1	1

Exhibit 19.5 Direct Labor Budget

317

payroll tax percentages, benefits, shift differential payments, and overtime expenses.

How Is the Overhead Budget Constructed?

A sample overhead budget is shown in Exhibit 19.6. In this exhibit, we see that the overhead budget is really made up of a number of subsidiary departments, such as maintenance, materials management, and quality assurance. If the budgets of any of these departments are large enough, it makes sense to split them off into a separate budget, so that the managers of those departments can see their budgeted expectations more clearly. Of particular interest is the valid capacity range noted on the far right side of the exhibit. This signifies the production activity level within which the budgeted overhead costs are accurate. If the actual capacity utilization were to fall outside of this range, either high or low, a separate overhead budget should be constructed with costs that are expected to be incurred within those ranges.

How Is the Cost of Goods Sold Budget Constructed?

A sample cost of goods sold budget is shown in Exhibit 19.7. This format splits out each of the product lines noted in the revenue budget for reporting purposes and subtracts from each one the materials costs that are noted in the purchases budget. This results in a contribution margin for each product line that is the clearest representation of the impact of direct costs (i.e., material costs) on each one. We summarize these individual contribution margins into a summary-level contribution margin and subtract the total direct labor and overhead costs (as referenced from the direct labor and overhead budgets) to arrive at a total gross margin. The statistics section also notes the number of production personnel budgeted for each quarterly reporting period, plus the average annual revenue per production employee— these statistics can be replaced with any operational information that management wants to see at a summary level for the production function, such as efficiency levels, capacity utilization, or inventory turnover.

		Overhead Budget for the Fiscal Year Ended xx/xx/10				
	Quarter 1	Quarter 2	Quarter3	Quarter 4	Totals	Valid Capacity Range
Supervision:						
Production Manager Salary	$ 16,250	$ 16,250	$ 16,250	$ 16,250	$ 65,000	—
Shift Manager Salaries	$ 22,000	$ 22,000	$ 23,500	$ 23,500	$ 91,000	40%–70%
Expense subtotal	$ 38,250	$ 38,250	$ 39,750	$ 39,750	$ 156,000	
Maintenance Department:						
Equipment Maint. Staff	$ 54,000	$ 56,500	$ 58,000	$ 60,250	$ 228,750	40%–70%
Facilities Maint. Staff	$ 8,250	$ 8,250	$ 8,500	$ 8,500	$ 33,500	40%–70%
Equipment Repairs	$225,000	$225,000	$275,000	$225,000	$ 950,000	40%–70%
Facility Repairs	$ 78,000	$ 29,000	$ 12,000	$ 54,000	$ 173,000	40%–70%
Expense subtotal	$365,250	$318,750	$353,500	$347,750	$1,385,250	
Materials Management Department:						
Manager Salary	$ 18,750	$ 18,750	$ 18,750	$ 18,750	$ 75,000	—
Purchasing Staff	$ 28,125	$ 18,750	$ 18,750	$ 18,750	$ 84,375	40%–70%
Materials Mgmt Staff	$ 28,000	$ 35,000	$ 35,000	$ 35,000	$ 133,000	40%–70%
Production Control Staff	$ 11,250	$ 11,250	$ 11,250	$ 11,250	$ 45,000	40%–70%
						(Continued)

Exhibit 19.6 Overhead Budget

Overhead Budget for the Fiscal Year Ended xx/xx/10

	Quarter 1	Quarter 2	Quarter3	Quarter 4	Totals	Valid Capacity Range
Quality Department:					$ 337,375	
Manager Salary	$ 13,750	$13,750	$ 13,750	$ 13,750	$ 55,000	—
Quality Staff	$ 16,250	$16,250	$ 16,250	$ 24,375	$ 73,125	40%–70%
Lab Testing Supplies	$ 5,000	$4,500	$ 4,500	$ 4,500	$ 18,500	40%–70%
Expense subtotal	$ 35,000	$34,500	$ 34,500	$ 42,625	$ 146,625	
Other Expenses:						
Depreciation	$ 14,000	$15,750	$ 15,750	$ 15,750	$ 61,250	—
Utilities	$ 60,000	$55,000	$ 55,000	$ 60,000	$ 230,000	40%–70%
Boiler Insurance	$ 3,200	$3,200	$ 3,200	$ 3,200	$ 12,800	—
Expense subtotal	$ 77,200	$73,950	$ 73,950	$ 78,950	$ 304,050	
Expense grand total	$601,825	$549,200	$585,450	$592,825	$2,329,300	

Exhibit 19.6 OVERHEAD BUDGET (CONTINUED)

Cost of Goods Sold Budget for the Fiscal Year Ended xx/xx/10					
	Quarter 1	Quarter 2	Quarter 3	Quarter 4	Totals
Product Line Alpha:					
Revenue	$ 210,000	$ 311,850	$ 370,000	$ 457,250	$1,349,100
Materials expense	$ 108,400	$ 108,400	$ 113,400	$ 155,216	$ 485,416
Contribution Margin $$	$ 101,600	$ 203,450	$ 256,600	$ 302,034	$ 863,684
Contribution Margin %	48%	65%	69%	66%	64%
Product Line Beta:					
Revenue	$1,048,000	$1,057,000	$1,061,000	$1,053,000	$4,219,000
Materials expense	$ 12,000	$ 14,000	$ 15,000	$ 13,250	$ 54,250
Contribution Margin $$	$1,036,000	$1,043,000	$1,046,000	$1,039,750	$4,164,750
Contribution Margin %	99%	99%	99%	99%	99%
Revenue—Product Line Charlie:					
Revenue	$ 563,000	$ 544,000	$ 562,000	$ 562,000	$2,231,000
Materials expense	$ 268,000	$ 200,000	$ 220,000	$ 230,000	$ 918,000
Contribution Margin $$	$ 295,000	$ 344,000	$ 342,000	$ 332,000	$1,313,000
Contribution Margin %	52%	63%	61%	59%	59%
Total Contribution Margin $$	$1,432,600	$1,590,450	$1,644,600	$1,673,784	$6,341,434
Total Contribution Margin %	79%	83%	83%	81%	81%
					(Continued)

Exhibit 19.7 Cost of Goods Sold Budget

Cost of Goods Sold Budget for the Fiscal Year Ended xx/xx/10					
	Quarter 1	Quarter 2	Quarter 3	Quarter 4	Totals
Product Line Alpha:					
Direct Labor Expense:	$ 125,702	$ 124,985	$ 140,441	$ 143,215	$ 534,343
Overhead Expense:	$ 601,825	$ 549,200	$ 585,450	$ 592,825	$2,329,300
Total Gross Margin $$	$ 705,073	$ 916,265	$ 918,709	$ 937,744	$3,477,791
Total Gross Margin %	39%	48%	46%	45%	44%
Statistics:					
No. of Production Staff*	23	22	22	23	
Ave. Annual Revenue per Production Employee	$ 316,696	$ 347,791	$ 362,364	$ 360,391	

* Not including general assembly staff

Exhibit 19.7 Cost of Goods Sold Budget (Continued)

How Is the Sales Department Budget Constructed?

The sales department budget is shown in Exhibit 19.8. This budget shows several ways in which to organize budget information. At the top of the budget is a block of line items that lists the expenses for those overhead costs within the department that cannot be specifically linked to a salesperson or region. In cases where the number of sales staff is quite small, *all* of the department's costs may be listed in this area.

An alternative is shown in the second block of expense line items in the middle of the sales department budget, where all of the sales costs for an entire product line are lumped together into a single line item. If each person on the sales staff is exclusively assigned to a single product line, it may make sense to break down the budget into separate budget pages for each product line and list all of the expenses associated with each product line on a separate page.

Another alternative is shown next in the exhibit, where we list a summary of expenses for each salesperson. This format works well when combined with the departmental overhead expenses at the top of the budget, since this accounts for all of the departmental costs.

A final option listed at the bottom of the exhibit is to itemize expenses by sales region. This format works best when many sales personnel within the department are clustered into a number of clearly identifiable regions. If there were no obvious regions or if there was only one salesperson per region, the better format would be to list expenses by salesperson.

How Is the Marketing Budget Constructed?

Exhibit 19.9 shows a sample marketing budget. This budget itemizes departmental overhead costs at the top, which leaves space in the middle for the itemization of campaign-specific costs. The campaign-specific costs can be lumped together for individual product lines, as is the case for product lines Alpha and Beta in the exhibit, or with subsidiary line items, as is shown for product line Charlie. A third possible format, which is to itemize marketing costs by marketing tool (e.g., advertising, promotional tour, coupon redemption, etc.) is generally not recommended if there is more than one product line, since

Sales Department Budget for the Fiscal Year Ended xx/xx/10

	Quarter 1	Quarter 2	Quarter 3	Quarter 4	Totals
Departmental Overhead:					
Depreciation	$ 500	$ 500	$ 500	$ 500	$ 2,000
Office supplies	$ 750	$ 600	$ 650	$ 600	$ 2,600
Payroll taxes	$ 2,945	$ 5,240	$ 5,240	$ 8,186	$ 21,611
Salaries	$ 38,500	$ 68,500	$ 68,500	$107,000	$282,500
Travel and entertainment	$ 1,500	$ 1,500	$ 1,500	$ 2,000	$ 6,500
Expense subtotal	$ 44,195	$ 76,340	$ 76,390	$118,286	$ 315,211
Product Line Alpha:	$ 32,000	$ 18,000	$ 0	$ 21,000	$ 71,000
Expenses by Salesperson:					
Jones, Milbert	$ 14,000	$ 16,500	$ 17,000	$ 12,000	$ 59,500
Smidley, Jefferson	$ 1,000	$ 9,000	$ 8,000	$ 12,000	$ 30,000
Verity, Jonas	$ 7,000	$ 9,000	$ 14,000	$ 12,000	$ 42,000
Expense subtotal	$ 22,000	$ 34,500	$ 39,000	$ 36,000	$ 131,500
Expenses by Region:					
East Coast	$ 52,000	$ 71,000	$ 15,000	$0	$ 138,000
Midwest Coast	$ 8,000	$ 14,000	$ 6,000	$ 12,000	$ 40,000
West Coast	$ 11,000	$ 10,000	$ 12,000	$ 24,000	$ 57,000
Expense subtotal	$ 71,000	$ 95,000	$ 33,000	$ 36,000	$ 235,000
Expense grand total	$137,195	$205,840	$148,390	$190,286	$ 681,711
Statistics:					
Revenue per salesperson	$607,000	$637,617	$664,333	$690,750	$2,599,700
T&E per salesperson	$ 500	$ 500	$ 500	$ 667	$ 2,167

Exhibit 19.8 SALES DEPARTMENT BUDGET

Marketing Budget for the Fiscal Year Ended xs/xx/10					
	Quarter 1	Quarter 2	Quarter 3	Quarter 4	Totals
Departmental Overhead:					
Depreciation	650	750	850	1,000	3,250
Office supplies	200	200	200	200	800
Payroll taxes	4,265	4,265	4,265	4,265	17,060
Salaries	$55,750	$55,750	$55,750	$55,750	223,000
Travel & entertainment	5,000	6,500	7,250	7,250	26,000
Expense subtotal	65,865	67,465	68,315	68,465	270,110
Campaign-Specific Expenses:					
Product Line Alpha	14,000	26,000	30,000	0	70,000
Product Line Beta	18,000	0	0	24,000	42,000
Product Line Charlie					0
Advertising	10,000	0	20,000	0	30,000
Promotional Tour	5,000	25,000	2,000	0	32,000
Coupon Redemption	2,000	4,000	4,500	1,200	11,700
Product Samples	2,750	5,250	1,250	0	9,250
Expense subtotal	51,750	60,250	57,750	25,200	194,950
Expense grand total	117,615	127,715	126,065	93,665	465,060
Statistics:					
Expense as percent of total sales	6.5%	6.7%	6.3%	4.5%	6.0%
Expense proportion by quarter	25.3%	27.5%	27.1%	20.1%	100.0%

Exhibit 19.9 Marketing Budget

there is no way to determine the impact of individual marketing costs on specific product lines.

How Is the General and Administrative Budget Constructed?

A sample general and administrative budget is shown in Exhibit 19.10. This budget can be quite lengthy, including such additional line items as postage, copier leases, and office repair. Many of these extra expenses have been pruned from the exhibit in order to provide a compressed view of the general format to be used. The exhibit does not lump together the costs of the various departments that are typically included in this budget but rather identifies each one in separate blocks; this format is most useful when there are separate managers for the accounting and human resources functions, so that they will have a better understanding of their budgets. The statistics section at the bottom of the page itemizes a benchmark target of the total general and administrative cost as a proportion of revenue. This is a particularly useful statistic to track, since the general and administrative function is a cost center and requires such a comparison to inform management that these costs are being held in check.

How Is the Staffing Budget Constructed?

A staffing budget is shown in Exhibit 19.11. This budget itemizes the expected headcount in every department by major job category. It does not attempt to identify individual positions, since that can lead to an excessively lengthy list. Also, because there may be multiple positions identified within each job category, the *average* salary for each cluster of jobs is identified. If a position is subject to overtime pay, its expected overtime percentage is identified on the right side of the budget.

How Is the Facilities Budget Constructed?

The facilities budget tends to have the largest number of expense line items. A sample of this format is shown in Exhibit 19.12. A statistics section at the bottom of this budget refers to the total amount of square feet occupied by the facility. A very effective statistic is the amount of unused square footage, which can be used to conduct an

		General and Administrative Budget for the Fiscal Year Ended xx/xx/10				
	Quarter 1	Quarter 2	Quarter 3	Quarter 4	Totals	Notes
Accounting Department:						
Depreciation	4,000	4,000	4,250	4,250	16,500	
Office supplies	650	650	750	750	2,800	
Payroll taxes	4,973	4,973	4,973	4,973	19,890	
Salaries	$65,000	$65,000	$65,000	$65,000	260,000	
Training	500	2,500	7,500	0	10,500	
Travel & entertainment	0	750	4,500	500	5,750	
Expense subtotal	75,123	77,873	86,973	75,473	315,440	
Corporate Expenses:						
Depreciation	450	500	550	600	2,100	
Office supplies	1,000	850	750	1,250	3,850	
Payroll taxes	6,598	6,598	6,598	6,598	26,393	
Salaries	$86,250	$86,250	$86,250	$86,250	345,000	
Insurance, business	4,500	4,500	4,500	4,500	18,000	
Training	5,000	0	0	0	5,000	
Travel & entertainment	2,000	500	500	0	3,000	
Expense subtotal	105,798	99,198	99,148	99,198	403,343	
					(Continued)	

Exhibit 19.10 General and Administrative Budget

General and Administrative Budget for the Fiscal Year Ended xx/xx/10

	Quarter 1	Quarter 2	Quarter 3	Quarter 4	Totals	Notes
Human Resources Department:						**0.4%**
Benefits programs	7,284	7,651	7,972	8,289	31,196	
Depreciation	500	500	500	500	2,000	
Office supplies	450	8,000	450	450	9,350	
Payroll taxes	2,869	2,869	2,869	2,869	11,475	
Salaries	$37,500	$37,500	$37,500	$37,500	150,000	
Training	5,000	0	7,500	0	12,500	
Travel & entertainment	2,000	1,000	3,500	1,000	7,500	
Expense subtotal	55,603	57,520	60,291	50,608	224,021	
Expense grand total	236,523	234,591	246,411	225,278	942,804	
Statistics:						
Expense as proportion of revenue	13.0%	12.3%	12.4%	10.9%	12.1%	
Benchmark comparison	11.5%	11.5%	11.5%	11.5%	11.5%	

Exhibit 19.10 GENERAL AND ADMINISTRATIVE BUDGET (CONTINUED)

Staffing Budget for the Fiscal Year Ended xx/xx/10					
	Quarter 1	Quarter 2	Quarter 3	Quarter 4	Average Salary	Overtime Percent
Sales Department:						
Regional Sales Manager	1	2	2	3	$120,000	0%
Salesperson	2	4	4	6	$65,000	0%
Sales Support Staff	1	1	1	2	$34,000	6%
Marketing Department:						
Marketing Manager	1	1	1	1	$85,000	0%
Marketing Researcher	2	2	2	2	$52,000	0%
Secretary	1	1	1	1	$34,000	6%
General and Administrative:						
President	1	1	1	1	$175,000	0%
Chief Operating Officer	1	1	1	1	$125,000	0%
Chief Financial Officer	1	1	1	1	$100,000	0%
Human Resources Mgr.	1	1	1	1	$80,000	0%
Accounting Staff	4	4	4	4	$40,000	10%
Human Resources Staff	2	2	2	2	$35,000	8%
Executive Secretary	1	1	1	1	$45,000	6%
Research Department:						
Chief Scientist	1	1	1	1	$100,000	0%
Senior Engineer Staff	3	3	3	4	$80,000	0%
Junior Engineer Staff	3	3	3	3	$60,000	0%
						(Continued)

Exhibit 19.11 STAFFING BUDGET

		Staffing Budget for the Fiscal Year Ended xx/xx/10			
	Quarter 1	Quarter 2	Quarter 3	Quarter 4	Average Salary
Overhead Budget:					
Production Manager	1	1	1	1	$65,000	0%
Quality Manager	1	1	1	1	$55,000	0%
Materials Manager	1	1	1	1	$75,000	0%
Production Scheduler	1	1	1	1	$45,000	0%
Quality Assurance Staff	2	2	2	3	$32,500	8%
Purchasing Staff	3	2	2	2	$37,500	8%
Materials Mgmt Staff	4	5	5	5	$28,000	8%
Total Headcount	39	42	42	48		

Exhibit 19.11 STAFFING BUDGET (CONTINUED)

Facilities Budget for the Fiscal Year Ended xx/xx/10					
	Quarter 1	Quarter 2	Quarter 3	Quarter 4	Totals
Facility Expenses:					
Contracted Services	$ 5,500	$ 5,400	$ 5,000	$ 4,500	$ 20,400
Depreciation	$29,000	$29,000	$28,000	$28,000	$114,000
Electricity Charges	$ 4,500	$ 3,500	$ 3,500	$ 4,500	$ 16,000
Inspection Fees	$ 500	$ 0	$ 0	$ 500	$ 1,000
Insurance	$ 8,000	$ 0	$ 0	$ 0	$ 8,000
Maintenance Supplies	$ 3,000	$ 3,000	$ 3,000	$ 3,000	$ 12,000
Payroll Taxes	$ 1,148	$ 1,148	$ 1,148	$ 1,186	$ 4,628
Property Taxes	$ 0	$ 5,000	$ 0	$ 0	$ 5,000
Repairs	$15,000	$ 0	$29,000	$ 0	$ 44,000
Sewage Charges	$ 250	$ 250	$ 250	$ 250	$ 1,000
Trash Disposal	$ 3,000	$ 3,000	$ 3,000	$ 3,000	$ 12,000
Wages—Janitorial	$ 5,000	$ 5,000	$ 5,000	$ 5,500	$ 20,500
Wages—Maintenance	$10,000	$10,000	$10,000	$10,000	$ 40,000
Water Charges	$ 1,000	$ 1,000	$ 1,000	$ 1,000	$ 4,000
Expense grand total	$85,898	$66,298	$88,898	$61,436	$302,528
Statistics:					
Total Square Feet	52,000	52,000	78,000	78,000	
Square Feet/Employee	839	813	1,219	1,099	
Unused Square Footage	1,200	1,200	12,500	12,500	

Exhibit 19.12 FACILITIES BUDGET

ongoing program of selling off, renting, or consolidating company facilities.

How Is the Research Department Budget Constructed?

The research department's budget is shown in Exhibit 19.13. It is most common to segregate the department-specific overhead that cannot be attributed to a specific project at the top of the budget and then cluster costs by project below that. By doing so, the management team can see precisely how much money is being allocated to each project. This may be of use in determining which projects must be canceled or delayed as part of the budget review process. The statistics section at the bottom of the budget notes the proportion of planned expenses between the categories of overhead, research, and development. These proportions can be examined to see if the company is allocating funds to the right balance of projects that most effectively meets it product development goals.

How Is the Capital Budget Constructed?

The capital budget is shown in Exhibit 19.14. This format clusters capital expenditures by a number of categories. For example, the first category, "bottleneck-related expenditures," clearly focuses attention on those outgoing payments that will increase the company's key production capacity. The payments in the third quarter under this heading are directly related to the increase in bottleneck capacity that were shown the production budget for the fourth quarter. The budget also contains an automatic assumption of $7,000 in capital expenditures for any net increase in non–direct labor headcount, which encompasses the cost of computer equipment and office furniture for each person. If the company's capitalization limit is set too high to list these expenditures on the capital budget, a similar line item should be inserted into the general and administrative budget, so that the expense can be recognized under the office supplies or some similar account.

An alternative to this grouping system is to list only the sum total of all capital expenditures in each category, which is used most frequently when there are far too many separate purchases to list on the budget. Another variation is to list only the largest expenditures on separate budget lines and cluster together all smaller ones. The

Research Department for the Fiscal Year Ended xx/xx/10					
	Quarter 1	Quarter 2	Quarter 3	Quarter 4	Totals
Departmental Overhead:					
Depreciation	500	500	400	400	1,800
Office supplies	750	2,000	1,500	1,250	5,500
Payroll taxes	9,945	9,945	9,945	11,475	41,310
Salaries	$130,000	$130,000	$130,000	$150,000	540,000
Travel and entertainment	0	0	0	0	0
Expense subtotal	141,195	142,445	141,845	163,125	588,610
Research-Specific Expenses:					
Gamma Project	20,000	43,500	35,000	12,500	111,000
Omega Project	5,000	6,000	7,500	9,000	27,500
Pi Project	14,000	7,000	7,500	4,500	33,000
Upsilon Project	500	2,500	5,000	0	8,000
Expense subtotal	39,500	59,000	55,000	26,000	179,500
Development-Specific Expenses:					
Latin Project	28,000	29,000	30,000	15,000	102,000
Greek Project	14,000	14,500	15,000	7,500	51,000
Mabinogian Project	20,000	25,000	15,000	10,000	70,000
Old English Project	6,250	12,500	25,000	50,000	93,750
Expense subtotal	68,250	81,000	85,000	82,500	316,750
Expense grand total	248,945	282,445	281,845	271,625	1,084,860

(Continued)

Exhibit 19.13 RESEARCH DEPARTMENT BUDGET

Research Department for the Fiscal Year Ended xx/xx/10					
	Quarter 1	Quarter 2	Quarter 3	Quarter 4	4
Statistics:					
Budgeted number of patent applications filed	2	0	1	1	
Proportion of expenses:					
Overhead	56.7%	50.4%	50.3%	60.1%	217.5%
Research	15.9%	20.9%	19.5%	9.6%	65.8%
Development	27.4%	28.7%	30.2%	30.4%	116.6%
Total Expenses	100.0%	100.0%	100.0%	100.0%	400.0%

Exhibit 19.13 RESEARCH DEPARTMENT BUDGET (CONTINUED)

Capital Budget for the Fiscal Year Ended xx/xx/10					
	Quarter 1	Quarter 2	Quarter 3	Quarter 4	Totals
Bottleneck-Related Expenditures:					
Stamping Machine			$150,000		$150,000
Facility for Machine			$ 72,000		$ 72,000
Headcount-Related Expenditures:					
Headcount Change × $7,000 Added Staff	$ 0	$ 21,000	$ 0	$42,000	$ 63,000
Profit-Related Expenditures:					
Blending Machine		$ 50,000			$ 50,000
Polishing Machine		$ 27,000			$ 27,000
Safety-Related Expenditures:					
Machine Shielding		$ 3,000	$ 3,000		$ 6,000
Handicapped Walkways	$8.5000	$ 5,000			$ 13,000
Required Expenditures:					
Clean Air Scrubber			$ 42,000		$ 42,000
Other Expenditures:					
Tool Crib Expansion				$18,500	$ 18,500
Total expenditures	$ 8,000	$106,000	$267,000	$60,500	$441,500

Exhibit 19.14 CAPITAL BUDGET

level of capital purchasing activity will determine the type of format used.

How Are the Budgeted Financial Statements Constructed?

All of the preceding budgets roll up into the budgeted income and cash flow statement, which appears in Exhibit 19.15. This format lists the grand totals from each preceding page of the budget in order to arrive at a profit or loss for each budget quarter. In the example, we see that a large initial loss in the first quarter is gradually offset by smaller gains in later quarters to arrive at a small profit for the year. However, the presentation continues with a cash flow statement that has less positive results. It begins with the net profit figure for each quarter, adds back the depreciation expense for all departments, and subtracts out all planned capital expenditures from the capital budget to arrive at cash flow needs for the year. This tells us that the company will experience a maximum cash shortfall in the third quarter. This format can be made more precise by adding in time lag factors for the payment of accounts payable and the collection of accounts receivable.

How Is the Financing Budget Constructed?

The final document in the budget is an itemization of the finances needed to ensure that the rest of the budget can be achieved. An example is shown in Exhibit 19.16, which carries forward the final cash position at the end of each quarter that was the product of the cash flow statement. This line shows that there will be a maximum shortfall of $223,727 by the end of the third quarter. The next section of the budget outlines several possible options for obtaining the required funds (which are rounded up to $225,000): debt, preferred stock, or common stock. The financing cost of each one is noted in the far right column, where we see that the interest cost on debt is 9.5%, the dividend on preferred stock is 8%, and the expected return by common stockholders is 18%.

The third section on of exhibit lists the existing capital structure, its cost, and the net cost of capital. The final section of the exhibit calculates any changes in the cost of capital that will arise if any of the three financing options are selected. In the exhibit, selecting additional debt as the

Income and Cash Flow Statement for the Fiscal Year Ended xx/xx/10					
	Quarter 1	Quarter 2	Quarter 3	Quarter 4	Totals
Revenue:	$1,821,000	$1,912,850	$1,993,000	$2,072,250	$7,799,100
Cost of Goods Sold:					
Materials	$ 388,400	$ 322,400	$ 348,400	$ 398,466	$1,457,666
Direct Labor	$ 125,702	$ 124,985	$ 140,441	$ 143,215	$ 534,343
Overhead					
Supervision	$ 38,250	$ 38,250	$ 39,750	$ 39,750	$ 156,000
Maintenance Department	$ 365,250	$ 318,750	$ 353,500	$ 347,750	$1,385,250
Materials Management	$ 86,125	$ 83,750	$ 83,750	$ 83,750	$ 337,375
Quality Department	$ 35,000	$ 34,500	$ 34,500	$ 42,625	$ 146,625
Other Expenses	$ 77,200	$ 73,950	$ 73,950	7 $5,950	$ 304,050
Total Cost of Goods Sold	$1,115,927	$ 996,585	$1,074,291	$1,134,506	$4,321,309
Gross Margin	$ 705,073	$ 916,265	$ 918,709	$ 937,744	$3,477,791
Operating Expenses					
Sales Department	$ 137,195	$ 205,840	$ 148,390	$ 190,286	$ 681,711
General and Admin. Dept.					
Accounting	$ 75,123	$ 77,873	$ 86,973	$ 75,473	$ 315,440
Corporate	$ 105,798	$ 99,198	$ 99,148	$ 99,198	$ 403,343
Human Resources	$ 55,603	$ 57,520	$ 60,291	$ 50,608	$ 224,021
Marketing Department	$ 117,615	$ 127,715	$ 126,065	$ 465,060	$ 465,060
Facilities Department	$ 85,898	$ 66,298	$ 88,898	$ 61,436	$ 302,528
(Continued)					

Exhibit 19.15 BUDGETED INCOME AND CASH FLOW STATEMENT

Income and Cash Flow Statement for the Fiscal Year Ended xx/xx/10				
	Quarter 1	Quarter 2	Quarter 3	Quarter 4	Totals
Research Department	$248,945	$282,445	$281,845	$271,625	$1,084,860
Total Operating Expenses	$826,176	$916,888	$891,609	$842,290	$3,476,963
Net Profit (Loss)	–$121,103	–$ 624	$ 27,100	$ 95,455	$ 828
Cash Flow:					
Beginning Cash	$100,000	$ 20,497	–$ 34,627	–$223,727	
Net Profit (Loss)	–$121,103	–$ 624	$ 27,100	$ 95,455	$ 828
Add Depreciation	$ 49,600	$ 51,500	$ 50,800	$ 51,000	$ 202,900
Minus Capital Purchases	–$ 8,000	–$106,000	–$267,000	–$ 60,500	–$ 441,500
Ending Cash	$ 20,497	–$ 34,627	–$223,727	–$137,772	

Exhibit 19.15 BUDGETED INCOME AND CASH FLOW STATEMENT (CONTINUED)

Financing Budget for the Fiscal Year Ended xx/xx/10					
	Quarter 1	Quarter 2	Quarter 3	Quarter 4	Financing Cost
Cash Position:	$20,497	–$34,627	–$223,727	–$137,772	
Financing Option One: Additional Debt		$225,000			9.5%
Financing Option Two: Additional Preferred Stock	$225,000				8.0%
Financing Option Three: Additional Common Stock	$225,000	$225,000			18.0%
Existing Capital Structure:					
Debt	$400,000				9.0%
Preferred Stock	$150,000				7.5%
Common Stock	$500,000				18.0%
Existing Cost of Capital	11.8%				
Revised Cost of Capital:					
Financing Option One	10.7%				
Financing Option Two	11.2%				
Financing Option Three	12.9%				

Note: Tax rate equals 38%

Exhibit 19.16 FINANCING BUDGET

preferred form of financing will result in a reduction in the cost of capital to 10.7%, whereas a selection of high-cost common stock will result in an increase in the cost of capital, to 12.9%.

  ## What Is a Flex Budget?

A *flex budget* itemizes different expense levels depending on changes in the amount of actual revenue. In its simplest form, the flex budget uses percentages of revenue for certain expenses rather than the usual fixed numbers. This allows for an infinite series of changes in budgeted expenses that are directly tied to revenue volume. However, this approach ignores changes to other costs that do not alter in accordance with small revenue variations. Consequently, a more sophisticated format will also incorporate changes to many additional expenses when certain larger revenue changes occur, thereby accounting for step costs. By making these changes to the budget, a company will have a tool for comparing actual to budgeted performance at many levels of activity.

The flex budget can be difficult to formulate and administer. One problem is that many costs are not fully variable, instead having a fixed cost component that must be included in the flex budget formula. Another issue is that a great deal of time can be spent developing step costs, which is more time than the typical controller has available, especially when in the midst of creating the standard budget. Consequently, the flex budget tends to include only a small number of step costs as well as variable costs whose fixed cost components are not fully recognized.

CHAPTER 20

CAPITAL BUDGETING

 What Is Capital Budgeting?

Capital budgeting is the process of choosing which fixed assets to acquire. There are typically many possible investments, so managers need a methodology for making investments that include such factors as production bottlenecks, capacity levels above and below the bottleneck, safety, legal requirements, and risk.

 What Are the Problems with Capital Budgeting Analysis?

The traditional capital budgeting approach involves reviewing a series of unrelated requests from throughout the company, each one asking for funding for various projects. Management decides whether to fund each request based on the discounted cash flows projected for each one. If there are not sufficient funds available for all requests having positive discounted cash flows, those with the largest cash flows or highest percentage returns are usually accepted first, until the funds run out.

There are three problems with this type of capital budgeting.

1. There is no consideration of how each requested project fits into the entire system of production. Instead, most requests involve the local optimization of specific work centers that may not contribute to the total profitability of the company.

2. There is no consideration of the bottleneck operation, so managers cannot tell which funding requests will result in an improvement to the efficiency of that operation.

3. Managers tend to inflate the forecasted cash flows in their requests, yielding inaccurate discounted cash

flow projections. Thus, the entire system of cash flow–based investments results in a suboptimal return on investment.

 ## Why Focus on Bottleneck Investments?

Pareto analysis holds that 20% of events cause 80% of the results. For example, 20% of customers generate 80% of all profits, or 20% of all production issues cause 80% of the scrap. The theory of constraints, when reduced down to one guiding concept, states that 1% of all events cause 99% of the results. This conclusion is reached by viewing a company as one giant system designed to produce profits, with one bottleneck controlling the amount of those profits. Since the total output of the system is restricted by the bottleneck, it can be considered the "drum" that sets the pace of operations.

Under the theory of constraints, all management activities are centered on management of the bottleneck operation, or constrained resource. A company will maximize its profits by focusing on making this resource more efficient and ensuring that all other company resources are oriented toward supporting it. The concept is shown in Exhibit 20.1, where the total production capacity of four work centers is shown, both before and after a series of efficiency improvements are made. Of the four work centers, the capacity of center C is the lowest, at 80 units per hour. Despite subsequent efficiency improvements to work centers A and B, the total output of the system remains at 80 units per hour, because of the restriction imposed by work center C.

This approach is substantially different from the traditional approach of local optimization, where *all* company

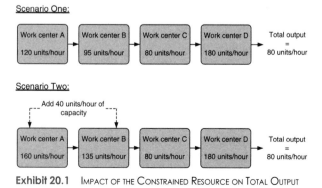

Exhibit 20.1 IMPACT OF THE CONSTRAINED RESOURCE ON TOTAL OUTPUT

operations are to be made as efficient as possible, with machines and employees maximizing their work efforts at all times. The key difference between the two methodologies is the view of efficiency: Should it be maximized everywhere, or just at the constrained resource? The constraints-based approach holds that any local optimization of a nonconstraint resource will simply allow it to produce more than the constrained operation can handle, which results in excess inventory.

EXAMPLE

A furniture company discovers that its bottleneck operation is its paint shop. The company cannot produce more than 300 tables per day, because that maximizes the capacity of the paint shop. If the company adds a lathe to produce more table legs, this will only result in the accumulation of an excessive quantity of table legs rather than the production of a larger number of painted tables. Thus, the investment in efficiencies elsewhere than the constrained operation will only increase costs without improving sales or profits.

The preceding example shows that not only should efficiency improvements *not* be made in areas other than the constrained operation but that it is quite acceptable to not even be efficient in these other areas. It is better to stop work in a nonconstraint operation and idle its staff than to have it churn out more inventory than can be used by the constrained operation.

When Should I Invest in a Bottleneck Operation?

In many cases, a company has specifically designated a resource to be its constraint, because it is so expensive to add additional capacity. Given the cost of additional investment, this decision is not to be taken lightly. The decision process is to review the impact on the incremental change in throughput caused by the added investment, less any changes in operating expenses. Because this type of investment represents a considerable step cost (where costs and/or the investment will jump considerably as a result of the decision), management usually must make its decision based on the perceived level of long-term throughput changes rather than on smaller expected short-term throughput increases.

What Capital Budgeting Application Form Should I Use?

The capital budgeting form shown in Exhibit 20.2 splits capital budgeting requests into three categories:

1. Bottleneck related
2. Risk related
3. Non–bottleneck related

The risk-related category covers all capital purchases for which the company must meet a legal requirement or

Capital Request Form

Project name: _____

Name of project sponsor: _____

Submission date: _____   Project number: _____

Bottleneck-Related Project	Approvals
Initial expenditure: $ _____	All _____
Additional annual expenditure: $ _____	Process Analyst
	$100,000 _____
Impact on throughput: $ _____	Supervisor
Impact on operating expenses: $ _____	$100,001– _____
	$1,000,000 President
Impact on ROI: $ _____	
(Attach calculations)	$1,000,000+ _____
	Board of Directors

Risk-Related Project	Approvals
Initial expenditure: $ _____	Corporate Attorney _____
Additional annual expenditure: $ _____	< $50,000 {
Description of legal requirement fulfilled or risk issue mitigated (attach description as needed):	Chief Risk Officer _____
_____	$50,001+ _____
	President
_____	$1,000,000+ _____
	Board of Directors

Non–Bottleneck-Related Project	Approvals
Initial expenditure: $ _____	All _____
Additional annual expenditure: $ _____	Process Analyst
☐ Improves upstream capacity? Attach justification of upstream capacity increase	<$10,000 _____
	Supervisor
☐ Other request Attach justification for other request type	$10,001– _____
	$100,000 President
	$100,000+ _____
	Board of Directors

Exhibit 20.2   BOTTLENECK-ORIENTED CAPITAL REQUEST FORM

for which there is a perception that the company is subject to an undue amount of risk if it does *not* invest in an asset. All remaining requests that do not clearly fall into the bottleneck-related or risk-related categories drop into a catch-all category at the bottom of the form. The intent of this format is to clearly differentiate between different types of approval requests, with each one requiring different types of analysis and management approval.

The approval levels vary significantly in this capital request form. Approvals for bottleneck-related investments include a process analyst (who verifies that the request will actually impact the bottleneck) as well as generally higher-dollar approval levels by lower-level managers—the intent is to make it easier to approve capital requests that will improve the bottleneck operation. Approvals for risk-related projects first require the joint approval of the corporate attorney and chief risk officer, with added approvals for large expenditures. Finally, the approvals for non–bottleneck-related purchases involve lower-dollar approval levels, so the approval process is intentionally made more difficult.

Should I Invest in Upstream Workstations?

The bottleneck operation should always have an adequate inventory buffer directly in front of it, so that it can maximize its production rate, irrespective of any upstream manufacturing problems. If there are severe upstream problems, the inventory buffer could be eliminated, leading to the shutdown of the bottleneck operation, which in turn directly reduces a company's profitability. Consequently, it is extremely important to have a sufficient amount of upstream production capacity to rapidly refill the inventory buffer in the event of a manufacturing problem. This production capacity is called *sprint capacity*.

To guard against a drop in sprint capacity, the management team should regularly monitor the capacity usage levels of upstream workstations and make selective investments in those workstations whose sprint capacity has dropped sufficiently to present a risk of imperiling the bottleneck operation's inventory buffer.

The inventory buffer trend report shown in Exhibit 20.3. The report shows an upper and lower boundary line, which represent tolerable boundaries for the percentage of all jobs where production problems caused the buffer to be eliminated. The small circles represent the daily

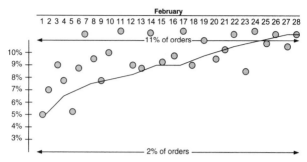

Exhibit 20.3   Inventory Buffer Trend Report

percentage of jobs causing buffer elimination, while the line running approximately through the center of the boundary limits is a multiday moving average of the percentage of expedited orders experienced. The report reveals that the buffer is being eliminated with increasing regularity and that roughly one-third of all days now result in buffer elimination levels exceeding the tolerable limit.

In the situation shown in the exhibit, it would be reasonable to invest in those upstream workstations where capacity problems are causing the inventory buffer elimination in front of the bottleneck operation.

Should I Invest in Downstream Workstations?

It is rarely necessary to invest in additional downstream capacity from the bottleneck operation, since doing so does nothing to increase a company's throughput. The only improvement would be to the efficiency of an operation that will still be controlled by the speed of the bottleneck operation. In reality, the situation is even worse, for the investment in such an operation has no return on investment (ROI) *at all* – so the company's total investment increases with no attendant improvement in its throughput.

Example

The industrial engineering manager of Circuit Board Corporation recommends that a $100,000 investment be made to improve the efficiency of the circuit board insertion machine, which is the next workstation in line after the bottleneck operation. This investment will double the speed of the machine. The projected results of this investment are shown in the table, where total corporate throughput remains the same while the total investment increases and the return on investment declines from 20% to 19%.

	Annual Throughput	Total Corporate Investment	Return on Investment
Before investment	$400,000	$2,000,000	20.0%
After investment	$400,000	$2,100,000	19.0%

The problem with the investment was that it increased the efficiency of a machine that is still only going to receive the same amount of work in process input from the bottleneck operation. Since its input has not changed, neither can its output, despite a higher level of efficiency.

Should I Lease an Asset or Buy It?

In a leasing situation, the company pays the lessor for the use of equipment that is owned by the lessor. Under the terms of this arrangement, the company pays a monthly fee; the lessor records the asset on its books and takes the associated depreciation expense while also undertaking to pay all property taxes and maintenance fees. The lessor typically takes back the asset at the end of the lease term, unless the company wishes to pay a fee at the end of the agreement period to buy the residual value of the asset and record it on the company's books as an asset.

A leasing arrangement tends to be rather expensive for the lessee, since it is paying for the lessor's profit and any differential between the interest rate charged by the lessor and the company's incremental cost of capital. However, leasing still can be a useful option, especially for those assets that tend to degrade quickly in value or usability and that would therefore need to be replaced at the end of the leasing period anyway. It is also useful when the company cannot obtain financing by any other means or wishes to reserve its available lines of credit for other purposes.

A. Lease Basis

Year	Pretax Lease Payments	Income Tax Savings (35% Rate)	After-Tax Lease Cost	Discount Factor (9%)	Net Present Value
1	280,000	98,000	182,000	0.9170	166,894
2	280,000	98,000	182,000	0.8420	153,244
3	270,000	94,500	175,500	0.7720	135,486
4	270,000	94,500	175,500	0.7080	124,254
5	120,000	42,000	78,000	0.6500	50,700
6	120,000	42,000	78,000	0.5960	46,488
7	120,000	42,000	78,000	0.5470	42,666
8	120,000	42,000	78,000	0.5020	39,156
9	120,000	42,000	78,000	0.4600	35,880
	1,700,000	595,000	1,105,000		794,768

B. Buy Basis

Year	Accelerated Cost Recovery	Income Tax Savings (35% Rate)	Discount Factor (9%)	Net Present Value
1	200,000	70,000	0.9170	64,190
2	200,000	70,000	0.8420	58,940
3	200,000	70,000	0.7720	54,040
4	200,000	70,000	0.7080	49,560
5	200,000	70,000	0.6500	45,500
6	—	—		—
7	—	—		—
8	—	—		—
9	—	—		—
	1,000,000	350,000		272,230

Exhibit 20.4 NET PRESENT VALUE CALCULATION FOR LEASE VERSUS BUY DECISION

The many factors used in calculating a lease payment (e.g., down payment, interest rate, asset residual value, and trade-in value) make it difficult to determine the cost of the underlying asset. Consequently, it is useful to use net present value analysis to independently verify the cost of a lease. An example is shown in Exhibit 20.4.

Based on the information in the exhibit, there is a net savings to be gained by buying the asset outright rather than leasing it. The net savings calculation is shown in the next table.

Present value of purchase	$1,000,000
Less: present value of related tax savings	272,230
Net purchase cost	$ 727,770
Net present value savings of purchase over lease:	
Present value of lease cost	$ 794,768
Net purchase cost (above)	727,770
Net savings	$ 66,998

By completing this analysis for each lease, one can determine the total cost difference between a lease and an outright asset purchase, which should be a part of management's approval process for acquiring an asset.

What Is Net Present Value?

The typical capital investment is composed of a number of both negative and positive cash flows that occur throughout the life of the asset. These cash flows are comprised of many things: the initial payment for equipment, continuing maintenance costs, salvage value of the equipment when it is eventually sold, tax payments, receipts from product sold, and so on.

Net present value is used to make all cash flows comparable for an analysis that is done in the present. Doing this requires the use of a discount rate (usually based on the cost of capital, as described in Chapter 18, *Metrics*) to reduce the value of a future cash flow into what it would be worth right now. By applying the discount rate to each anticipated cash flow, we can reduce and then add them together, which yields a single combined figure that represents the current value of the entire proposed capital investment. This is known as its net present value.

For an example of how net present value works, Exhibit 20.5 lists the cash flows, both in and out, for a capital investment that is expected to last for five years. The year is listed in the first column, the amount of the cash flow in the second column, and the discount rate in the third column. The final column multiplies the cash flow from the second column by the discount rate in the third column to yield the present value of each cash flow. The grand total cash flow is listed in the lower right corner of the table.

Notice that the discount factor in Exhibit 20.5 becomes progressively smaller in later years, since cash flows farther in the future are worth less than those that will be

Year	Cash Flow	Discount Factor*	Present Value
0	-$100,000	1.000	-$100,000
1	+25,000	.9259	+23,148
2	+25,000	.8573	+21,433
3	+25,000	.7938	+19,845
4	+30,000	.7350	+22,050
5	+30,000	.6806	+20,418
		Net Present Value	+$6,894

* Note: Discount factor is 8%.

Exhibit 20.5 NET PRESENT VALUE EXAMPLE

received sooner. The discount factor is published in present value tables, which are listed in many accounting and finance textbooks. They are also a standard feature in midrange handheld calculators. Another variation is to use the next formula to manually compute a present value:

Present value of a future cash flow

$$= \frac{\text{(Future cash flow)}}{(1 + \text{Discount rate}) \text{ (squared by the number of periods of discounting)}}$$

Using this formula, if we expect to receive $75,000 in one year, and the discount rate is 15%, the calculation is:

$$\text{Present value} = \frac{\$75,000}{(1 + .15)^1}$$

$$\text{Present value} = \$65,217.39$$

 ## What Cash Flows Are Included in a Net Present Value Calculation?

Here are the most common cash flow line items to include in a net present value analysis:

○ *Cash inflows from sales.* If a capital investment results in added sales, all throughput (sales minus totally variable expenses) attributable to that investment must be included in the analysis.

○ *Cash inflows and outflows for equipment purchases and sales.* There should be a cash outflow when a product is purchased as well as a cash inflow when the equipment is no longer needed and is sold off.

○ *Cash inflows and outflows for working capital.* When a capital investment occurs, it normally involves the use of some additional inventory. If there are added sales, there will probably be additional accounts receivable. In either case, these are additional investments that must be included in the analysis as cash outflows. Also, if the investment is ever terminated, the inventory will presumably be sold off and the accounts receivable collected, so there should be line items in the analysis, located at the end of the project time line, showing the cash inflows from the liquidation of working capital.

○ *Cash outflows for maintenance.* If there is production equipment involved, there will be periodic maintenance needed to ensure that it runs properly.

○ *Cash outflows for taxes.* If there is a profit from new sales that are attributable to the capital investment, the incremental income tax that can be traced to those incremental sales must be included in the analysis. Also, if there is a significant quantity of production equipment involved, the annual personal property taxes that can be traced to that equipment should also be included.

○ *Cash inflows for the tax effect of depreciation.* Depreciation is an allowable tax deduction. Accordingly, the depreciation created by the purchase of capital equipment should be offset against the cash outflow caused by income taxes. Although depreciation is really just an accrual, it does have a net cash flow impact caused by a reduction in taxes and so should be included in the net present value calculation.

What Is Investment Payback?

Investment payback is the period of time required to recoup the amount of the original investment. The net present value method does not fully explain *investment risk,* which is the chance that the initial investment will not be earned back or that the rate of return target will not be met. Discounting can be used to identify or weed out such projects, simply by increasing the hurdle rate. For example, if a project is perceived to be risky, an increase in the hurdle rate will reduce its net present value, which makes the investment less likely to be approved by management. However, management may not be comfortable dealing with discounted cash flow methods when looking at a risky investment—it just wants to know how long it will take until the company gets its invested funds back; the payback method is the solution.

There are two ways to calculate the payback period. The first method is to divide the capital investment by the average annual cash flow from operations. For example, in Exhibit 20.6, we have a stream of cash flows over five years that is heavily weighted toward the time periods that are farthest in the future. The sum of those cash flows is $8,750,000, which is an average of $1,750,000 per year. We will also assume that the initial capital investment was $6,000,000. Based on this information, the payback period is $6,000,000 divided by $1,750,000, which is 3.4 years. However, if we review the stream of cash flows in Exhibit 20.7, it is evident that the cash inflow did not cover the investment at the 3.4-year mark. In fact, the actual cash inflow did not exceed $6,000,000 until shortly after the end of the fourth year. What happened? The stream of cash flows in the example was so skewed toward future periods that the annual *average* cash flow was not representative of the annual actual cash flow. Thus, we can use the averaging method only if the stream of future cash flows is relatively even from year to year.

Year	Cash Flow
1	$1,000,000
2	1,250,000
3	1,500,000
4	2,000,000
5	3,000,000

Exhibit 20.6   STREAM OF CASH FLOWS FOR A PAYBACK CALCULATION

The second approach is to manually calculate the payback period. To do so, we deduct the total expected cash inflow from the invested balance, year by year, until we arrive at the correct period. For example, we have re-created the stream of cash flows from Exhibit 20.6 in Exhibit 20.7, but with an extra column that shows the net capital investment remaining at the end of each year. We can use this format to reach the end of year 5; we know that the cash flows will pay back the investment sometime during year 5, but we do not have a month-by-month cash flow that tells us precisely when. Instead, we can assume an average stream of cash flows during that period, which works out to $250,000 per month ($3,000,000 cash inflow for the year, divided by 12 months). Since there was only

Year	Cash Flow	Net Investment Remaining
0	0	$6,000,000
1	$1,000,000	5,000,000
2	1,250,000	3,750,000
3	1,500,000	2,250,000
4	2,000,000	250,000
5	3,000,000	—

Exhibit 20.7   STREAM OF CASH FLOWS FOR A MANUAL PAYBACK CALCULATION

$250,000 of net investment remaining at the end of the fourth year, and this is the same monthly amount of cash flow in the fifth year, we can assume that the payback period is 4.1 years.

CHAPTER 21

CONTROL SYSTEMS

What Are the Controls for a Computerized Accounts Payable System?

*T*he accounts payable process flow is shown in Exhibit 21.1. This process takes advantage of the basic features of a computerized accounting system, including the minimum set of controls needed to ensure that it operates properly.

The controls noted in the flowchart are described in the next bullet points, in sequence from the top of the flowchart to the bottom.

- *Automatic duplicate invoice number search.* The accounting software automatically checks to see if a supplier's invoice number has already been entered, and warns the user if this is the case, thereby avoiding the need for manual investigation of potentially duplicate invoices.
- *Conduct 3-way match.* The payables staff compares the pricing and quantities listed on the supplier invoice to the quantities actually received, as per receiving documents, and the price originally agreed to, as noted in the company's purchase order.
- *Print report showing payables by due date.* Since the computer system stores the invoice date and number of days allowed until payment, it can report to the user the exact date on which payment must be made for each invoice, thereby eliminating the need to manually monitor this information.
- *Check stock from locked storage.* Unused check stock should always be kept in a locked storage cabinet. In addition, the range of check numbers used should be stored in a separate location and cross-checked against the check numbers on the stored checks, to

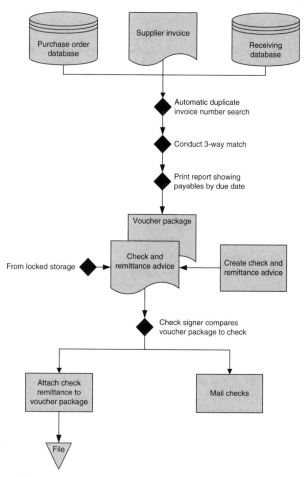

Exhibit 21.1 Controls for Computerized Accounts Payable

verify that no checks have been removed from the locked location.

○ *Check signer compares voucher package to check.* The check signer must compare the backup information attached to each check to the check itself, verifying the payee name, amount to be paid, and the due date. This review is intended to spot unauthorized purchases, payments to the wrong parties, or payments being made either too early or too late. This is a major control point for companies not using purchase orders, since the check signer represents the only supervisory-level review of purchases.

What Are the Controls for Procurement Cards?

The key procurement card controls are enumerated in Exhibit 21.2. The first control calls for card users to itemize

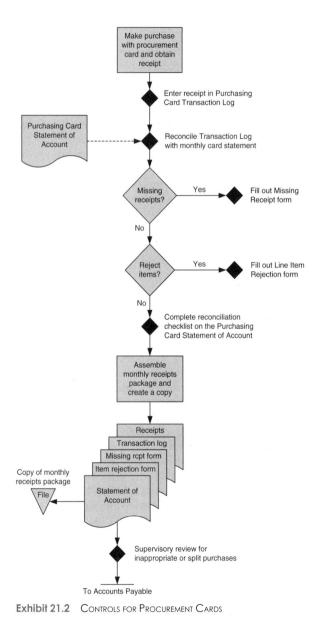

Exhibit 21.2   CONTROLS FOR PROCUREMENT CARDS

each of their purchases in a separate log, which they reconcile against the monthly card statement, noting missing receipts and rejected line items as part of the reconciliation. They assemble this information into a packet of receipts and forms and have a supervisor review it for inappropriate or split purchases. Then this supervisor forwards the packet to the accounts payable department for payment.

The controls noted in the flowchart are described in the next bullet points, in sequence from the top of the flowchart to the bottom.

- *Enter receipt in procurement card transaction log.* When employees use procurement cards, there is a danger that they will purchase a multitude of items and not remember all of them when it comes time to approve the monthly purchases statement. By maintaining a log of purchases, the card user can tell which statement line items should be rejected.

- *Reconcile transaction log with monthly card statement.* Each card holder must review monthly purchases, as itemized by the card issuer on the monthly card statement.

- *Fill out missing receipt form.* Each card user should attach original receipts to the statement of account in order to verify that he or she has made every purchase noted on the statement. If people do not have a receipt, they should fill out a missing receipt form, which itemizes each line item on the statement of account for which there is no receipt. The department manager must review and approve this document, thereby ensuring that all purchases made are appropriate.

- *Fill out line item rejection form.* There must be an organized mechanism for card holders to reject line items on the statement of account. A good approach is to use a procurement card line item rejection form, which users can send directly to the card issuer.

- *Complete reconciliation checklist.* The statement of account reconciliation process requires multiple steps, some of which card holders are likely to inadvertently skip from time to time. Accordingly, a standard reconciliation checklist that they must sign is a useful way to ensure that the procedure is followed.

- *Supervisory review for inappropriate or split purchases.* There must be a third-party review of all purchases made with procurement cards. An effective control is to hand this task to the person having budgetary responsibility for the department in which the card holder works. By doing so, the reviewer is more likely to conduct a detailed review of purchases that will be charged against his or her budget.

What Are the Controls for Order Entry, Credit, and Shipping?

The order entry, credit, and shipment process flow is shown in Exhibit 21.3. The process flow includes controls that take advantage of the ability of the computer system to automatically verify such information as on-hand inventory balances and product pricing. The only paperwork generated by this process is the bill of lading, which is required for shipment.

The controls noted in the flowchart are described at greater length in the next bullet points, in sequence from the top of the flowchart to the bottom.

○ *Verify approved buyer.* Even if the order entry staff receives an ostensibly complete purchase order document from a customer, it is possible that the person who completed and signed the purchase order is not authorized to do so by the customer's management team.

○ *Check on-hand inventory status.* If the order entry computer system is linked to the current inventory balance, the system should warn the order entry staff if there is not a sufficient quantity in stock to fulfill an order and will predict the standard lead time required to obtain additional inventory. This is a control over the company's ability to ship within its standard shipping period.

○ *Automatic price matching.* The computer automatically compares the entered price against the standard corporate price book. If the information in the price book varies from the price listed on the purchase order, the order entry staff must either obtain a supervisory override to use the alternative price or discuss the situation with the customer.

○ *Set up complex billing terms.* If a sale requires unusually complex billing and payment terms, the best place to set up this information is during the initial order entry point, so the information will be available to all users of the order entry database.

○ *Online review by credit department.* If the order entry system has workflow management, any orders entered by the order entry staff will be routed to the

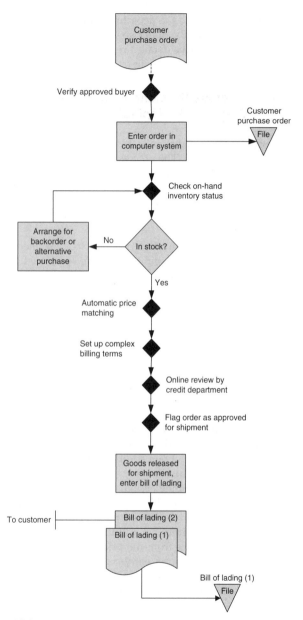

Exhibit 21.3 Controls for Order Entry, Credit, and Shipping

credit department as soon as the orders are entered. This control not only speeds up the credit review process but also ensures that every order entered will be routed to the credit department. This control is typically modified, so that orders falling below a minimum threshold are automatically approved.

○ *Flag order as approved for shipment.* Once reviewed, the credit department can issue an online approval of a customer order, which the computer system routes to the shipping department for fulfillment.

What Are the Controls for Drop-Shipped Orders?

A company may not keep a product in stock for delivery to customers. Instead, it routes customer orders directly to its supplier, which in turn ships the goods directly to the customer. This is known as drop shipping. Additional controls are needed to ensure that customer orders are sent to and received by the supplier. It is also necessary to ensure that notification of delivery is received from the supplier in a timely manner, so the company can issue an invoice to the customer. These controls are shown in Exhibit 21.4. In the exhibit, other controls related to the general process flow have been removed in order to make room for those controls used only for drop-shipped orders.

The controls noted in the flowchart are described at greater length in the next bullet points, in sequence from the top of the flowchart to the bottom.

○ *Verify receipt of customer order by supplier.* The area of greatest risk in the process flow is simply ensuring that the supplier has received a copy of the customer order, which can be confirmed in a number of ways: through an automatic electronic receipt message if Electronic Data Interchange (EDI) is used, or a simple e-mail, fax, or phone call.

○ *Match supplier's bill of lading to customer order.* The company needs a method for determining what has shipped, so it can create customer invoices. When the supplier creates a bill of lading for its own records and the customer, it should create an additional copy for the company, which is matched to the open customer order and sent to the billing staff for invoice creation.

○ *Investigate old open orders.* By default, the preceding matching process leaves all the unmatched orders on file, which the order entry staff uses to create a report of all old open orders. With this report, it follows up with the supplier to determine when remaining orders are expected to be shipped.

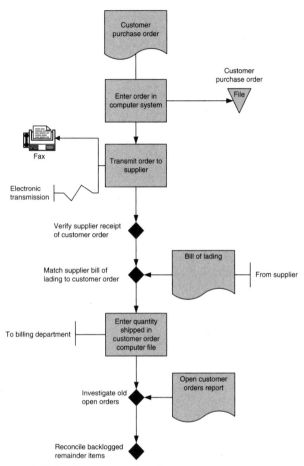

Exhibit 21.4 Controls for Drop Shipping

○ *Reconcile backlogged remainder items.* Once a customer order is largely completed, there may be a small number of items remaining on backlog. If so, the order entry staff should regularly follow up on these items to see if the supplier is still able to ship them or if the customer wants them.

What Are the Controls for a Perpetual Inventory Tracking System?

In a computerized perpetual inventory environment, warehouse employees typically enter all transactions on the fly, using radio frequency bar code scanners as they move inventory around the warehouse. The system of controls for such a system is shown in Exhibit 21.5.

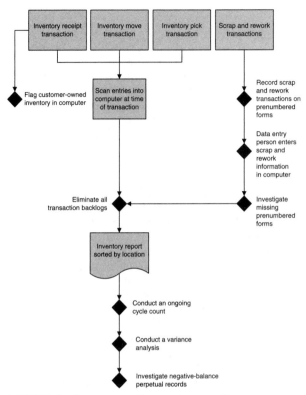

Exhibit 21.5   Controls for a Perpetual Inventory System

The controls noted in the flowchart are described at greater length in the next bullet points, in sequence from the top of the flowchart to the bottom.

○ *Flag customer-owned inventory.* In situations where customers send inventory to a company for inclusion in a finished product, there is a significant risk that the company will inadvertently include the customer-owned inventory in its own inventory valuations. When inventory records are maintained in a computer system, the easiest way to handle this inventory is to flag it in the computer record as being customer-owned, which assigns it a zero cost.

○ *Record scrap and rework transactions on prenumbered forms.* A startling amount of materials and associated direct labor can be lost through the scrapping of production or its rework. The manufacturing staff should be well trained in the use of transaction forms that record these actions, so that the inventory records will remain accurate.

○ *Data entry person enters scrap and rework information in computer.* Since the production staff typically has no experience with data entry, it is better to send all completed scrap and rework forms to the warehouse clerk, who enters the information. This tends to result in significantly lower data entry errors.

○ *Investigate missing prenumbered forms.* Any missing scrap or rework form could represent a valid transaction that has not been included in the computer database. Accordingly, the data entry person should use the computer to print a list of missing form numbers and conduct a search for the documents.

○ *Eliminate all transaction backlogs.* A major ongoing difficulty for any inventory handling operation is when inventory-related transactions (e.g., receipts, put-aways, picks, etc.) are not recorded as soon as they occur. When this happens, anyone counting the inventory will arrive at a total inventory quantity that varies from what the current record states and will post an adjusting entry to alter the supposedly incorrect record balance to match what was just counted. Then, when the late transaction entry is made, the record balance will differ from the physical quantity on hand. One control over this problem is to ensure that there is never a backlog of unrecorded transactions.

○ *Conduct an ongoing cycle count.* Because the materials handlers not only move inventory but also record their own transactions, it is mandatory to conduct an ongoing cycle counting program to ensure that they have correctly entered transactions.

○ *Conduct a variance analysis.* Whenever either a physical or cycle count uncovers a variance between the actual and book quantity, it is mandatory that the variance be fully investigated and the underlying cause be corrected. Otherwise, the reason for the error will continue to cause errors in the future.

○ *Investigate negative-balance perpetual records.* A record in the perpetual inventory card file contains a running balance of the current on-hand inventory quantity, usually in the far-right column. If this number ever reaches a negative balance, always investigate to determine what transaction or counting error caused the problem, and take steps to ensure that it does not happen again.

What Are the Controls for Billing?

When creating invoices, the level of control needed over the process varies based on the use of paper-based or computer records for the information that is used in the billing process. If there is complete computerized integration with the order entry, credit, and shipping functions, considerably fewer controls are needed in the billing process. Both scenarios are shown in Exhibit 21.6, along with the necessary primary control points.

Under Scenario A in the exhibit, the computerization of the billing process means little, because all inputs to the

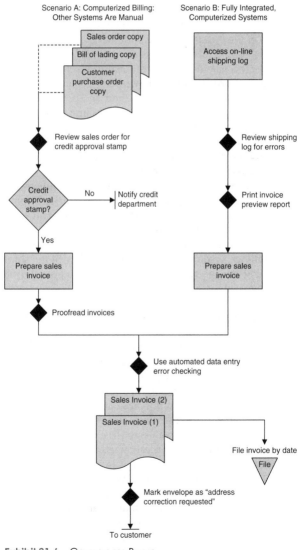

Exhibit 21.6 Controls for Billing

process are still on paper, requiring complete reentry of all information from the source documents and subsequent proofreading of the resulting invoice. The only advantage of using the computer is that it automatically creates a sequential invoice number on each invoice, so there is no need for prenumbered invoice forms. Scenario B takes much greater advantage of complete system integration, since all information previously entered in the computer system by the order entry staff can be copied directly into the invoice.

The controls noted in the flowchart are described at greater length in the next bullet points, in sequence from the top of the flowchart to the bottom.

- ○ *Review sales order for credit approval stamp.* All customer orders should have been reviewed by the credit department and received an approval stamp prior to being forwarded to the billing department. Thus, this control should spot few missing credit approval stamps. Any such instances represent a control breach, so the credit department should be notified of the problem at once.

- ○ *Review shipping log for errors.* In a fully integrated system, the billing clerk accesses the online shipping log each day to see what has been shipped and automatically prints invoices in a single batch for all shipped items. A reasonable control is to have the billing person conduct a cursory review of the shipping log to ensure that all items noted should be invoiced.

- ○ *Print invoice preview report.* Though the preceding control may be sufficient for verifying the quantity of goods shipped, it does not reveal pricing information. To access that information, print a preview report of all invoices and review it for accuracy prior to printing the actual invoices.

- ○ *Proofread invoices.* Some invoices are so complex, involving the entry of purchase order numbers, many line items, price discounts, and other credits, that it is difficult to create an error-free invoice. If so, customers reject the invoices, thereby delaying the payment process. To correct this problem, assign a second person to be the invoice proofreader. This person has not created the invoice and so has an independent view of the situation and can provide a more objective view of invoice accuracy.

- ○ *Use automated data entry error checking.* The billing staff may make a number of common errors on an invoice, such as the wrong price, product or service description, and customer name. In a computerized system, automated data checking methods can be used to reduce the frequency of these problems. There can also be required fields that must have a valid entry or else the invoice cannot be completed, such as the customer purchase order number field.

○ *Mark envelope as "address correction requested."* Customers regularly move to new locations, and the company needs a simple mechanism to track them. One such approach is to mark the words "Address Correction Requested" on each envelope mailed. If the customer has moved and filed a forwarding address with the U.S. Postal Service, the Postal Service will forward the mail to the new address and also notify the company of the new address, which can be used to update the customer address file.

What Are the Controls for Collections?

The flowchart in Exhibit 21.7 shows a basic process flow for collections, including the controls needed to ensure that the process operates correctly. The most common type of control is a supervisory review to take the next collection step, such as approving a special payment plan, sending a receivable to a collection agency, suing a customer, or writing off an account balance.

The controls noted in the flowchart are described at greater length in the next bullet points, in sequence from the top of the flowchart to the bottom.

○ *Assign account ownership.* Clearly define responsibility for who collects every customer account. Otherwise, collections activity may not occur at all, resulting in greatly delayed payments.

○ *Periodically reassign account responsibility.* Collections personnel can become too familiar with a long-standing set of customers, resulting in such a high degree of identification with customer problems that they allow more slack in making payments. Long-term relationships can also increase the risk of collusion between customers and the collections staff. To avoid these problems, periodically reassign account responsibility to different collections personnel.

○ *Segregate the cash recordation and write-off functions.* If the same person is able to record cash receipts and

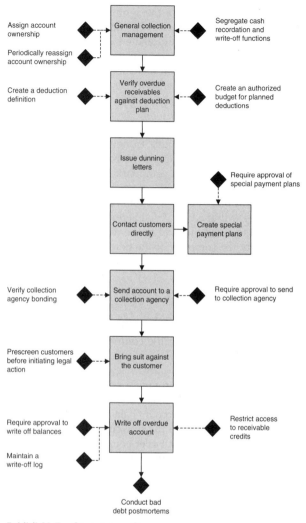

Exhibit 21.7 CONTROLS FOR COLLECTIONS

write off receivable balances, it is possible for that person to pocket incoming cash and write off the related receivable. To prevent this, always segregate the two functions.

○ *Create a deduction definition.* Customers sometimes deliberately misinterpret a company's deduction authorizations in order to take larger deductions. To mitigate this problem, identify all payment deductions caused by deduction authorization violations and refine the deduction definition to exclude the problem deductions. Then meet with the offending customers to discuss the enhanced deduction definition.

○ *Create an authorized budget for planned deductions.* A portion of collection issues arise from deductions taken by customers, some of which are authorized under special marketing plans, such as cooperative advertising, rebates, and mark-down allowances. When created, these plans should be budgeted, approved by both the marketing director and controller, and distributed to the collections staff. Ideally, the plans should identify the approximate amount of deductions expected from each customer, which the collections staff can use as evidence to verify deductions taken.

○ *Require approval of special payment plans.* It is possible that the collections staff may allow delinquent customers to use alternative payment plans, such as extended payments or the return of merchandise. Some of these solutions may be unexpectedly onerous for the company, so a supervisor should authorize these plans.

○ *Require approval to send to collection agency.* Collection agencies are usually paid about one-third of all collected amounts, so the cost of referring accounts to them is considerable. To keep an excessive proportion of receivables from being sent to collection, have a supervisor approve them in advance. This control can be avoided for smaller balances.

○ *Verify collection agency bonding.* A collection agency usually requires a customer to send payment to the agency, which extracts its fee from the payment and forwards the remaining funds to the company. This arrangement puts the company at risk of not being paid by the collection agency. To mitigate this risk, verify each year that the collection agency is fully bonded.

○ *Prescreen customers before initiating legal action.* Initiating legal action against a customer is an enormously expensive and prolonged undertaking. In addition, even if the court awards a substantial settlement, there may not be enough assets to collect. To improve the cost/benefit situation, always prescreen a customer's financial circumstances before initiating a legal action. This can include a review of all judgments and tax liens already filed against it as well as outstanding debt.

○ *Require approval to write off balances.* A lazy collections person could write off a large amount of receivables rather than attempt to collect them.

○ *Maintain a write-off log.* The collections staff could forge a supervisor's signature on write-off approval forms. To prevent this, the authorizing supervisor should maintain a log of all write-offs approved and keep it in a secure location. There should also be a monthly or quarterly review process that compares the contents of the log to actual recorded credits.

○ *Restrict access to receivable credits.* Employees could record unauthorized credits in the accounts receivable subledger, thereby eliminating open receivables. To prevent this, lock down access to the screen in the accounts receivable subledger that allows access to the creation of credits.

○ *Conduct bad debt postmortems.* It is possible that large receivable write-offs could have been prevented through an adjustment of the underlying credit-granting policies and procedures. It is useful to conduct a formal postmortem analysis on larger write-offs to discuss what systemic changes or new controls can be implemented to reduce the likelihood of their reoccurrence.

What Are the Controls for Check Receipts?

The control system for the processing of check receipts is shown in Exhibit 21.8. Despite the presumed use of a computerized accounting system, this is still a very labor-intensive process.

The controls noted in the flowchart are described at greater length in the next bullet points, in sequence from the top of the flowchart to the bottom.

○ *Mailroom prepares check prelist.* As soon as the mail arrives, the mailroom staff should open all envelopes and prepare a list of checks that itemizes from whom checks were received and the dollar total on each check. Then the staff copies this check prelist, sending the original to the cashier and the copy to the accounts receivable clerk. A slight improvement in the control is to make an additional copy of the check prelist and retain it in a locked cabinet in the mailroom, thereby providing evidence of initial receipt in case both the cashier and

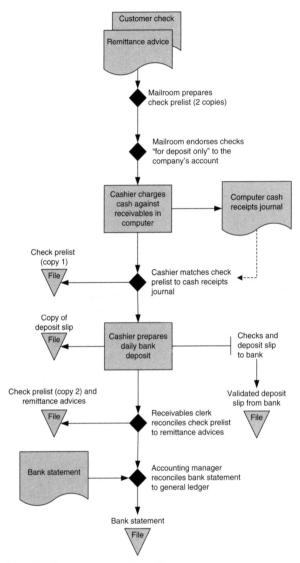

Exhibit 21.8 CONTROLS FOR CHECK RECEIPTS

receivables clerk are in collusion and have destroyed their copies.

○ *Mailroom endorses checks "for deposit only."* By immediately stamping checks as "for deposit only" upon their arrival in the company, it becomes much more difficult for anyone in the accounting department to remove a check and cash it for their own use.

○ *Cashier matches check prelist to cash receipts journal.* Once the cashier has recorded the amounts of all received checks in the cash receipts journal, this person should compare entries to the check prelist. By doing so, she can locate any errors in her entries.

○ *Receivables clerk reconciles check prelist to remittance advices and cash receipts journal.* This control is frequently excluded in a computerized environment, because the receivables clerk is no longer involved in data entry — this person's role has devolved into a cross-examination of work done by the cashier. Nonetheless, it is still a useful control, since the cashier will realize that the receivables clerk is conducting an independent review of all steps in the cash receipts process.

○ *Accounting manager reconciles bank statement to general ledger.* Upon receipt of the monthly bank statement, the accounting manager should reconcile it to the general ledger cash account, using the computerized bank reconciliation module in the accounting software. This control provides an independent review of both cash receipts and payable checks processed and detects the removal of cash after it has been entered in the accounting system (i.e., larceny). This task should be performed by the accounting manager rather than anyone in the cash-handling or recording processes.

What Are the Controls for Investments?

The process of issuing funds for an investment is unique in that every step in the process is a control point. Without regard to controls, the only step required to make an investment is for an authorized person to create and sign an investment authorization form (itself a control point) and deliver it to the bank, which invests the company's funds in the designated investment. However, as shown in the flowchart in Exhibit 21.9, there are a number of additional steps, all designed to ensure that there is an appropriate level of control over the size and duration of the investment and that the earnings from the investment vehicle are maximized.

The controls noted in the flowchart are described at greater length in the next bullet points, in sequence from the top of the flowchart to the bottom.

○ *Create and approve a cash forecast.* There must be some basis for both the size and duration of an investment. Otherwise, a mismatch can develop between

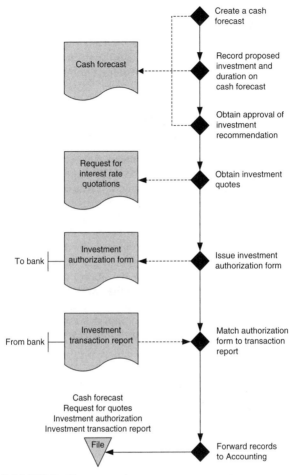

Exhibit 21.9 CONTROLS FOR INVESTMENTS

the need for cash and its availability, resulting in liquidity problems or an excessive amount of underutilized cash. By requiring that a cash forecast be completed and approved by an authorized person, there is less risk of these problems occurring.

○ *Record proposed investment and duration on the cash forecast.* Though the cash forecast alone should be a sufficient control over the determination of the correct size and duration of an investment, it helps to formally write this information directly on the cash forecast, so there is no question about the details of the proposed investment.

○ *Obtain approval of investment recommendation.* A manager should sign off on the proposed investment. By placing the approval signature line directly on the cash forecast, the approver can review the accuracy of the forecast as well as the resulting investment recommendation, giving sufficient information for the approver to determine if the recommendation is correct.

○ *Obtain and document quotes for each investment.* An investment officer may have a favorite bank and may continue to invest with it, even if its rates are not competitive. It is also common for the investment staff to not want to go to the effort of obtaining multiple quotes on a regular basis. By requiring them to complete a quotation sheet, this control ensures that the best investment rate is obtained.

○ *Issue a signed investment authorization form to the issuer.* Banks will not invest funds without a signed investment authorization form from the company. From the company's perspective, a signed authorization also ensures that the appropriate level of management has approved the investment.

○ *Match authorization form to transaction report.* The bank may unintentionally invest funds incorrectly or neglect to invest at all. By matching the signed authorization form to any investment transaction report issued by the bank, the company can verify what action the bank took as a result of the authorization.

○ *Forward records to accounting for storage.* There is some risk that a person in the investment department will alter investment authorization documents after the fact to hide evidence of inappropriate investments. To reduce this risk, require people in the investment department to immediately forward a set of supporting documents to the accounting department for storage in a locked location. The accounting staff should stamp the receipt date on each set of documents received, which the internal auditors can use to determine if any documents were inappropriately delayed.

What Are the Controls for Payroll?

The basic process flow for payroll processing is shown in Exhibit 21.10. It assumes that a computerized timekeeping system is linked to the payroll processing software, so that a great deal of time card review and compilation is avoided.

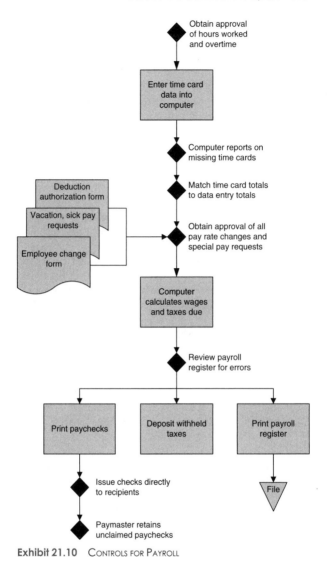

Exhibit 21.10 CONTROLS FOR PAYROLL

The controls noted in the flowchart are described at greater length in the next bullet points, in sequence from the top of the flowchart to the bottom.

- *Obtain approval of hours worked and overtime.* Employees may pad their timesheets with extra hours. Alternatively, they may have fellow employees clock them in and out on days when they are not working. Supervisors should review and initial all timesheets to ensure that hours have been worked.

○ *Computer reports on missing time cards.* It is not necessary to manually determine which current employees have not submitted time cards, since this information can be provided by the computer system itself. However, it may still be necessary to conduct a periodic audit of the employee master file to ensure that all employees listed as active have not actually been terminated (possibly indicating the presence of ghost employees).

○ *Match time card totals to data entry totals.* It is quite possible to incorrectly keypunch the time reported on time cards into the payroll software. To detect these errors, have someone besides the data entry person compare the employee hours loaded into the payroll software to the amounts listed on employee timesheets.

○ *Obtain approval of all pay rate changes and special pay requests.* Pay changes can be made quite easily through the payroll system if there is collusion between a payroll clerk and any other employee. This can be spotted through regular comparisons of pay rates paid to the approved pay rates documented in employee records.

○ *Review payroll register for errors.* The computer system will print a payroll register once it has completed all payroll processing, which makes this an ideal source document for comparison to authorizing wage and deduction documents as well as the total hours listed on timecards.

○ *Issue checks directly to recipients.* A common type of fraud is for the payroll staff either to create employees in the payroll system (ghost employees) or to carry on the pay of employees who have left the company and pocket the resulting paychecks. This practice can be stopped by ensuring that every paycheck is handed to an employee who can prove his or her identity. The person handing out checks can compare the payroll register to the checks to ensure that all checks are being given to the employees.

In cases where there are outlying locations for which it is impossible to physically hand a paycheck to an employee, a reasonable alternative is to have the internal audit staff periodically travel to these locations with the checks on an unannounced basis and require physical identification of each recipient before handing over a check.

○ *Paymaster retains unclaimed paychecks.* The person who physically hands out paychecks to employees is sometimes called the *paymaster*. This person does not prepare the paychecks or sign them, and his or her sole responsibility in the payroll area is to hand out paychecks. If an employee is not available to accept a paycheck, the paymaster retains that person's check in a secure location until the employee is personally available to receive it. This approach avoids the risk of giving the paycheck to a friend of the employee who might cash it and also keeps the payroll staff from preparing a check and cashing it themselves.

PART V

PUBLIC COMPANY ACCOUNTING

CHAPTER 22

SEC FILINGS

What Is the Form 8-K?

A public company is required to file a Form 8-K to report a material, undisclosed event. The form must be filed within four business days of the event. If the event occurs on a weekend or holiday, the four-day rule shall begin on the next business day thereafter. A moderately active company will find itself filing this form quite frequently, possibly more than all other forms combined.

The Securities and Exchange Commission (SEC) defines a number of types of material events that must be reported in a Form 8-K; they are described in the next table. For the more common Form 8-K disclosures, an example is also provided.

Section 1—Company's Business and Operations

Item 1.01   *Entry into a material definitive agreement.* This is for a material definitive agreement not made in the ordinary course of business. Disclose the date of the agreement, the parties involved, and a brief description of the agreement.
Example: On [date] we entered into an amendment to our senior secured credit facility with ABC Bank. which amends the borrowing base definition. Under the terms of the amendment, the percentage of receivables to be included in the borrowing base is changed from 70% to 80%.

Item 1.02   *Termination of a material definitive agreement.* This is for the termination of a material definitive agreement not made in the ordinary course of business. Disclose the termination date, the parties involved, and a brief description of the agreement as well as the circumstances surrounding the termination and any material early termination penalties incurred by the company.
Example: On [date] the Company terminated its previously announcement Agreement and Plan of Merger, dated as of [date], with XYZ Company. The Company's board of directors did not believe that the merger could be finalized.

(Continued)

(Continued)

Item 1.03   *Bankruptcy or receivership*. This is for a company's entry into bankruptcy or receivership. Identify the proceeding, the identity of the court, the date that jurisdiction was assumed, and the identity of the receiver. If a plan of reorganization or liquidation has been entered, disclose the court, confirmation date, and the material features of the plan.
Example: On [date], ABC Company filed a voluntary petition for relief under Chapter 11 of the United States bankruptcy code in the United States Bankruptcy Court, Southern District of New York (case number 01234). The Debtors will continue to operate the business as "debtors-in-possession" under the jurisdiction of the Court and in accordance with applicable provisions of the Bankruptcy Code and orders of the Court. The filing is attached hereto.

Section 2—Financial Information

Item 2.01   *Completion of acquisition or disposition of assets*. For the purchase or sale of a significant amount of assets, disclose the transaction date, the other party, the amount of consideration involved, and the source of funds used for an acquisition.
Example: On [date], stockholders of ABC Company ("ABC") approved and adopted the Agreement and Plan of Merger, dated as of [date] by and among XYZ Company ("XYZ") and ABC, which contemplated that XYZ will merge with and into ABC, with ABC surviving the Merger as a wholly owned subsidiary of XYZ. On [date], the Merger was consummated. Pursuant to the terms of the Merger Agreement, former ABC common stockholders are entitled to receive $1.15 in cash in exchange for each share of ABC common stock, outstanding immediately prior to the effective time of the Merger.

Item 2.02   *Results of operations and financial condition*. Note the date of the release of any material, nonpublic information regarding the company's results of operations or financial condition and attach the text of the release.
Example: On [date], the Company announced its financial results for the quarter ended September 30, 20XX. The full text of the press release issued in connection with the announcement is furnished as an exhibit to this Form 8-K.

Item 2.03   *Creation of a direct financial obligation or an obligation under an off–balance sheet arrangement of a company*. When the company enters into a material obligation, disclose the transaction date and the amount and terms of the obligation.
Example: ABC Company ("ABC") will become obligated on material direct financial obligations pursuant to the Credit Agreement dated as of [date], among ABC and Big Bank ("Big"). Under the terms of the Credit Agreement, Big will make available to ABC up to a $100,000,000 term loan commitment and up to a $50,000,000 revolving loan commitment. Proceeds of the credit agreement may be used for general corporate purposes. The principal amount outstanding of all term loans and revolving loans is due and payable on [date]. Loans will bear interest at Big's base rate plus an applicable margin ranging from 0% to .2%, based upon ABC's

credit rating. Interest on base rate loans is payable on a quarterly basis on the last day of March, June, September and December, and interest is payable at the end of the applicable interest period.

Item 2.04   *Triggering events that accelerate or increase a direct financial obligation or an obligation under an off–balance sheet arrangement.* If a triggering event occurs, note the date of the event and provide a brief description of it, as well as the amount of the obligation.
Example: On [date], the Company received notices from ABC Advisors, holder of the Company's convertible debentures, claiming that the Company was in default of the terms of the debentures for failure to maintain current financial statements in the registration statement relating to the sale of the Company's common stock issuable upon conversion of one of those debentures, and as a result that ABC Advisors was exercising its right to accelerate payment of the full principal amount of the debentures. Approximately $25 million, including interest, is currently outstanding on the debentures.

Item 2.05   *Costs associated with exit or disposal activities.* If the company commits to an exit or disposal plan, note the date of the commitment, the course of action to be taken, and the expected completion date. For each major type of cost, also estimate the range of amounts expected to be incurred.
Example: On [date], the Company committed to a restructuring plan that includes a reduction in force of approximately 500 positions. The restructuring plan is intended to improve operational efficiencies. The Company anticipates that it will complete the restructuring by [date]. In connection with the restructuring, the Company expects to incur total expenses relating to termination benefits of $21 million to $24 million, all of which represent cash expenditures. The Company expects to record the majority of these restructuring charges in the quarter ending December 31, 20XX.

Item 2.06   *Material impairments.* If the company concludes that one or more of its assets are impaired, disclose the date of the decision, describe the asset, and note the circumstances leading to the conclusion. Also note the amount of the impairment.
Example: During the quarter ended September 30, 20XX, as part of the Company's ongoing strategic review of the business, an impairment analysis was performed on the Aerospace segment goodwill and intangible assets. On [date] the Company concluded that noncash goodwill and intangible asset impairment charges of $10 million were required and such charges were recorded in the quarter ended September 30, 20XX.

Section 3—Securities and Trading Markets

Item 3.01   *Notice of delisting or failure to satisfy a continued listing rule or standard; transfer of listing.* Disclose the date when the company received notice from a national exchange that a class of its common equity does not satisfy its continued listing or that the exchange expects to delist it. Also note the rule being violated that led to the notification and the action the company expects to take in response. If
(Continued)

(Continued)

the company has caused an exchange listing to be withdrawn, describe the action taken and the date of the action.

Example: ABC Company today announced it has received notice from Nasdaq that its common stock is subject to potential delisting from the Nasdaq Capital Market because the bid price of the Company's common stock closed below the minimum $1.00 per share requirement for 30 consecutive business days prior to [date]. The Company has been granted an initial 180 calendar days, or until [date], to regain compliance.

Item 3.02   *Unregistered sales of equity securities.* In the event of an unregistered security sale, state the date of sale, the type and amount of securities sold, the consideration paid, the type of exemption from registration being claimed, and any convertibility terms. This report needs to be filed only if the shares issued are more than 1% of the shares outstanding. For a smaller reporting company, the reporting threshold is 5% of the shares outstanding.

Example: On [date], accredited investors purchased an aggregate of 25,000,000 shares of common stock at $2.00 per share for an aggregate purchase price of $50,000,000 from ABC Company ("ABC"). The funds raised will be utilized by ABC for working capital and research purposes. The shares were offered and sold to the accredited investors in a private placement transaction made in reliance upon exemptions from registration pursuant to Section 4(2) under the Securities Act of 1933. Each of the Investors are accredited investors as defined in Rule 501 of Regulation D promulgated under the Securities Act of 1933.

Item 3.03   *Material modification to rights of security holders.* Disclose the date of modification, the type of security involved, and the effect of the modification on the rights of the security holders.

Example: On [date], ABC Company entered into an amendment to its Preferred Stock Rights Agreement dated [date] with XYZ Trust Company to amend the exercise price of a right to purchase one share of its Series A Preferred Stock to $25.00 per share and to make certain conforming changes related to the change in exercise price.

Section 4—Matters Related to Accountants and Financial Statements

Item 4.01   *Changes in the company's certifying accountant.* If the company's auditor resigns or is dismissed, disclose whether the change was a resignation or dismissal, and whether the auditor's report for either of the past two years contained an adverse opinion or disclaimer of opinion, or was qualified. Also state whether the change was recommended or approved by the company's board of directors or its audit committee and whether there were any disagreements with the auditor during the two most recent fiscal years that were not resolved to the satisfaction of the auditor.

Example: On [date], our client-auditor relationship with XYZ Auditor ("XYZ") ceased. As of that date, ABC Company (the "ABC") had no disagreements with XYZ on any matter of accounting principles or practices, financial statement disclosure, or auditing scope or procedure. We have provided XYZ with a copy of the disclosures we are making in response to this Item 4.01. XYZ has furnished us with a letter dated [date], addressed to the Commission, and stating that it agrees with the statements made herein.

Item 4.02   *Nonreliance on previously issued financial statements or a related audit report or completed interim review.* If the company concludes that any previously issued financial statements cannot be relied on because of an error, disclose the date of this decision and describe the facts underlying the decision. There are multiple additional steps to be taken besides filing this Form 8-K.
Example: On [date], management of the Company, with concurrence of the Audit Committee of the Company's Board of Directors (the "Audit Committee"), concluded that the Company's previously issued financial statements for the three months ended March 31, 20XX (the "Financials") incorrectly valued an allowance against deferred tax assets. As a result, the Financials should no longer be relied upon. The Company intends to file amended financial statements in a Form 10-Q/A for the three month period ended March 31, 20XX no later than May 31, 20XX. During the first quarter of 20XX, in accordance with Statement of Financial Accounting Standards No. 109, "Accounting for Income Taxes" ("FAS 109"), the Company recorded a valuation allowance of $125 million to reduce certain net deferred tax assets to their anticipated realizable value. The Company later realized it had incorrectly determined the valuation allowance against deferred tax assets. The Company and its auditors have reached a preliminary conclusion that an additional valuation allowance of $45 million should have been recorded at March 31, 20XX.

Section 5—Corporate Governance and Management

Item 5.01   *Changes in control of the company.* Identify the person acquiring control of the company and the date of the change, and describe the transaction resulting in the change of control. Also note the amount of consideration used to effect the change and the source of the person's funds to do so.
Example: On [date], Current Investor, the controlling shareholder of ABC Company ("ABC"), entered into a Securities Purchase and Sale Agreement with XYZ Company ("XYZ"). Pursuant to the Securities Purchase and Sale Agreement, Current Investor agreed to sell all of his shares of the Company's common stock to XYZ. Upon the closing of the Securities Purchase and Sale Agreement on [date] (the "Closing"), a change in control of the Company occurred. Pursuant to the Securities Purchase and Sale Agreement, XYZ has acquired 5,000,000 shares of the Company's common stock from Current Investor. XYZ paid $15,000,000 to acquire such shares. Funds for the acquisition were from the working capital of XYZ. XYZ now owns 80% of ABC's issued and outstanding shares.

Item 5.02   *Departure of directors or certain officers; election of directors; appointment of certain officers.* If a director resigns, is removed, or refuses to stand for reelection because of a disagreement with the
(Continued)

(Continued)

company, note the date of the event and the director's committee positions held and describe the disagreement. If the director has provided any written correspondence related to the disagreement, this must be attached as an exhibit.
Example: Mr. Alfred Director resigned as a director of ABC Company ("ABC"), effective on [date]. Mr. Director was a member of ABC's audit committee and governance committee. He gave no reason for his resignation.

Item 5.03   *Amendments to articles of incorporation or bylaws; change in fiscal year.* For such amendments that were not previously disclosed in a proxy statement, disclose the amendment date and describe the change.
Example: On [date], ABC Company filed with the Secretary of State of the State of New York a Certificate of Amendment to its Certificate of Incorporation establishing the terms of a new class of Series A Preferred Stock.

Item 5.04   *Temporary suspension of trading under the company's employee benefit plans.* For such a suspension, note the reason for the blackout period, the plan transactions to be suspended, the class of equity securities affected, and the duration of the blackout period.
Example: On [date], the Audit Committee of the Board of Directors of ABC Company ("ABC") concluded that the Company's financial statements for one or more prior periods will likely need to be restated in conjunction with revising its sales return reserve calculations. Because of the potential restatement of this information and in order to ensure compliance with applicable securities laws, participants in the ABC Company 401(k) Plan (the "Plan") will be temporarily subject to a blackout period during which they will be precluded from acquiring beneficial ownership of additional interests in the Company's common stock fund under the 401(k) plan. During the blackout period, Plan participants will be unable to direct investments into the Company's stock fund under the Plan. The blackout period began at 7:00 a.m. Eastern time on [date] and is currently anticipated to end at 7:00 a.m. Eastern time on the day immediately following the day on which the restated financial statements are filed with the Securities and Exchange Commission.

Item 5.05   *Amendment to company's code of ethics, or waiver of a provision of the code of ethics.* Note the date of any change that applies to the company's chief executive officer, chief financial officer, or principal accounting officer and the name of the person to whom it was granted; and describe the nature of the waiver.
Example: On [date], the Board of Directors of the Company approved a Code of Business Conduct and Ethics, which covers all employees and directors of the Company. The new Code of Business Conduct and Ethics encompasses and supersedes the Code of Business Conduct and Ethics for the Company's Senior Officers, which has been posted on the Company's Web site.

Item 5.06   *Change in shell company status.* If a company is no longer a shell company, disclose the material terms of the transaction.
Example: The disclosure regarding the reverse merger in Item 2.01 above is hereby incorporated by reference. Prior to the effective time of the reverse merger, ABC Company was a shell company.

Section 6—Asset-Backed Securities (ABS)

Item 6.01   *ABS informational and computational materials.* Report any information and computational material filed in, or as an exhibit to, this report.

Item 6.02   *Change of servicer or trustee.* If a servicer or trustee has resigned or been removed, or if a new servicer has been appointed, state the event date and the circumstances of the change.

Item 6.03   *Change in credit enhancement or other external support.* If the company becomes aware of any material enhancement or support regarding one or more classes of asset-backed securities, identify the parties to the agreement causing the change, and describe its date, terms, and conditions.

Item 6.04   *Failure to make a required distribution.* If a required distribution to holders of asset-based securities is not made, identify the failure and state the nature of the failure.

Item 6.05   *Securities Act updating disclosure.* If any material pool characteristic of the actual asset pool at the time of issuance differs by 5% or more from the description of the asset pool in the prospectus, disclose the characteristics of the actual asset pool.

Section 7—Regulation FD

Item 7.01   *Regulation FD disclosure.* Disclose under this item only information that the company elects to disclose pursuant to Regulation FD.
Example: On [date], ABC Company ("ABC") will make a presentation to potential lenders. A copy of the slides to be used in the presentation is furnished herewith as an Exhibit.

Section 8—Other Events

Item 8.01   *Other events.* Disclose under this category any events that the company considers to be of importance to its securities holders.
Example: On [date], ABC Company ("ABC") entered into a Settlement Agreement with the United States Department of Justice to settle all outstanding federal suits against ABC in connection with claims related to the Company's alleged off-label marketing and promotion of its ABC Product® to pediatricians (the "Settlement Agreement"). The settlement is neither an admission of liability by ABC nor a concession by the United States that its claims are not well founded. Pursuant to the Settlement Agreement, the Company will pay approximately $10 million to settle the matter between the parties. The Settlement Agreement provides that, upon full payment of the settlement fees, the United States releases ABC from the claims asserted by the United States. As of [date], ABC accrued a loss contingency of $10 million for this matter.

What Information Is Included in the Annual and Quarterly Reports?

Financial statements and supporting disclosures must be filed by publicly held companies with the SEC on a quarterly basis. Those statements issued for the first, second, and third quarters of a company's fiscal year are called 10-Q reports; the year-end report is called a 10-K report. The 10-Q and 10-K reports include a company's basic financial statements as well as the disclosures shown in the next table. *All* items must be included in the 10-K, and *indicated* items must be included in the 10-Q.

Item Header	Include in 10-Q	Description
Item 1. Business		Describes the company's general purpose, its history, business segments, customers, suppliers, sales and marketing operations, customer support, intellectual property, competition, and employees. It is designed to give the reader a grounding in what the company does and the business environment in which it operates.
Item 1A. Risk factors	Yes	Is an exhaustive compilation of all risks to which the company is subjected. Serves as a general warning to investors of what actions might negatively impact their investments in the company.
Item 1B. Unresolved staff comments		If an accelerated or large accelerated filer received written comments from the SEC at least 180 days before its fiscal year-end and those comments are unresolved, disclose all material unresolved issues.
Item 2. Properties		Describes the company's leased or owned facilities, including square footage, lease termination dates, and lease amounts paid per month.

Item Header	Include in 10-Q	Description
Item 3. Legal proceedings	Yes	Describes current legal proceedings involving the company and the company's estimate of the likely outcome of those proceedings.
Item 4. Submission of matters to a vote of security holders	Yes	Describes any matters submitted to shareholders for a vote during the fourth quarter of the fiscal year.
Item 5. Market for company stock		Notes where the company's stock trades, the number of holders of record, and high and low closing prices per share, by quarter.
Item 6. Selected financial data		Provides, in tabular comparative format for the last five years, selected information from the company's income statement and balance sheet.
Item 7. Management's discussion and analysis (MD&A)	Yes	Involves multiple areas of required commentary, including opportunities, challenges, risks, trends, key performance indicators, future plans, and changes in revenues, cost of goods sold, other expenses, assets, and liabilities.
Item 7A. Quantitative and qualitative disclosures about market risk	Yes	Quantifies the market risk as of the end of the last fiscal year for its market risk-sensitive instruments. Several presentation formats are available.
Item 8. Financial statements and supplementary data	Yes	Includes all disclosures required by generally accepted accounting principles, including descriptions of acquisitions, discontinued operations, fixed assets, accrued liabilities, related party transactions, income taxes, stock options, segment information, and many other possibilities, depending on the nature of a company's transactions.

(Continued)

Item Header	Include in 10-Q	Description
Item 9. Changes in and disagreements with accountants on accounting and financial disclosure		States the existence and nature of any disagreement with the company's auditors when the company elects to account for or disclose transactions in a manner different from what the auditors want.
Item 9A. Controls and procedures	Yes	Generally describes the company's system of internal controls, testing of controls, changes in controls, and management's conclusions regarding the effectiveness of controls.
Item 10. Directors, executive officers, and corporate governance		Identifies executive officers, directors, promoters, and control persons.
Item 11. Executive compensation		Itemizes various types of compensation received by company executives.
Item 12. Security ownership of certain beneficial owners and management and related stockholder matters		Notes the number of shares of all types owned or controlled by certain beneficial owners and management.
Item 13. Certain relationships and related transactions, and director independence		Describe any transactions with related parties during the past fiscal year involving amounts greater than $120,000.
Item 14. Principal accountant fees and services		Discloses the aggregate fees billed for each of the last two fiscal years for professional services rendered by the company's auditor for reviews and audits, for audit-related activities, taxation work, and all other fees.
Item 15. Exhibits and financial statement schedules	Yes	Item 601 of Regulation S-K requires the attachment of numerous exhibits to the 10-K, including such issues as a company's code of ethics, material contracts, articles of incorporation, bylaws, and acquisition purchase agreements.

When Must Annual and Quarterly Reports Be Filed?

The 10-K filing deadline depends on the size of the company, as noted next:

- File within 60 days of the end of the fiscal year if the company is a *large accelerated filer*. This type of company must have an aggregate market value owned by nonaffiliated investors of at least $700 million as of the last business day of the company's most recent second fiscal quarter.
- File within 75 days of the end of the fiscal year if the company is an *accelerated filer*. This type of company must have an aggregate market value owned by nonaffiliated investors of at least $75 million, but less than $700 million, as of the last business day of the company's most recent second fiscal quarter.
- File within 90 days of the end of the fiscal year for all other companies.

The 10-Q filing deadline uses the same definitions to determine when the report must be filed.

- Large accelerated filers and accelerated filers file within 40 days of the end of the fiscal quarter.
- All other companies file within 45 days of the end of the fiscal quarter.

What Is the Form S-1?

The Form S-1 is the default stock registration form to be used if no other registration forms or exemptions from registration are applicable. The 17 main informational contents of the Form S-1 are described next.

1. *Forepart of the registration statement.* Includes the company name, the title and amount of securities to be registered, and their offering price. Also describes the market for the securities and a cross-reference to the risk factors section.
2. *Summary information.* Provides a summary of the prospectus contents that contains a brief overview of the key aspects of the offering as well as contact information for the company's principal executive offices.
3. *Risk factors.* Discusses the most significant factors that make the offering speculative or risky, and explains how the risk affects the company or the securities being offered.

4. *Ratio of earnings to fixed charges.*

5. *Use of proceeds.* States the principal purpose for which proceeds from the offering are intended.

6. *Determination of offering price.* Describes the factors considered in determining the offering price, both for common equity and for warrants, rights, and convertible securities.

7. *Dilution.* Discloses book value per share information before and after the distribution.

8. *Selling security holders.* For those securities being sold for the account of another security holder, names each security holder as well as each person's relationship with the company within the past three years.

9. *Plan of distribution.* Describes information about underwriters, how securities are to be distributed, compensation paid to the sellers of securities, and stabilization transactions.

10. *Description of securities to be registered.* Describes such issues as the voting, liquidation, dividend, and conversion rights associated with the securities.

11. *Interests of named experts and counsel.* Identifies any experts and counsel who are certifying or preparing the registration document or providing a supporting valuation, and the nature of their compensation relating to the registration.

12. *Information with respect to the registrant.* This section comprises the bulk of the document and includes a description of the business and its property, any legal proceedings, the market price of the company's stock, financial statements, selected financial data, and management's discussion and analysis of the company's financial condition and its results of operations. It also requires disclosure of any disagreements with the company's auditors, market risk analysis, and several ownership and governance issues.

13. *Material changes.* Describes material changes that have occurred since the company's last-filed annual or quarterly report.

14. *Other expenses of issuance and distribution.* Itemizes the expenses incurred in connection with the issuance and distribution of the securities to be registered.

15. *Indemnification of directors and officers.* Notes the effect of any arrangements under which the company's directors and officers are insured or indemnified against liability.

16. *Recent sales of unregistered securities.* Identifies unregistered securities sold by the company within the past three years and the use of proceeds.

17. *Exhibits and financial statement schedules.* Provides exhibits for such items as the underwriting agreement, consents, and powers of attorney.

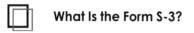 ## What Is the Form S-3?

The Form S-3 allows a company to incorporate a large amount of information into the form by reference, which is generally not allowed in a Form S-1. Specifically, the company can incorporate the information already filed in its latest Form 10-K, subsequent quarterly 10-Q reports, and 8-K reports, thereby essentially eliminating the "information with respect to the registration" that is needed for the Form S-1. The Form S-3 is restricted to those companies meeting these four eligibility requirements:

1. It is organized within and has principal business operations within the United States; and

2. It already has a class of registered securities, or has been meeting its periodic reporting requirements to the SEC for at least the past 12 months; and

3. It cannot have failed to pay dividends, sinking fund installments, or defaulted on scheduled debt or lease payments since the end of the last fiscal year; and

4. The aggregate market value of the common equity held by nonaffiliates of the company is at least $75 million.

If a company has an aggregate market value of common equity held by nonaffiliates of less than $75 million, it can still use Form S-3, provided that:

1. The aggregate market value of securities sold by the company during the 12 months prior to the Form S-3 filing is no more than one-third of the aggregate market value of the voting and nonvoting common equity held by its nonaffiliated investors; and

2. It is not a shell company, and has not been one for the past 12 months; and

3. It has at least one class of common equity securities listed on a national securities exchange.

In addition, if the form is to be used to register nonconvertible securities, they must be rated "investment-grade securities" by one of the nationally recognized statistical rating organizations.

What Is the Form S-8?

The Form S-8 allows a company to register securities that it offers to its employees and consultants under an employee benefit plan. Such a plan can involve a broad array of securities-related issuances, such as common stock, stock options, restricted stock units, and purchases under an employee stock purchase plan. People covered by this type of registration include employees, officers, directors, general partners, and consultants. Securities issued to consultants can be registered through a Form S-8 only if the consultants provide bona fide services to the company, and those services are not related to the sale of its securities or making a market in them. Family members are also covered, if they received company securities through an employee gift.

The form has the dual advantages of being effective immediately upon filing and of being extremely simple to complete. The company must merely state that its regular periodic filings are incorporated by reference and note the manner in which the company indemnifies its officers and directors. There are a few other requirements that are generally not applicable. The principle accompanying document is the employee benefit plan.

This form of registration is available only if a public company has been current with its filing requirements for at least the past 12 months and has not been a shell company for at least the preceding 60 days.

What Forms Require a Payment to the SEC?

Most ongoing informational reports filed with the SEC, such as the Forms 10-Q, 10-K, and 8-K, require no fee. However, stock registration forms, such as the Forms S-1 and S-3, require a payment to the SEC. The SEC will not accept such filings if payment has not yet been received. Payments are made through the Fedwire system.

To calculate the fee to be paid to the SEC, the form instructions for every form requiring a payment begins with a table with calculation information, entitled "Calculation of Registration Fee." In it, the company itemizes the amount of securities to be offered, the proposed maximum aggregate offering price, and the amount of the registration fee. A sample table is presented next.

Title of Each Class of Securities to Be Registered	Amount to Be Registered	Proposed Maximum Offering Price per Unit	Proposed Maximum Aggregate Offering Price	Amount of Registration Fee
Common stock, no par value under the ABC Company: 20XX Employee Stock Purchase Plan	1,000,000	$2.50	$2,500,000	$100

To ensure that a company has paid in enough funds to process a filing, it should submit a test filing; the test will return whether there are sufficient funds on hand to complete the filing.

How Do I Make a Fedwire Payment?

To issue a wire transfer to the SEC, include in the wire instructions the American Bankers Association number for U.S. Bank, which is 081000210. Then include the SEC's account number at U.S. Bank, which is 152307768324, as well as the company's central index key (CIK). The SEC assigns a CIK to every company when it initially begins filing activities. The "CIK" designation should precede the CIK number; for example, the wiring instructions could read CIK0123456789. An example of the wiring instructions to the SEC is shown next.

Amount: $10,000
Receiving bank ABA number: 081000210
Receiving bank name: U.S. Bank
Receiving account number: 152307768324
Receiving account name: Securities and Exchange Commission
Originator to beneficiary information: CIK0123456789

It is also possible to pay the SEC by check. To do so, make the check payable to the Securities and Exchange Commission. On the front of the check, include the SEC's account number (152307768324) and the company's CIK number. To send checks by overnight delivery service, mail to this address:

U.S. Bank
Government Lockbox 979081
1005 Convention Plaza
SL-MO-C2-GL
St. Louis, MO 63101

To send checks by regular mail delivery, mail to this address:

Securities and Exchange Commission
P.O. Box 979081
St. Louis, MO 63197-9000

The SEC occasionally changes these payment instructions, so be sure to verify the most recent information on the SEC Web site, at www.sec.gov/info/edgar/fedwire. htm.

CHAPTER 23

PUBLIC COMPANY ACCOUNTING TOPICS

When Is Interim Reporting Required?

*I*nterim reporting refers to a requirement by the Securities and Exchange Commission (SEC) for all publicly held companies to file quarterly information on the Form 10-Q. The intent of this requirement is to provide users of the financial statements with more current information.

What Is the Integral View of Interim Reporting?

Under the *integral view* view, each interim period is considered to be an integral part of the annual accounting period. As such, annual expenses that may not specifically arise during an interim period are nonetheless accrued within *all* interim periods, based on management's best estimates. This heightened level of accrual usage will likely result in numerous accrual corrections in subsequent periods to adjust for any earlier estimation errors. It also calls for the use of the estimated annual tax rate for all interim periods, since the annual tax rate may vary considerably from the rate in effect during the interim period if the company is subject to graduated tax rates

A number of expenses can be assigned to multiple interim reporting periods, even if they are incurred only in one interim period. The key justification is that the costs must clearly benefit all periods in which the expense is recorded. Examples of such expenses are:

- Advertising expense
- Bonuses (if they can be reasonably estimated)
- Contingencies (that are probable and subject to reasonable estimation)

- Contingent rental expense (if the contingent expense appears probable)
- Income taxes (based on the estimated annual effective tax rate)
- Profit sharing (if it can be reasonably estimated)
- Property taxes

What Is the Discrete View of Interim Reporting?

Under this view, each interim period is considered to be a discrete reporting period and as such is *not* associated with expenses that may arise during other interim periods of the reporting year. A result of this type of reporting is that an expense benefiting more than one interim period will be fully recognized in the period incurred rather than being recognized over multiple periods.

How Are Changes in Accounting Principle and Estimate Accounted for in Interim Periods?

Any change in accounting *principle* must be applied to all interim periods presented in the financial statements, which may call for retrospective application. However, a change in accounting *estimate* is to be accounted for only on a go-forward basis, so no retrospective application is allowed.

When Is Segment Information Required?

Segment information is required only for public companies. It is reported in order to provide the users of financial information with a better knowledge of the different types of business activities in which a company is involved. The general requirement for segment reporting is that the revenue, profit or loss, and assets of each segment be reported, as well as a reconciliation of this information to the company's consolidated results. In addition, the company must report the revenues for each product and service, and by customer, as well as revenues and assets for domestic and foreign sales and operations. This information is to be accompanied by disclosure of the methods used to determine the composition of the reported segments.

A *reportable segment* is a distinct revenue-producing component of a business entity for which separate financial information is produced internally and whose results are regularly reviewed by the chief operating decision maker.

How Are Reportable Segments Determined?

A segment is considered to be reportable if it is significant to the company as a whole. Significance is assumed if its passes any one of these three tests:

1. Segment revenue is at least 10% of consolidated revenue.
2. Segment profit or loss, in absolute terms, is at least 10% of the greater of the combined profits of all operating segments reporting a profit or the combined losses of all operating segments reporting a loss.
3. Segment assets are at least 10% of the combined assets of all operating segments.

When evaluating a segment's reportability with these tests, a segment should not be reported separately if it becomes reportable only due to a one-time event. Conversely, a segment should be reported, even if it does not currently qualify, if it did qualify in the past and is expected to do so again in the future.

In addition, the combined revenue of the segments designated as reportable must be at least 75% of consolidated revenue. If not, additional segments must be designated as reportable. Finally, it is generally best to limit the number of reported segments to no more than 10; similar segments thereafter should be aggregated for reporting purposes.

EXAMPLE

The next table shows how the three 10% tests and the 75% test may be conducted. The first table shows the operating results of six segments of a reporting entity.

Segment Name	Revenue	Profit	Loss	Assets
A	$101,000	$5,000	$—	$60,000
B	285,000	10,000	—	120,000

(Continued)

(Continued)

Segment Name	Revenue	Profit	Loss	Assets
C	130,000	—	(35,000)	40,000
D	500,000	—	(80,000)	190,000
E	440,000	20,000	—	160,000
F	140,000	—	(5,000)	50,000
Totals	$1,596,000	$35,000	$(120,000)	620,000

Because the total reported loss of $120,000 exceeds the total reported profit of $35,000, the $120,000 is used for the 10% profit test. The tests for these segments are itemized in the next table, where test thresholds are listed in the second row. For example, the total revenue of $1,596,000 shown in the preceding table is multiplied by 10% to arrive at the test threshold of $159,600 that is used in the second column. Segments B, D, and E all have revenue levels exceeding this threshold, so an "X" in the table indicates that their results must be separately reported. After conducting all three of the 10% tests, the table shows that segments B, C, D, and E must be reported, so their revenues are itemized in the last column. The last column shows that the total revenue of all reportable segments exceeds the $1,197,000 revenue level needed to pass the 75% test, so that no additional segments must be reported.

Segment Name	Revenue 10% Test	Profit 10% Test	Asset 10% Test	75% Revenue Test
Test Threshold	$159,600	$12,000	$62,000	$1,197,000
A				
B	X		X	$ 285,000
C		X		130,000
D	X	X	X	500,000
E	X	X	X	440,000
F				
			Total	$1,355,000

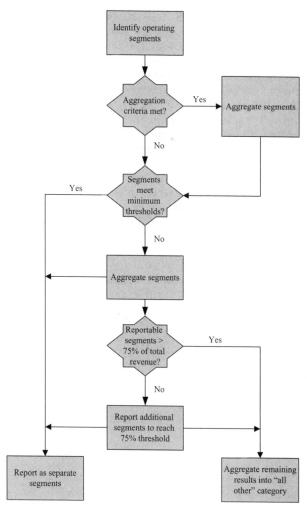

Exhibit 23.1   DECISION TREE FOR DETERMINING REPORTABLE SEGMENTS

The decision tree in Exhibit 23.1 shows how to determine which segments must be separately reported, which segments should be aggregated, and which ones can be summarized into the "all other" segments category.

How Is Basic Earnings per Share Calculated?

Basic earnings per share (EPS) is calculated for a simple capital structure, where there are no potential common shares, such as options, restricted stock units, and warrants. The basic EPS calculation is income available to common stockholders (the numerator) divided by the weighted-average number of common shares outstanding (the denominator) during the period.

The income available to common stockholders used as the numerator in any of the EPS computations must be reduced by any preferential claims against it by other securities. These other securities are usually in the form of preferred stock, and the deduction from income is the amount of the dividend declared (whether paid or not) during the year on the preferred stock. If the preferred stock is cumulative, the dividend is deducted from income (added to the loss) whether declared or not.

The number of shares outstanding under a simple capital structure can be determined using the rules shown in Exhibit 23.2.

Transaction	Effect on EPS Computation
Common stock outstanding at the beginning of the period	Included in number of shares outstanding
Issuance of common stock	Increase number of shares outstanding by number of shares issued times the portion of the year outstanding
Conversion into common stock	Increase number of shares outstanding by number of shares converted times the portion of the year outstanding
Reacquisition of common stock	Decrease number of shares outstanding by number of shares reacquired times portion of the year since reacquisition
Stock dividend or split	Increase number of shares outstanding by number of shares issued for the dividend or resulting from the split retroactively as of the beginning of the earliest period presented
Reverse split	Decrease number of shares outstanding by decrease in shares retroactively as of the beginning of the earliest period presented
Business combination	Increase number of shares outstanding by number of shares issued times portion of year since acquisition

Exhibit 23.2   EPS Calculations for Various Equity Transactions

How Is Diluted Earnings per Share Calculated?

A complex capital structure is one that includes securities granting rights with the potential to be exercised and reduce earnings per share (dilutive securities). Examples of dilutive securities are convertible debt, convertible preferred stock, options, warrants, participating securities, two-class common stocks, and contingent shares. The common stock outstanding and all other dilutive securities are used to compute diluted earnings per share (DEPS). DEPS represents the earnings attributable to each share of common stock *after* giving effect to all potentially dilutive securities that were outstanding during the period. The computation of DEPS requires that these two steps be performed:

1. Identify all potentially dilutive securities.
2. Compute dilution, the effects that the other dilutive securities have on net income and common shares outstanding.

Any antidilutive securities (those that *increase* EPS) are not included in the computation of EPS.

What Methods Are Used for Calculating Diluted Earnings per Share?

The *treasury stock method*, which is used for the exercise of most warrants or options, requires that diluted earnings per share (DEPS) be computed as if the options or warrants were exercised at the beginning of the period (or actual date of issuance, if later) and that the funds obtained from the exercise were used to purchase (reacquire) the company's common stock at the average market price for the period.

The *if-converted method* is used for those securities that are currently sharing in the earnings of the company through the receipt of interest or dividends as preferential securities but that have the potential for sharing in the earnings as common stock (e.g., convertible bonds or convertible preferred stock). The if-converted method recognizes that the convertible security can share in the earnings of the company only as one or the other, not both. Thus, the dividends or interest less income tax effects applicable to the convertible security as a preferential security are not recognized in income available to common stockholders used to compute DEPS, and the weighted-average number of shares is adjusted to reflect the assumed conversion as of the beginning of the year (or actual date of issuance, if later).

How Should Non-GAAP Information Be Disclosed?

The SEC requires that a company issuing information about a non–generally accepted accounting principles (GAAP) financial measure accompany that presentation with this information:

- ○ A presentation of the most directly comparable financial measure, calculated and presented in accordance with GAAP
- ○ A reconciliation of the differences between the non-GAAP financial measure with the most comparable financial measure as calculated and presented in accordance with GAAP

The SEC defines a non-GAAP financial measure as one that excludes amounts that are included in the most directly comparable GAAP measure or that includes amounts excluded from the most directly comparable GAAP measure.

INDEX